D0468134

TIMELINES
OF WORLD HISTORY

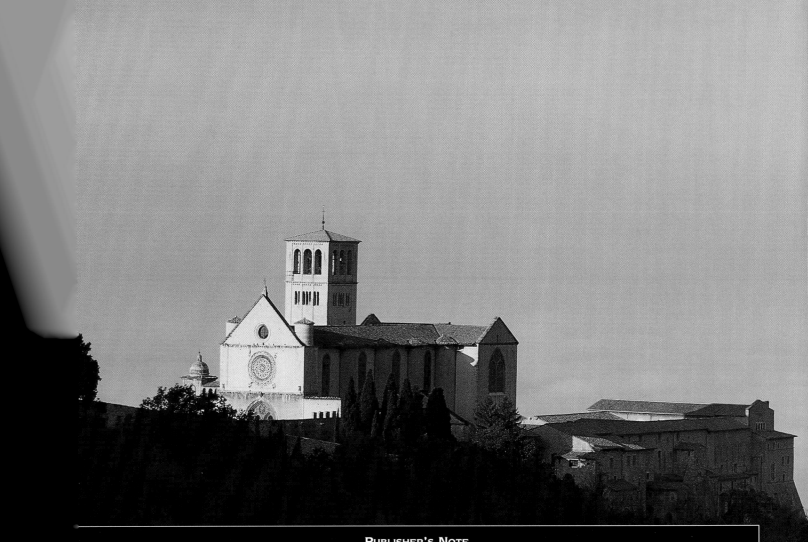

PUBLISHER'S NOTE
The following abbreviations are used in the text: b. = born, d. = died, r. = reigned,
c. = circa (about), f. = flourished. The adoption of the terms BC/AD in the text
rather than BCE/CE is the decision of the publishers and not the responsibility of
either the contributors or the consultant.

General editor • Fleur Robertson
Additional editing • Ron Hawkins, Martyn Bramwell
History consultant • Professor Kevin Repp
Americanization • Dr Susan Imhoff
Initial design concept, jacket and title pages • Phillip Clucas
Design concept and design • Nerissa Davies, Sue Mims
Additional design TT Designs • Design assistance • John O'Hara
Picture research • Phillip Clucas, Fleur Robertson
Production • Neil Randles, Karen Staff, Ruth Arthur

5008 Timelines of World History
Published in 1998 by CLB, an imprint of Quadrillion Publishing Ltd,
Godalming Business Centre, Woolsack Way, Godalming, Surrey, GU7 1XW, England
Distributed in the US by Quadrillion Publishing Inc., 230 Fifth Avenue, New York, NY 10001

Copyright © 1998 Quadrillion Publishing Ltd
All rights reserved. No part of this publication may be reproduced, stored in a
retrieval system or transmitted by any means, electronic, mechanical, photocopying
or otherwise, without the prior permission of the publisher.

ISBN 1-85833-854-9

Printed and bound in Dubai

TIMELINES
OF WORLD HISTORY

MAIN CONTRIBUTORS
Dr Susan Imhoff • Dr Ailbhe MacShamhráin
Richard Killeen

ADDITIONAL CONTRIBUTORS
Nigel Rodgers • Dr J. Aaron Frith
Professor Abebe Zegeye

CONSULTANT
Professor Kevin Repp
of Yale University History Faculty

CLB

CONTENTS

FOREWORD

It is a pleasure to introduce *Timelines of World History*, an impressive, colorful, and informative survey of the political, economic, social, intellectual, and cultural history of five diverse regions of the world that will be both interesting and useful for the general reader. The "equal time" allotted to culture and politics allows an especially rich tapestry of personalities and events to unroll from a variety of spreads, which are still more distinctive in lavishing attention on non-Western cultures. Something of a trailblazer in these respects, *Timelines of World History* seems to point the way not only for other books of its kind, but even for some world history textbooks that, despite a decade and a half of committed research and pedagogical experiments, still occasionally fall short of a balanced treatment one would like to see. In both structure and substance the present volume strives admirably toward this goal within its own bounds and, as a model of "edutainment," will prove fascinating as well as fortifying for inquisitive readers of all ages.

Professor Kevin Repp
Department of History, Yale University
Consultant for *Timelines of World History*

AFRICA

THE EMERGENCE OF MAN

Available evidence suggests that the African continent provided the earliest home for mankind. Africa escaped all five glaciations of the Ice Age, experiencing instead pluvial or wet periods interspaced with drier phases. Such climatic conditions perhaps favored the development of hominids, proto-human beings related to the ape but possessing a brain twice the size of that of their simian cousins. The ability of these proto-humans to stand and walk led modern anthropologists to classify the species concerned as *Homo erectus*. One advantage of an erect posture was that the hominids' hands were free for use. In addition, brain development meant that they could store and retrieve information. Unlike the ape, who might use a stick or stone to meet a passing need, the hominid could preplan and chose an implement in advance of the task. Besides, he could adapt the implement to better serve its purpose: mankind could invent! Many anthropologists classify hominids at this stage of development as *Homo habilis*, or "handy man." The capacity of these earliest humans to fashion tools is illustrated by certain African finds. While hominid skulls have been discovered at several locations from Kenya to Zambia to South Africa, the most significant finds are from Olduvai Gorge, Tanzania, where, at an occupation site some 1,750,000 years old, skeletal remains were associated with typologically early "chopper-tools." Apparently, these worked stones were mainly used for breaking up carcasses and scraping vegetation from the ground. The spread of this elementary technology from East Africa can be traced, chopper-tools being found at later sites in South Africa and, north of the Sahara, in Algeria and Morocco. After the Günz Glaciation, 500,000 years ago, chopper-tool manufacture spread into the adjacent continents of Europe and Asia.

THE LOWER PALEOLITHIC IN AFRICA

Long before this, around 600,000 years ago, the earliest recognizable Lower Paleolithic (Old Stone Age) culture emerged in East Africa and is represented at the higher levels of Olduvai Gorge. This Acheulian culture is characterized by the "hand axe," an all-purpose tool of flint used to cut down saplings, cut up meat, skin carcasses or root out vegetables. This tool had no handle, and was probably held in a wad of grass to protect the palm. These early East African people, still at a *Homo habilis* stage of development, camped on the plains where they hunted a range of animals including bison and deer. Gathering of vegetation for food was very much a secondary activity. The warm climate meant there was little need for clothing. Acheulian culture would survive in parts of East Africa for several hundred thousand years, as evidenced by finds from Kalambo Falls on the Tanzanian-Zambian border. Meanwhile, hand-axe technology spread northwestwards, broadly following the earlier route of the chopper-tools, being found at Oran in Algeria and Casablanca in Morocco. Some 250,000

Lower Paleolithic hand axe from Kathu Pan, South Africa.

years ago or more, hunter-toolmakers in North Africa had adopted the Levalloisian technique. This involved preparing a flint core so that, when struck, a single large oval flake with sharp edges could be removed. As the technique developed, the flakes became thinner and more blade-like. The preparation of animal-hides could now be more effective.

AFRICA'S MIDDLE AND UPPER PALEOLITHIC

Before the northern hemisphere's Würm Glaciation some 160,000 years ago, a Middle Paleolithic Levalloiso-Mousterian culture emerged in North Africa. Its technology, which included hand axes and scrapers, with pointed and knife-like implements, parallels the Mousterian cultures of Europe although it is not necessarily related. Similar cultures on other continents are associated with a "proto" *Homo sapiens* type which, on the evidence of ritual burials, already had some notion of religion. By Upper Paleolithic times, *Homo sapiens* proper had appeared in North Africa and is attested at the Haua Fteah cave in eastern Libya. The Dabba culture, which flourished in this region from about 100,000 years ago, with its range of tools including backed blades and *burins* for engraving, anticipates the Aurignacian found elsewhere. Later, perhaps 35,000 years ago, the Stillbay industries of south and east Africa would produce leaf-shaped spearheads and a variety of wooden-handled tools.

THE MESOLITHIC IN AFRICA

Climatic change, as the Ice Age drew to a close about 12,000 years ago, promoted forest growth. As open plains contracted, great herds of animals dwindled and hunting alone was less able to meet man's food requirements. With populations gravitating towards major river valleys, fishing and fowling gradually increased in importance along with the gathering of roots, fruits and wild cereals. Archaeologists term this stage of development the Mesolithic, or "Middle Stone Age," a phase which can sometimes be difficult to distinguish from the later Paleolithic. Prehistoric art appears somewhat late in Africa; carvings and rock paintings of the bubalu (buffalo) in the Sahara region and engravings of oxen in the Tassili mountains date to about 7000 BC. The Sandawe culture of Tanzania produced rock paintings of ritual significance, with male simbo dancers performing a shamanistic dance in which participants entered a trance-like state and saw visions of animals, ensuring success in the hunt. Northeast Africa was geographically advantaged, however, being closest to the Middle East, where the Natufian culture was already pioneering cereal cultivation and domestication of animals by *c.* 7000 BC, even if the production of pottery still lay in the future. As it happens, wild cattle and pigs were already present in North Africa. The stage was set for the introduction of Neolithic ("New Stone Age") cultures, characterized by food production, into the Nile Valley.

This hominid skull from Olduvai Gorge, Tanzania—over 1,750,000 years old—was found in association with chopper-tools.

7

5000	2000	1000	500	AD1	400	600

WESTERN AND CENTRAL ASIA

NEANDERTHALERS IN WESTERN ASIA AND EUROPE

The archaic humans called Neanderthalers (after a site in modern Germany) flourished in western Asia as well as Europe between 100,000 and 40,000 years ago. Recent evidence suggests that although they share a common ancestor, *Homo neanderthalensis* is not a direct predecessor of *Homo sapiens*, or modern humans, as was once thought. Nor were the Neanderthalers the clownish brutes of popular imagination: in fact, they are associated with the increasingly sophisticated technology of the Mousterian, or Middle Paleolithic, period of prehistoric culture. The Neanderthalers developed stone tools suited to a variety of tasks, such as cutting and preparing meat, scraping hides, and working with wood. With their skills, they were able to live in inhospitable regions previously uninhabited by humans.

Even more intriguing, a Neanderthal site at Shanidar in modern Iraq, dating from about 60,000 years ago, shows evidence of ritual practice and careful burial of the dead, suggesting early religion and perhaps belief in an afterlife. Some Neanderthal burials are those of aged or handicapped persons who must have been supported by the rest of the community, evidence perhaps of a sophisticated sense of social responsibility, or perhaps even of respect for the wisdom of the old or infirm. Whether such sentiments were communicated in "words" is debatable: anthropologists are divided over whether the vocal chords of Neanderthalers were sufficiently developed to permit true human speech.

NEOLITHIC CULTURES

The transitional Mesolithic period, characterized by the addition of some agricultural practices to nomadic life, is associated in western Asia with the Natufian people of Palestine and Syria. The earliest known Neolithic culture in the world, distinguished by the development of settled agriculture, domestication of animals, and pottery, was developed by the Natufians (or perhaps their successors) between 8000 and 6000 BC. Another Neolithic culture flourished in villages and towns in ancient Anatolia (Asia Minor, or the Asiatic portion of modern Turkey). Remains of textiles, stone and clay statuettes, wooden vessels, shrines, and houses with beautiful wall paintings at the Anatolian site of Çatal Hüyük suggest a highly developed culture, dated about 7000 BC. Evidence of Neolithic cultures from about 6000 BC has also been found near the Zagros Mountains in Iran, and from about 5000 BC along the shores of the Caspian Sea. Very little is known of the earliest cultures of Arabia.

Remains of Mesolithic and Neolithic cultures have been found scattered throughout modern India and Pakistan, dated as early as the sixth millennium BC. In southern India, Neolithic peoples made pottery using a potter's wheel, hollowed timbers, dressed skins, and made ornaments of conch shells, pearls, and gold beads. They farmed jungle clearings and domesticated dogs, oxen and goats. India, like Japan, did not have a true bronze age, but unlike Japan, this was not because metalworking culture was imported. Rather, in the south, iron came into use, and in the north, the people who eventually built the cities of Harappa and Mohenjo-Daro worked with copper instead of bronze.

LANGUAGES AND PEOPLES

The ancient Sumerian language that gave the world its first writing system appears to be unrelated to any of the languages that borrowed that system, such as the Semitic Akkadian languages (Old Akkadian, Assyrian, Babylonian), which belong to the Afroasiatic language group. Israeli Hebrew and modern Arabic are among the few languages of this group that survive in Asia. The many languages found throughout western and central Asia include representatives of the Indo-European and Altaic language groups. On the vast Indian subcontinent and neighboring islands, in addition to these, three or four more ancient language groups are represented, including the Dravidian languages now found only in southern India and Sri Lanka. The populations of Asia are as complex as their languages. In India alone, elements of almost every human type can be found in various admixtures, ranging from the darkest to the fairest skin color and with many distinctive physical characteristics.

CULTURE VS. GEOGRAPHY

India, like China, can lay claim to having one of the oldest continuous civilizations in the world. Unlike China, however, whose different peoples and successive ruling elites, even those of different ethnic origins, were linked by a common writing system (which also spread to Japan and Korea) and, later, by the Confucian principles that infused the unusually durable state bureaucracy, India remained diverse, and difficult, if not impossible, to unify. The very ancient Hindu religion provided some cohesion among the Indian regions, as did, to a lesser extent, the later Buddhist faith, but there was no single "state" language until the period of British rule in the nineteenth century.

Nonetheless, the great ancient civilization in India, like that of China in the east, came to dominate its surrounding regions. Along their borders these two dominant cultures mixed with local traditions as well as with each other. Tibet provides one example of an interesting native culture that was also influenced by each of its powerful neighbors. The old-fashioned notions of "further India" and "Indochina," which do not fully acknowledge the distinctive indigenous cultures of the region now called Southeast Asia, were nonetheless based on undeniable historical influences. These historical cultural influences sometimes take precedence in this book over any strict geographical boundaries between "Western and Central" and "East" Asia.

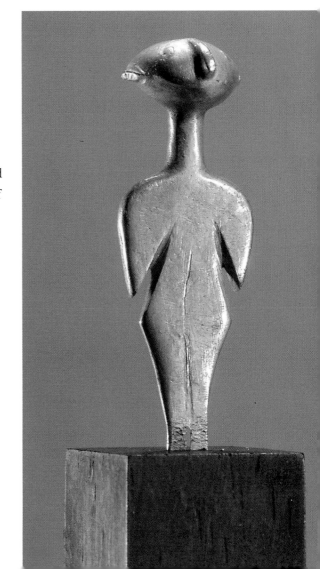

A type of female figurine from Neolithic Anatolia called a "bird-goddess" or "star-gazer."

5000	2000	1000	500	AD1	400	600

EAST ASIA AND THE PACIFIC

EARLY HUMANS IN EAST ASIA AND THE PACIFIC

Ancient skeletal remains of *Homo erectus*, a possible evolutionary precursor of modern humans, have been found southwest of Peking (Beijing) as well as on the Indonesian island of Java. Peking Man and Java Man lived about 500,000 years ago, used bone and stone tools, had knowledge of fire, and buried their dead. *Homo erectus* in China hunted dangerous game such as saber-toothed tigers, wild boars, and elephants; and split human marrow bones suggest cannibalism. *Homo sapiens*, or direct ancestors of modern humans, appeared at the beginning of the last ice age, perhaps as early as 65,000 BC, eventually displacing *Homo erectus*.

Human origins in Japan remain a mystery. Japan was once connected to the Asian mainland, as fossilized remains of ancient continental mammals make evident. Discovery of Paleolithic stone tools in the 1940s dramatically rewrote Japanese prehistory, suggesting that humans as well as animals may have used this ancient land bridge, instead of arriving much later by sea, as was previously thought. Some ancient peoples probably did arrive by sea, although the dates and routes are uncertain. The ancestors of the Ainu people of northern Japan, of different ethnic stock from the ancestors of the Chinese and Japanese peoples, may have arrived from Indonesia. Possibly these were the Jōmon people, whose relationship with their Paleolithic predecessors is unknown. Japanese Shintō myths share certain similarities with the mythologies of Indonesia and New Zealand, and there are resemblances between early Japanese and Polynesian architecture and marriage customs.

At least four different ancient peoples from Asia are known to be the ancestors of the inhabitants of the Pacific, including the possible relatives of the Ainu. Early migrations, from the Malay peninsula to Indonesia and some of the further islands, including New Guinea and other islands of Melanesia and Micronesia, would have been aided by land bridges or involved relatively easy sea journeys. The earliest inhabitants of Australia are usually thought to be *Homo sapiens* who arrived perhaps 50,000 years ago, but recent controversial dating of stone artifacts in northern Australia suggests the possibility that these first colonizers may have arrived much earlier, and may even have been *Homo erectus*.

PREHISTORIC CULTURAL PHASES

In east Asia, as in Europe, different regions passed at different times through the phases of increasing technological sophistication used by archaeologists to characterize prehistoric human development. It is usual, for example, to distinguish between Paleolithic and subsequent Mesolithic cultures by different methods of making tools and implements. However, in east Asia, as in the Americas, the identification of these phases is not quite as informative as it is for European and western Asian cultures, which provided nineteenth-century archaeologists with their initial models of cultural development. This is especially true of the later phases: Japan, for example, had no true bronze age, since metalworking culture was simply imported from the Asian mainland, while the natives of Australia and New Guinea never had a bronze age at all. Some of these natives, especially in remote regions, still live more or less as their Paleolithic ancestors did.

In China, the shift from Paleolithic to Mesolithic cultures is indistinct, although more sophisticated stone blades were produced in the north (Mongolia), and in the south early pottery appeared. The transition to the Neolithic phase is defined by settled agricultural development and domestication of animals. Agriculture may have begun as early as 6800 BC, with rice farming in Thailand, but it is usual to consider the Huang He (Yellow River) valley of northern China as the earliest east Asian agricultural center. The land here was covered with a fine yellow dust blown in from central Asian deserts near the end of the last ice age. This *loess* was easy to work and fertile when watered, and agriculture may have begun as early as 4000 BC. The loess is also easily transformed into unstable and impassable mud; both the ease and the difficulties of handling this soil have typified northern Chinese farming for centuries.

Neolithic Chinese farmers domesticated many animals, including dogs, pigs, and goats. They lived in sturdy thatched houses, partly underground, with stoves, ovens, and plaster or beaten earth floors. Spindles for weaving have been found, as well as cut silkworm cocoons, evidence that silkworm-breeding in China is extremely ancient. Community leaders were evidently women: their comparatively richer burial sites suggest a matriarchal culture, which also seems to have been the case in early Korea and Japan.

LANGUAGES

The cultural variety of Asia and the Pacific is suggested by the number of ancient language groups. In contrast to Europe, where most languages derive from one ancient language group, Indo-European, there are at least three groups in Asia. The Sino-Tibetan group comprises the various languages of modern China, Tibet, Thailand, Laos, most of Burma, and perhaps Vietnam. The Altaic group includes the languages of the northern nomads, such as Turkish, Mongolian, and Tungusic; Japanese and Korean may also be in this group. In mainland Southeast Asia, some Sinitic languages are spoken, but there are also languages belonging to the Malayo-Polynesian or Austronesian group: these are spoken in the Philippines, Indonesia, and Malaysia, as well as by the original inhabitants of Taiwan. The Cambodian Khmer were thought until recently to belong to yet another language group; but their language may be distantly related to Vietnamese. Australian aboriginal languages, Papuan languages, and the language of the Ainu are apparently unrelated any of these groups or to each other.

A NOTE ON TRANSCRIPTION

There are various methods of transcribing Asian languages into English. Transcriptions of Chinese are particularly varied; the older Wade-Giles system (e.g., "Peking") has in some cases been superseded by the Pinyin system (e.g., "Beijing") developed during the Cultural Revolution, and intended to more accurately reflect current pronunciation. Wherever possible, alternative spellings are given; but usage in this book has been dictated by an admittedly subjective sense of familiarity for native English speakers. For example, the older spelling "Ch'in" has been preferred to the Pinyin "Jin" in the discussion of the dynasty that gave rise to the English name "China."

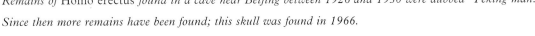

Remains of Homo erectus *found in a cave near Beijing between 1926 and 1930 were dubbed "Peking man." Since then more remains have been found; this skull was found in 1966.*

5000	2000	1000	500	AD1	400	600

EUROPE

MAN'S ARRIVAL IN EUROPE: THE LOWER PALEOLITHIC

It seems reasonable that earliest humans reached Europe from Africa and from Asia, crossing from Morocco into Iberia and also making their way up the Danube Valley. Some vague indications of early Paleolithic occupation, including flint flakes, have been noted at Vallonet Cave in southeast France. It has been suggested that this occupation dates back some 500,000 years, but the evidence is inconclusive. Chopper-tool industries had made their way into Europe by the time of the Günz Glaciation. A rather late chopper-tool phase was centered around Budapest during an interstadial (or mild period) in the Riss Glaciation 200,000 years ago or more. A curious aspect of this particular phase is that it appears to be associated not with *Homo habilis*, but with an early form of *Homo sapiens*. By the end of the Riss, about 190,000 years ago, the Lower Paleolithic Acheulian culture had begun to spread throughout Europe. Although the term has been broadly applied to technologically similar cultures characterized by the production of hand axes and cleavers, including hand-axe cultures originating in other continents, the Acheulian in its "classical" sense owes its name to the site of St. Acheul in northern France. By the same token, the Levalloisian technique of striking flakes from prepared cores is so named from a French site. Nomadic hunter-cultures using hand-axe technology of Acheulian type spread across Atlantic Europe, from the Iberian peninsula through France to southern England, and along the Mediterranean, via Italy and Greece, reaching as far as Turkey. Penetration into northern Europe, however, was limited.

THE MIDDLE AND UPPER PALEOLITHIC IN EUROPE

In Europe the Mousterian culture, which had begun to flourish about 150,000 years ago, is associated with a relatively developed human type which, from an occupation site in Germany, has been termed *Homo neanderthalensis*. Hunters and cave-dwellers, who had to endure colder climates than many of their contemporaries on other continents, the Neanderthals produced a range of flint tools. In addition to hand-axes, the prevalence of pointed flints and rounded scrapers may reflect a need to prioritize the preparation of animal skins for clothing. For the first time, there are indications of religion or at least of belief in an afterlife. At several locations, human remains have been found buried in dwelling caves. At Monte Circeo in Italy, a skull which shows signs of deliberate opening seems to suggest ritual cannibalism. In some modern primitive societies it was believed that a chieftain who consumed part of his predecessor's brain would inherit the latter's qualities. It appears that Middle Paleolithic Europeans had already discovered warfare: at least one Neanderthal skeleton bears marks of a

The "Venus figurine" from Willendorf (lower Austria), 4¹/₄ in. in height, is carved from limestone. It is believed to be some 20,000 years old.

spear wound in its side. The arrival of Upper Paleolithic cultures into Europe from Asia, including the Aurignacian with its "steep" scrapers and the Gravettian with its backed blades, is difficult to pinpoint, but dates of around 40,000 BC have been suggested. Both cultures feature the *burin*, or engraving tool. Europe's Upper Paleolithic sequence is best illustrated in France, culminating in the Magdalenian culture which lasted until about 10,000 BC. These hunter peoples continued to work in flint but expanded their range of tools and weapons through bone-working, producing spearheads and harpoons. The development of basic sewing techniques using bone needles and leather thongs meant that clothing could be produced more effectively. Art in the form of cave paintings has been found at Altamira in Spain and at several locations in France including Niaux and Lascaux; at the latter site, discovered in 1940, the artist's subjects included bulls, deer and horses. Typically, these paintings were executed in deep cave recesses which were difficult to access and where the work could only have been carried out by artificial light. In all likelihood, this was provided by "candles" fashioned from reeds dipped in fat. The occurrence of heavily indented footprints in front of some paintings has prompted archaeologists to suggest that the artwork was the focus of ritual dances aimed at bringing success in the hunt. Another art medium, figure carving, also features in Upper Paleolithic Europe. Produced in a variety of materials from bone to limestone, these sculptures included representations of animals, such as the horse head from La Madeleine, and female figurines like those from Dolni Vestonice, Moravia, or Willendorf, Austria. Often grotesque with exaggerated hips and breasts, these so-called "Venus figurines" are thought to be the products of a fertility cult.

THE MESOLITHIC IN EUROPE

Climatic change from about 10,000 BC and the gradual encroachment of forest promoted, as it did in other continents, the emergence of Mesolithic cultures with a greater emphasis on fishing and the gathering of wild vegetation. As elsewhere, population groups gravitated towards coasts and river valleys. In northern Europe the Maglemosian culture, evidenced at such sites as Klosterlund in Denmark and Star Carr in England, was at least equally concerned with fishing as with hunting. Harpoons are amongst the most common Maglemosian finds, while some locations have produced bows and arrows. Antler headgear has also been found, but whether these represent ritual or status head-dress, or hunting disguises, is not certain. Further south, in the Mediterranean region, the Mesolithic manifested itself in the Tardenoisian culture. Primarily hunter-gatherers like their northern contemporaries, the Tardenoisians had begun by about 6000 BC to domesticate animals. These developments, however, would be overtaken by the introduction to Europe of Late Stone Age, or Neolithic, farming cultures.

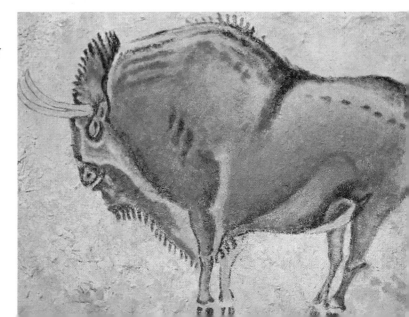

Part of the cave-painting from Altamira, Spain, discovered in 1878. Featuring a bison, the painting is of Upper Paleolithic date (21,000 to 13,000 BC).

5000	2000	1000	500	AD1	400	600

THE AMERICAS

EARLY HUMANS IN THE AMERICAS

All the skeletal remains of ancient humans that have been found in the Americas are those of *Homo sapiens*, or direct ancestors of modern humans. It is now generally agreed that the first discoverers of the Americas crossed over the ancient land bridge (sometimes called Beringia) that once connected northern Asia with North America. There is little agreement, however, about when this discovery took place or whether it was one migratory wave or several. Certainly the date of arrival continues to recede into the past. One of the earliest proposed dates is 50,000 years ago, and some archaeological evidence suggests dates of between 40,000 and 30,000 years ago. The most conservative estimates place the arrival or arrivals between 20,000 and 10,000 years ago.

One recent theory proposes that humans of three distinct Asian ethnic stocks migrated to the Americas, of which only one reached Mesoamerica. Of these particularly venturesome hunter-gatherers, only a few continued further south into South America. This theory may offer some explanation for similar distinctive cultural features among otherwise very different South American peoples. Recent controversial dating of a site in Brazil places humans there as early as 32,000 years ago. There is more general agreement that humans had reached the southern tip of South America by about 9000 BC.

LITHIC AND ARCHAIC CULTURES

In the Americas, as in parts of Asia, the archaeological phases of culture systematized in the nineteenth century from European and western Asian examples are sometimes inadequate characterizations of American developments. For example, the Archaic Old Copper culture of the Great Lakes region (*c.* 4000-1500 BC), made tools and ornaments of copper, but is not considered a Bronze Age metalworking culture, as the Harappan culture of ancient northern India sometimes is, even though the Harappans too worked in copper (rather than bronze). Unlike the Harappans, the Old Copper peoples are not associated with urbanization and increasing social stratification. Another example is the difficulty of classifying peoples who were hunter-gatherers but who lived a settled existence rather than a migratory one, as did several ancient peoples in South America.

In the Americas, therefore, somewhat different systems of prehistorical classification are used. The earliest period is called Lithic or Paleo-Indian. Paleo-Indians were migratory hunters of woolly mammoths, mastodons, saber-toothed tigers, horses, and other game until about 8000 BC, or just after the end of the last Ice Age. Many of the animals hunted by the Paleo-Indians

An ancient carved stone head found in the area of the Salish peoples of the Fraser River Valley in northwestern North America.

disappeared, perhaps because of climatic changes or excessive hunting or both. During the most ancient Lithic phase, Paleo-Indians used implements of stone and bone, and wooden spears without stone points. The second phase of the Lithic period was characterized by new stone technologies (including stone spear points) with distinctive regional styles. The oldest of these cultures in North America are the southwestern Sandia culture and the more widespread Clovis culture. These were superseded after about 8000 BC by the Folsom peoples, who probably invented the *atlatl*, or spear-thrower, which became widely used. The Plano or Plainview peoples of the Great Plains developed means of preserving meat with animal fat and berries, and the Desert Indians were skillful basketmakers. In South America remains at Monte Verde in Chile that are about 13,000 years old show a culture of hunter-gatherers who may have used slingshots armed with stones as well as ancient bolas, and who lived in wooden dwellings clustered near a wooden ceremonial center.

During the Archaic period, which lasted from about 6000 to 1000 BC, American Indians adapted at different times and in different ways to the post-glacial environment, and increasingly developed regional characteristics. The Archaic period is roughly comparable to the transitional Mesolithic period in Europe: foraging and hunting was supplemented by some agriculture, domestication of some animals (such as the dog), and more settled life in communities. Archaic Indians also made ornaments and practiced elaborate rituals and burials. In North America, the Mississippi River divided the cultures of the lush Eastern Woodlands, such as the Old Copper culture, from the traditions of the more barren West, such as the Cochise Desert culture in what is now New Mexico and Arizona. The Cochise peoples, coping with a harsh environment, were the ancestors of the sophisticated Mogollon, Hohokum, and Anasazi peoples. Another intriguing Archaic culture in North America is that of the Red Paint people of what is now New England and northeastern coastal Canada, who buried their dead in graves lined with finely ground red hematite.

AGRICULTURE

The oldest domesticated plants in the Americas, found in a cave in the Andes, are about ten thousand years old, and may have been raised to provide materials for clothing, bedding, shelter and the like, rather than for food. Agriculture is generally considered to have begun in Mesoamerica, perhaps as early as 7000 BC, and to have spread northwards (and perhaps southwards) from there. Villages and city-states also eventually developed in Mesoamerica, generally recognized signs of increasingly complex social organization. Yet other Indians, such as the peoples of the Pacific Northwest, also developed highly complex social organizations without an agricultural base.

LANGUAGES

The many different American Indian languages do not belong to any one language group. In fact, nowhere in the world is there such diversity of languages as in the Americas. At least ten different language groups have been identified in the Americas, each containing a number of languages. Some early pictographic and ideographic writing systems developed in Mesoamerica, but these were rare. Alternative means of communicating were developed, such as the *quipu* knot system used by the Incas, or the sign language used as a *lingua franca* by the different peoples of the North American plains. Many American Indian languages are still spoken today.

15

5000	2000	1000	500	AD1	400	600

- *c.* 5000 BC Chincoros culture in north Chile; mummification techniques.

- *c.* 4500 BC Stone Age ends in Egypt, as copper is first used for ornaments and weapons.

- *c.* 4000 BC Domestication of horses on the steppes north of the Black Sea.

- *c.* 4000-1500 BC Old Copper Culture around North American Great Lakes.

- *c.* 3500 BC Sumerian civilization in Lower Mesopotamia.

- *c.* 3500 BC Union of various kingdoms to form single kingdom of Upper Egypt.

- *c.* 3250 BC Sumerians invent the wheel and later the chariot.

- *c.* 3200 BC Earliest surviving evidence of writing in temple at Uruk in Mesopotamia.

- *c.* 3100 BC Menes, king of Egypt, the first historical figure whose name is known to us.

- *c.* 3000 BC First evidence of the plow in Egypt and Mesopotamia.

- *c.* 3000 BC Foundation of the cities of Harappa and Mohenjo-Daro in the Indus Valley.

- *c.* 3000-1000 BC Ancestors of Aleuts and Eskimos voyage to North America from East Asia.

- *c.* 2700 BC Early Minoan period in Crete (-2000).

- *c.* 2630 BC First Egyptian step pyramids built in reign of Pharaoh Djoser.

- *c.* 2600 BC Huang Ti founds the Chinese nation and becomes its first emperor.

- *c.* 2500 BC First dynasty of Ur in Sumeria.

- *c.* 2500 BC Zenith of Egyptian Old Kingdom; pyramids of Giza and Great Pyramid of Khufu.

- 2330 BC b. Sargon the Great (d. 2305), conquers Sumeria and creates Akkadian empire.

- *c.* 2300 BC Mongoloid people settle Korea.

- 2230 BC Death of Naram Sin, grandson of Sargon, signals decline of Akkadian empire.

- *c.* 2180 BC Guti peoples destroy Akkadian capital, ending world's first empire.

- *c.* 2100 BC Beginning of Egyptian Middle Kingdom (-1784).

"Sage-kings" and Shamans

The beginnings of civilization in east Asia are lost to time. According to tradition, the clan-based farming villages of China's northern plain first united in 2600 BC under the "Yellow Emperor" Huang-Ti, who was one of the eight "sage-kings" or "culture heroes." In 2205 BC, the last of these legendary rulers, Yu the Great, supposedly founded China's first dynasty, the Hsia (or Xia). Archaeologists have found no trace of the Hsia's actual existence, however, and the origins of the Chinese nation remain enshrouded in myth. We can say even less about Australia's nomadic aborigines, who were apparently linked by vast trade networks during this period. Aboriginal societies, which survived essentially intact for another 4000 years, had no centralized power structures. They rested instead on kinship and ritual—although

some individuals may have attained localized authority as shamans who enjoyed access to a spiritual plane called the Dreaming.

Petroglyph incised in the rock at an aboriginal sacred site, Australia.

Early Egypt

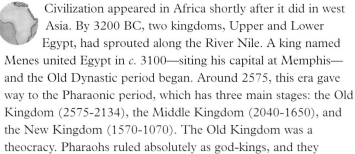

Civilization appeared in Africa shortly after it did in west Asia. By 3200 BC, two kingdoms, Upper and Lower Egypt, had sprouted along the River Nile. A king named Menes united Egypt in *c.* 3100—siting his capital at Memphis—and the Old Dynastic period began. Around 2575, this era gave way to the Pharaonic period, which has three main stages: the Old Kingdom (2575-2134), the Middle Kingdom (2040-1650), and the New Kingdom (1570-1070). The Old Kingdom was a theocracy. Pharaohs ruled absolutely as god-kings, and they commanded an elite of priests, nobles and civil servants. Most Egyptians, though, were peasants who supplied labor for the pharaohs' massive building projects, the most impressive being Khufu's Great Pyramid at Giza in 2500. Around 2134, the Old Kingdom ended in revolution, and there followed a century of chaos called the First Intermediate Period, during which political authority was fragmented among local monarchs.

Khufu's Great Pyramid and the mysterious Sphinx at Giza.

800	1000	1200	1400	1600	1800	2000

A detail from the so-called "Standard of Ur". The top panel shows a banquet; the bottom, drovers driving livestock.

The Sumerians

Around 3500 BC, the first civilization, Sumer, arose between the Tigris and Euphrates rivers in southern Mesopotamia, or modern Iraq. Early Sumer consisted of independent city-states organized around temples and ruled by a priestly class. Chronic warfare between the city-states, however, gave rise to warrior-kings who vied for control of Sumer. In 2500, the king Mesanepada founded the First Dynasty of Ur and established his city as the Sumerian capital. Later, the legendary Gilgamesh made Uruk ascendant. But in 2330, Sargon the Great of Akkad conquered Sumer's cities to create the world's first empire. Akkadian rule collapsed in 2230 when Akkad fell to mountain peoples called the Gutians. In 2100, king Ur-Nammu established the Third Dynasty of Ur (little is known of the Second Dynasty) and produced the earliest known lawbook. Ur stood as a wealthy center of commerce and worship until the Elamites razed it around 1900 BC.

Stonehenge

Agriculture reached southeastern Europe during the sixth millennium BC and spread throughout the continent by about 3500 BC. As a result, farming villages sprang up all across Europe, ranging from the Sesklo and Dimini in Thessaly to the Iberian and Beaker cultures of southern England. These societies were preliterate, and so their political configurations are difficult to ascertain. Like other Neolithic peoples, they probably organized into patrilineal kin groups and were ruled by chieftains and shamans. The profoundly religious orientation of early Europeans—as well as their impressive engineering and mathematical skill—can be seen in the great megaliths they constructed, the most famous of which is Stonehenge in England. Built of stones weighing up to twenty-five tons, these monuments were possibly used to observe the stars and predict the passage of the seasons—an ability that may have bestowed both spiritual and temporal authority on certain individuals.

Stonehenge, possibly a prehistoric solar observatory, Salisbury Plain, southern England.

Settled Agriculture and the Growth of Villages

By 2000 BC, many peoples in the Americas had begun to lay the groundwork for large-scale civilization by making the crucial transition from hunting-gathering to settled agriculture. Although tribes in Arctic regions and the Great Plains retained a nomadic lifestyle, the cultivation of crops such as maize, squash and sunflowers allowed villages to flourish in diverse regions, from Mesoamerica and the Central Andes to the Northwest, Southwest, and Eastern Woodlands of the present-day United States. In most cases, these settlements were governed by councils of elders, who represented local families. The elders in turn selected a chief – usually a man but sometimes a woman – to preside over the council. Commonly, several villages banded together to form a loose alliance, and families often linked across villages as clan groups. Native American villages also gave rise to full-time religious leaders and the construction of shrines, totems and permanent temples.

Section of a totem pole from the American northwest.

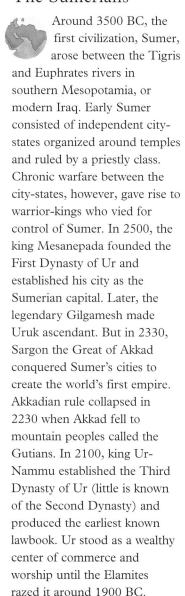

5000	2000	1000	500	AD1	400	600

Neolithic Farmers

From about 4000 BC, economic and cultural developments characteristic of the Neolithic, or New Stone Age, were carried into Europe from Africa and Asia Minor along the waterways of the Mediterranean and the Danube. adopting agricultural techniques, Europeans began to cultivate crops and to domesticate goats, sheep and cattle. Settlements of a more permanent character replaced the hunter-gatherer camps: some communities built rectangular log houses, others lakeside dwellings composed of circular thatched huts raised on wooden platforms. As with neighboring continents at an earlier date, steady food supply promoted stability and facilitated specialization of labor. Stone axe-heads were shaped, polished and fitted with handles. These Neolithic farmers produced Europe's earliest pottery. By about 3500 BC, the custom of erecting massive stone structures for funerary and ceremonial purposes was already extending into western Europe. Built from gigantic stones, or megaliths, tombs enclosing cremated remains and goods are evidence of formal religion, and suggest a highly organized society. Various megalithic monuments, including Stonehenge in Britain dating from about 2000 BC, are aligned with the midsummer (or midwinter) solstice.

A Neolithic lake dwelling at Lake Zurich, after a painting by W. Kranz.

Egyptian Old Kingdom

The fifth millennium BC saw Neolithic cultures emerge in Northeast Africa, as knowledge of agriculture diffused from the Middle East. Hunter-gatherers settled along the Nile and learned irrigation methods, utilizing canals and the *shaduf* for lifting water buckets. They grew corn and raised goats, sheep and cattle; the cow-goddess Hathor was worshipped by early Nile farmers. Settlements like Memphis and Thebes evolved into cities heralding the earliest high civilization of Africa, the Old Kingdom of Egypt. Tradition claims that Menes united the kingdoms of Upper and Lower Egypt *c.* 3100 BC, establishing his capital at Memphis. Already, metallurgy was known: bronze chisels cut blocks for the step-pyramid of Pharaoh Djoser *c.* 2700 BC. Later, mathematical advances facilitated the construction of true pyramids. Craftsmen produced wheel-turned pottery and woven cloth: plain white kilts for men and long gowns for women. By this time, Egyptians had developed picture writing—hieroglyphics—mainly for temple inscriptions. Knowledge of farming was carried southwest to the Niger by *c.* 2000 BC and westwards across the northern Sahara, where rock paintings record scenes of daily life.

The step-pyramid of Maidum, built for Pharaoh Snefru of the Fourth Dynasty.

Early Chinese Civilization

Neolithic cultures can be dated to the sixth millennium BC in China, where agriculture apparently developed independently in at least three regions. Near the bend of the Yellow River (Huang He) in north China, the principal crops were millet, hemp, and mulberries (for silkworms); in the lower Yangtze River valley, the major crop was rice; and on the southeast coast early farmers grew tubers and roots. The Yang-Shao culture in the Wei River valley in the northern region produced painted pottery with geometric designs in red, white and black; further east and somewhat later, the Lung Shan culture produced elegant glossy black pottery. Although there is disagreement about which agricultural region may have produced the first "civilization" in East Asia—as characterized by, for example, the formation of cities and the development of writing—the northern plain is usually considered the birthplace of Chinese civilization. Flourishing about the second millennium BC, later than the civilizations which emerged in Egypt, Mesopotamia, and the Indus Valley, the Chinese civilization is still one of the oldest in the world. In contrast to these other ancient cultures, Chinese civilization has also proven remarkably durable, retaining much of its essential identity for present-day inhabitants of China.

The Yang-Shao people made pottery in a variety of shapes, painted with geometric designs or stylized representations of human faces and of fish.

800	1000	1200	1400	1600	1800	2000

The First Cities

The world's first cities, differentiated from villages by specialized occupations and the presence of an elite of warriors, priests, and administrators, appeared in Mesopotamia between about 3500 and 3200 BC. Ancient Mesopotamia was situated between the Tigris and Euphrates rivers, a fertile plain subject to periodic flooding but needing irrigation for regular farming. Planning and overseeing the necessary labor for building and maintaining canals was undoubtedly a part of the social development that led to the growth of cities in southern Mesopotamia, in a region known as Sumer. Here, about 3200 BC, the earliest forms of writing were invented. This alone would make the ancient Sumerians memorable, but they also invented the wheel and the lunar calendar. The independent "city-states" of Sumer, such as Uruk, Ur, and Lagash, were eventually unified into one realm about 2320 BC by the warrior king Sargon the Great from Akkad in northern Mesoptamia. About this time, the Mesopotamians also traded with the Indus Valley civilization (in modern Pakistan), whose achievements appear to rival those of Mesopotamia and Egypt. The ruins of the principle cities, Mohenjo-Daro and Harappa, show sophisticated urban construction and also yield small, graceful figurines as well as seals with a still-undeciphered script.

The head of a bearded golden bull ornaments a stringed instrument found in a king's tomb in the ancient city of Ur.

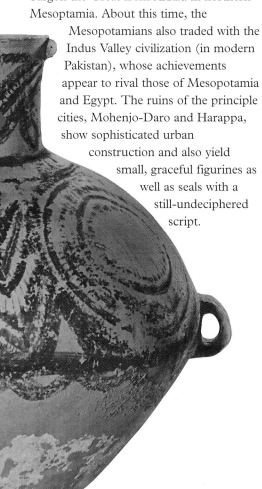

Archaic Americans

Changes in early American cultures about 5000 BC (or earlier) marked the shift from the Lithic to the Archaic or Foraging period, characterized by different hunting techniques (following the extinction of the great mammals), gathering and early domestication of plants, and elaborate burial rituals. Archaic peoples used specialized tools made of available regional materials, such as wood, stone, bone, ivory, shell, and plant fibers. The people of the Old Copper culture (*c.* 4000-1500 BC) near the Great Lakes were unique among northern Indians in making tools and ornaments of copper. Aleuts and Inuits migrated from Siberia to North America in small boats between 3000 and 1000 BC. In Mesoamerica, cultivation of plants such as maize (corn), squash, pumpkins, and peppers began earlier than in more northerly regions, spreading as far as the Cochise people of present-day New Mexico by about 3500 BC. Mesoamericans also began to make pottery, which by 2000 BC had spread to much of North America. Among South Americans, the sophisticated Chincoros fisherfolk of northern Chile began living in settled communities about 5000 BC

and were the first people in the world to artificially mummify their dead. Their process reached its full complexity by the third millennium BC, or about the time the Egyptians began their own mummification procedures.

Bannerstones such as these from the Eastern Woodlands peoples of North America were used to weight wooden spear-throwers called atlatls. Use of this new hunting weapon became widespread in the Americas during the Archaic period.

ANCIENT EMPIRES

I am yesterday; I know tomorrow.
from the Egyptian *Book of the Dead*

Historians like to say that "History begins in Sumer." In one sense, this refers to the invention of writing in Mesopotamia, which quite literally created the boundary between the prehistorical world of archaeological research and the historical world of documented narrative. Yet the invention of writing is only one aspect of the extraordinary transformation that occurred first in the lower valley of Mesopotamia, between the Tigris and Euphrates rivers, and was soon echoed in many other regions of the globe. With amazing rapidity, relatively speaking, humans moved from simple agricultural settlements and early cities to complex civilizations with highly sophisticated social organization. The architectural achievements of the centers of these civilizations were often so imposing that even the ruins still astound modern observers.

Impressive as they are architecturally, these monuments are perhaps more intriguing for what they represent: the central administration of extensive political, military, religious and economic organization of a kind far surpassing the social cooperation needed to construct the earliest cities. The development of writing led to the ability to track, record and control the allocation of resources over a wide region from one location, where an elite class of priests and scribes served a single powerful ruler, often regarded as semi-divine or even as a deity. Laws, codified in written form, could be standardized and administered over an extended territory. Large armies could be raised and commanded from this central location, and religious, literary, and artistic influences disseminated easily. The earliest of these ancient empires, or "palace-centered cultures," as they are sometimes called, emerged *c.* 3000 BC in Sumer and Egypt. Within a short time, other cultures,

distinctive but with similar features, arose in other regions: the Indus Valley civilization, about 2700 BC; the Minoans of Crete, about 2200 BC; the Shang civilization of China, about 1766 BC; and the Olmecs in the Americas, about 1200 BC.

TURMOIL IN MESOPOTAMIA AND STABILITY IN EGYPT

The remarkable inventions of Sumerian culture, including their cuneiform system of writing, were adopted by neighboring peoples to the north, east, and west as far as the Mediterranean, even though these peoples spoke different languages from the Sumerians. Sumerian city-states, walled for protection, had magnificent palaces and multi-tiered temples (*ziggurats*) that inspired imitation by their neighbors when they did not simply take them over or demolish and rebuild them along similar lines. For these reasons Sumerian culture persisted long past the time when the Sumerians themselves were powerful. The first significant invasion, and the first unification of the independent city-states of Sumer, was led by a warrior king called Sargon the Great from Akkad, north of Sumer, about 2320 BC. According to legend, he washed his weapons in the waters of the Arabian Gulf when he arrived there, to signify the end of warfare. It was short-lived; the history of Mesopotamia is one of successive conquest by various peoples. The Sargonid dynasty was soon followed by the Amorites, then by the Assyrians, the Hittites, and the Chaldeans. All of them, however, owed something of their cultures to the early Sumerians.

By the time Sargon achieved his conquest, Egyptians had constructed many of the monuments that continue to fascinate the modern world. The regions of upper and lower Egypt (not, as a modern reader might assume, northern and southern Egypt, but

the reverse, following the flow of the Nile to the Mediterranean Sea) were first united by a king known as Menes, who is also credited with founding the city of Memphis and initiating the first dynasty, about 2920 BC. Little is known about the pharaohs of the first two dynasties, but the founder of the Third Dynasty, Djoser (Zoser), is remembered for ordering the construction of the first Egyptian pyramid. Called the Step Pyramid from its tiered design, it was constructed about 2630 BC. During the Fourth Dynasty (c. 2575-2465 BC), Egyptian culture experienced a brilliant flowering. The pyramids of Giza and the monumental Sphinx, with its implacable visage of the pharaoh Khafre, were completed. Hieroglyphic writing, which first appeared about 3000 BC, was in common usage among the elite. Fine arts, literature, and trade also flourished.

CONTACT BETWEEN EMPIRES AND ISOLATED EMPIRES

Some ancient empires were linked to each other by trade. The Sumerians traded with the Indus Valley civilization in modern Pakistan and northern India. The people of the Indus civilization constructed cities such as Harappa and Mohenjo-Daro. Each was planned on a grid pattern, with a citadel and a residential section with sophisticated plumbing. Similarities in artistic representation suggest that the Indus religion may have influenced the earliest development of Hinduism. In the Mediterranean, Egyptians sailed from the Nile delta across the sea to trade with the Minoans on Crete, whose civilization blossomed after *c.* 2000 BC. Protected by their island location, the Minoans were, like the Egyptians, a peaceable people, whose cities boasted beautiful palaces and whose religion was matriarchal. Their script, like that of the Indus civilization, remains incompletely deciphered.

The Egyptian pyramids at Giza, an unparalleled feat of architecture completed during the Fourth Dynasty (c. 2575 - 2465 BC). The largest pyramid, the Great Pyramid of Cheops, is one of the Seven Wonders of the Ancient World.

Completely isolated from these cultures, but about the time of the mysterious destruction of the Indus Valley cities *c.* 1750 BC (perhaps by Aryan invaders, perhaps by natural disaster), the Shang civilization developed in China. Shang rulers commanded large armies whose generals rode in horse-drawn war chariots. The bronze-casting techniques of the Shang have never been surpassed, and their written language is unique among ancient languages in still being legible to modern Chinese readers. The youngest of the ancient empires, that of the Olmecs of Mexico, arose *c.* 1200 BC, also in isolation. Their ceremonial centers were unusual in not being urban. Olmec traditions influenced many later Mesoamerican peoples, including the Maya. Indeed, all these ancient empires set standards for social organization that have been guiding principles for later generations. *S.I.*

21

5000	2000	1000	500	AD1	400	600

- *c.* 2000 BC Mainland Mongols invade Japan, displacing primordial Ainu people.

- *c.* 2000 BC Indo-European peoples spread their languages from Bengal to Ireland.

- *c.* 2000 BC Rise of Dong-Son culture in Vietnam; spreads across Southeast Asia.

- *c.* 2000 BC First bronze casting, Western Asia.

- *c.* 2000 BC Middle Minoan period on Crete: palace at Knossos.

- *c.* 2000 BC Rise of Old Babylon.

- *c.* 2000 BC Emergence of Pre-Classical Mayan civilization.

- *c.* 1900 BC Aryans begin to push into India, displacing their Dravidian predecessors.

- *c.* 1766 BC Rise of Shang dynasty in north-eastern China.

- *c.* 1600 Hittites from Anatolia penetrate northern borders of Babylonian empire.

- *c.* 1600 BC Mycenaean civilization rises to dominate eastern Mediterranean.

- 1570 BC Egyptian New Kingdom (-1070).

- *c.* 1500 BC Rise of Olmec civilization, Mexico.

- *c.* 1500 BC Destruction of Minoan civilization; eruption of Thera.

- *c.* 1469 BC Megiddo in Palestine, first recorded battle in history.

- *c.* 1400 BC Earliest known Native American town established near Vicksburg, Mississippi.

- *c.* 1400 BC Construction begins at Sechín Alto, the Andes, the largest monumental site in early American architecture.

- *c.* 1400 BC Iron Age in Western Asia and India.

- *c.* 1400 BC Development of Hindu culture of the Ganges valley.

- *c.* 1380 BC Hittite empire under Suppiluliumasi.

- 1304 BC Accession of Rameses II, whose kingdom stretched from Nubia to the Delta.

- *c.* 1300 BC Assyria gradually supplants Babylon.

- 1271 BC Egyptian-Hittite border between Palestine and Syria.

- *c.* 1250 BC Moses leads the Jewish people in flight from Egypt into Palestine.

- *c.* 1200 BC End of Mycenaean civilization.

- *c.* 1200 BC Siege of and destruction of Troy VIIa, probably the Troy of *The Illiad*.

- 1116 BC Tiglathpileser I establishes Assyrian power from the Gulf to the Mediterranean.

The Olmecs

 The first major civilization in the Americas was the Olmec, situated along the Gulf Coast of modern Mexico. Emerging around 1200 BC, the Olmecs had four urban centers—San Lorenzo, La Venta, Laguna de los Cerros, and Tres Zapotes—which may have succeeded one another as the seat of government. The details of Olmec political organization are unknown, but the *stelae*, or stone carvings, these peoples left behind seemingly depict their rulers as gods, suggesting a theocracy. At any rate, the construction of large stone altars and ceremonial platforms almost certainly indicates that power was concentrated in the hands of an elite few who directed the labors of the many, and it is likely that a caste system based on lineage and wealth ordered Olmec society. Through trade, diplomacy and possibly even warfare, the Olmecs stimulated social and cultural development throughout Mesoamerica

The Middle and New Kingdoms

Ancient Egypt's Middle Kingdom period began in 2040 BC when Mentuhotep II restored order and established a new capital at Thebes. Over the next four centuries, pharaohs again reigned as god-kings and Egypt expanded southwards to include Nubia and Kush. But in the seventeenth century BC, invaders from western Asia—the Hyksos, driving iron-fitted chariots—won control of the Nile Delta. Disorder ensued in a time known as the Second Intermediate period. Ahmose I of Thebes ousted the Hyksos around 1570, and the New Kingdom period commenced. Ahmose consolidated royal power by rebuilding the state bureaucracy, maintaining a standing army, and declaring a state religion (the temple of Amon). However, later pharaohs—including Tutankhamun and Ramses the Great—contended with economic decline, religious unrest, political intrigue, and foreign invasion by the Hittites and "Sea Peoples." By 1070 BC, the New Kingdom—indeed, the Egyptian empire—had crumbled.

Wall painting from the tomb of Nakht, a scholar-priest of c. 1400 BC; here he hunts with his family.

800	1000	1200	1400	1600	1800	2000

The Shang Dynasty

The first Chinese dynasty for which we have reliable historical evidence is the Shang. According to Chinese annals, the Shang overthrew the Hsia in 1766 BC. Their kingdom soon occupied much of the Yellow River Basin and 40,000 square miles of northern Honan. Shang emperors presided from several different capitals, including An-yang, and power, which was absolute, transferred from brother to brother or from father to son. Shang society was highly stratified: the emperor ruled through a gentry of warrior-landlords, who claimed divine ancestry and exercised great control over a large peasant class. This hierarchical social order was further reinforced by the development of a writing system, which was used only by priests called the *shih* to record affairs of state and practice arcane skills of divination. The Shang governed China for 600 years but fell to the Chou people of the Wei Valley in 1122 BC.

Waterfall at Taishan, one of China's five sacred mountains, Shandong province, once part of the Shang kingdom.

Bronze ritual vessel with gold sheet overlay from the Shang dynasty in China.

Minoan Crete

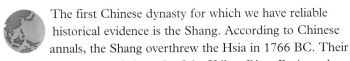

Around 2000 BC the first European civilization emerged in the Cretan palaces of Knossos, Phaistos and Malia. The palaces were unfortified, suggesting unusual peacefulness: unplanned, growing around a central courtyard, and remarkably sophisticated, boasting running water and proper bathrooms. Minoan Cretans developed three systems of writing, but only one, Linear B, has been deciphered. Records reveal a bureaucratic society, but Minoan art suggests a light-hearted culture with women playing a prominent role. Minoan culture spread around the Aegean, influencing the Mycenaean Greeks who had occupied mainland Greece in *c.* 1900 BC. When *c.* 1500 BC a tidal wave damaged the Knossos palace the Mycenaeans occupied and rebuilt it. Combining Minoan-style bureaucracy with military prowess, Mycenaeans dominated the Mediterranean sea-routes, building resplendent palaces at Mycenae, Tiryns and Pylos, but their power collapsed for unknown reasons after 1200 BC, ushering in a dark age.

The Throne Room of the Minoan Palace at Knossos, Crete.

Babylon: the First Law Code

Babylon was the successor of the Sumerian and Akkadian empires in the rich river valleys of Lower Mesopotamia. The greatest of the early Babylonian warrior-kings was Hammurabi, who greatly extended his power but is remembered principally as the world's earliest law-giver. His codification of the laws of Babylon in 282 sections is the first such exercise in history and a crucial moment in the development of stable, civilized life. Primitive societies rely on the vendetta or some other form of revenge to settle disputes; settled societies need the impartiality, finality and neutrality of the law to avoid the endless spiral of revenge that accompanies the vendetta. All the common forms of criminal and civil matters, from murder to family disputes, are covered in the code.

This stele, made of diorite, contains Hammurabi's code in cuneiform lettering. It shows the king standing before the god Shamash.

5000	2000	1000	500	AD1	400	600

Mycenae and Urnfield

Knowledge of metalworking reached Europe early in the second millennium BC, again from Asia Minor and North Africa, via the same Mediterranean and Danubian waterways as previously. Already with a developed agriculture and an increasingly complex social order, Europeans had experienced a Chalcolithic phase, learning how to hammer copper into decorative pendants and bracelets. Now, with new knowledge, they could exploit local tin to make bronze tools and weapons. By the Middle Bronze Age, c. 1500 BC, Danube Valley craftsmen had perfected techniques to decorate ceremonial items with intricate engraving. Gold-working meant that the status of royals was enhanced by a growing range of prestige ornaments, including collars and bracelets, while items interpreted as dress fasteners suggest cloth production by this time. Crete and Mycenae during this period in effect represented the earliest European civilizations; they had cities with palaces like Knossos, and had devised a form of linear writing. Royal burials took the form of inhumations with rich grave goods. Further west in Central Europe, the Urnfield culture dominated; hillforts were developing as ritual centers and ruling aristocrats were cremated and buried in urns.

Danube Valley: a Middle Bronze Age ceremonial axe-head (c. 1500-1250 BC), Romania.

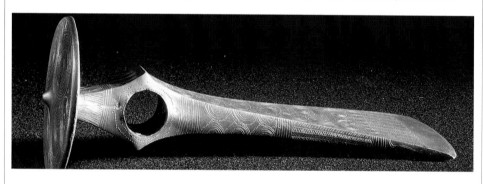

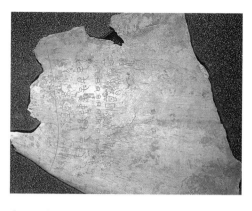

Some characters etched on "oracle bones" are easily identified by modern Chinese readers. To understand the antiquity of Chinese writing, one might imagine modern Egyptians still using a system of hieroglyphics.

The Shang Dynasty in China

The very early history of China was long considered almost entirely legendary. The first rulers in ancient accounts are larger-than-life "culture heroes" who are credited with the development of the calendar, writing and medicine. An early empress is said to have invented silk production. However, archaeological evidence has confirmed the actual existence of China's second traditional dynasty, the Shang emperors, who apparently replaced the earlier Hsia dynasty about 1766 BC and ruled until about 1122 BC, when they were overthrown by their neighbors, the Chou. The Shang people built fortified cities, used horse-drawn chariots in warfare (defending their cities against Mongolian nomads), domesticated many animals, and made bronze artifacts using very sophisticated techniques. Emperors ruled a highly stratified society with the help of priests skilled in astronomy, astrology, and mathematics. Shang religious practice involved animal and sometimes human sacrifice, and also the practice of divination by heating pieces of cattle bone or tortoise shell until they cracked. Some of these "oracle bones" provide the earliest examples of Chinese writing, already well developed by this period. It is essentially pictographic, and recognizably the ancestor of the Chinese writing system still in use today: evidence of extraordinary longevity.

Hinduism

Hinduism originated from the mixture of indigenous beliefs with the religion of the Indo-Aryan peoples who displaced the Indus Valley civilization about 1500 BC. Immensely diverse, Hinduism remains the predominant religion of India to this day. Its principal tenets are contained in the collection of poems, prayers and incantations known as the Four Vedas. The oldest is the *Rig Veda* ("verses of wisdom"), composed between 1500 and 900 BC. The Vedas culminate with the philosophical dialogues of 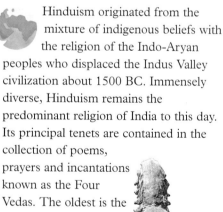 the *Upanishads*. In addition to these sacred texts, popular tales evolved into two enduring Hindu epics, the *Mahabharata* and the *Ramayana*, which developed about the same time as the Homeric epics in Greece. Although Hinduism recognizes many deities, three of the oldest are associated with basic life principles: Brahma is the personification of creation, Vishnu of preservation, and Shiva of destruction. These personifications became very complex: Vishnu has many incarnations, including the popular Krishna; and Shiva is the god of intellect and learning as well as destruction. Often, the female consorts (*shakti*) of the gods are needed to initiate their actions, which may explain the popularity of goddesses among Hindus. The beginnings of the caste system are also associated with the origins of Hinduism.

The Hindu god Shiva in his teaching pose.

800	1000	1200	1400	1600	1800	2000

Egyptian Middle Kingdom

Egypt's Middle Kingdom, which by *c.* 2000 BC extended from Nubia (modern north Sudan) to Canaan (modern Israel), had a highly developed social order and economy. Hieroglyphics evolved into a priestly script and a popular form of writing to facilitate commercial records. Scholarship included secular poetry and prose, mathematics, medicine and surgery. Laws were codified and a sun calendar devised. Religion was structured with deities including Osiris, who judged souls, Isis his wife and Ra the sun-god. The pharaoh, or king, was also considered divine. Although the pyramids of the Old Kingdom were abandoned, pharaohs were buried in splendid tombs with elaborate grave goods. Mural paintings illustrate many aspects of domestic life. Craftsmen produced fine gold, turquoise and glass ornaments and built houses of mud brick. Egyptians learned how to weave colored fabrics and, partly because dust storms and flies caused eye disease, heavy eye make-up was worn by men and women. Travel was commonly by river, but *c.* 1500 BC the horse was introduced and chariots became popular. By this time, having conquered Canaan, the Egyptians came into closer contact with Semitic peoples, including the Jews, who were then nomadic shepherds.

An Egyptian mural depicting a goldsmith working on a bowl (fifteenth century BC).

The Olmecs in Mesoamerica

The Archaic period of Indian life gave way, at different times in different regions, to the Formative period, which lasted until contact with Europeans. In Mesoamerica the early Formative period is sometimes called "Preclassic." It is characterized there by permanent agricultural villages with irrigation systems, from which eventually rose the great Olmec civilization along the Mexican Gulf coast. This civilization, often called the "Mother Culture" of Mesoamerica, was defined not so much by the development of cities, as in Mesopotamia at an earlier date, but by a stratified theocratic society, extensive trade, great ceremonial centers, and sophisticated art and architecture. The Olmecs also used a glyphic protoalphabet and established a calendar. The earliest of the important Olmec centers developed at San Lorenzo about 1200 BC and flourished until about 900 BC, when the dominant center became La Venta, home of the largest Olmec pyramid. Perhaps the most famous Olmec monuments are enormous basalt heads, which may represent chiefs or kings, wearing headgear for the ceremonial ball game important in Mesoamerican cultures. Other Olmec artifacts are stone stelae, perhaps thrones, and small human-jaguar figurines with snarling faces, often carved in jade. The plumed serpent who later became known as Quetzalcoatl is also represented. Olmec influence lingered in many later Mesoamerican cultures.

Some of the huge carved basalt heads of the Olmecs weigh as much as twenty tons. The stone, not always found near the ceremonial centers, was transported overland (without the use of wheels) and floated down rivers.

5000	2000	1000	500	AD1	400	600

Carthage

Carthage, one of the great cities of antiquity, was founded by Phoenician traders in the eighth century BC. Occupying an easily defended site with two fine natural harbors, it quickly became a vital link in the Phoenicians' Mediterranean trading system. By subduing the inland tribes it also became the major land power on the central North African coast. By the sixth century BC it had expanded to control the Mediterranean islands, including the Balearics and most of Sicily, and all of the North African coast west of Egypt. In later centuries it colonized eastern Spain. But all this expansion brought it up against the rising power of Rome. The two cities fought each other to a finish in the three Punic Wars, of which the second (219-210 BC) was the most important. After the third Punic War (146 BC) Carthage was destroyed and the site plowed with salt by the victorious Romans.

A Phoenician ivory plaque dating from the eighth century BC.

Early Mound Builders

Between 1000 and 500 BC, when the Olmec still dominated south-central Mexico, sophisticated societies emerged in other parts of the Americas. In the Andes of South America, a regional temple center at Chavín de Huantar was built around 800 BC, marking the appearance of a theocratic culture that would expand dramatically outward after 400. And in the Ohio and Mississippi Valleys of North America, the Adena surfaced. The Adena were the first native American peoples to construct large earthen mounds. These mounds—such as the Serpent Mound in Ohio—were the funerary monuments of important persons (perhaps chiefs or shamans) and may also have served as sites of religious ceremony. As such, the mounds surely played a key role in the political organization of the Adena, but their precise function remains unknown. Other mound-building cultures followed the Adena, including the highly successful Hopewells (200 BC-700 AD).

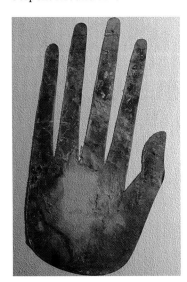

A Hopewell culture mica hand found buried in Ohio, 400 miles from the nearest mica source.

Assyrians and Persians

In the eighth century BC, Assyrian armies swept across western Asia, sacking Israel, Babylon, Cilicia, Syria, and parts of Elam. From resplendent Nineveh, Assyrian kings ruled their empire with brute force. They conscripted soldiers and removed the peoples of conquered territories. But their hegemony proved short-lived. In 612 BC, the Chaldeans and Medes joined forces to destroy Nineveh. The Chaldeans founded New Babylon—ruled most famously by Nebuchadnezzar II, who wrecked Jerusalem in 586—while the Medes dominated Persia. Around 550, the Persian prince Cyrus the Great threw over the Medes, and in 539 captured Babylon, thereby founding the Persian empire, the most extensive the world had known. Cyrus's grandson, Darius the Great (521-486), divided the realm into twenty provinces ruled by satraps, who were often local nobles. With authority so dispersed, Persian emperors relied on good roads and an early postal system to watch over their far-flung empire.

A staircase leading to the Tripylon at Persepolis, the Persian capital, shows a procession of the Medes and Persians.

Early Japan

The original people of Japan had been called the Ainu but from about 2000 BC onwards they were displaced by Mongol invaders from the Asian mainland as well as by Malay or Polynesian people pushing up from the south. By 700 BC, according to the ancient chronicles, the country was united in a single state by the warlord Jimmu Tenno, who founded the first imperial house based on his stronghold in Honshu, and gradually extended his power throughout the whole archipelago. There are no authentic historical sources for any of this and its sole status is that of creation myth. Nonetheless, there was an established imperial power structure in place long before reliable records begin in the fifth century AD. Moreover, Shintō—the state religion—is very ancient; its mythic origins are also linked to Jimmu. The most sacred of all Shintō shrines, at Ise near Kyoto, contains a mirror that the sun goddess is supposed to have given him.

800	1000	1200	1400	1600	1800	2000

1000 BC David, king of Judah, establishes his capital at Jerusalem.

c. **1000 BC** Western Chou dynasty in China.

c. **1000** Mound-Builders appear in the Ohio valley.

c. **1000** Maya Middle Pre-Classic period begins in lowland jungles of Central America.

935 BC Re-establishment of the Assyrian empire under Assurdan II.

c. **900 BC** Rise of Damascus as center of power and trade.

c. **900 BC** Foundation of Sparta.

884 BC Centralized rule in Assyria.

814 BC Phoenicians found Carthage.

c. **800 BC** Occupation of site at Chavin de Huantar, north Peru, the earliest mature Andes civilization.

771 BC Eastern Chou dynasty (-256) nominally in control but in fact local magnate-warlords ascendant in China.

753 BC Foundation date of the city of Rome.

c. **750 BC** Homer composes *The Iliad* and *The Odyssey*.

745 BC Tiglathpileser III, a usurper, ushers in the last phase of the Assyrian empire.

722 BC Kingdom of Israel destroyed by Assyrians.

c. **700 BC** Attica under Athenian control.

c. **700 BC** First coins used in Lydia, Turkey.

c. **700 BC** Jimmu Tenno, warlord, forms first united Japanese empire.

c. **650 BC** According to Herodotus, Phoenician sailors circumnavigate Africa.

612 BC Destruction of Assyrian capital of Nineveh by Medes, Babylonians and Scythians who found the New Babylonian empire.

605 BC Accession of Nebuchadnezzar II, the Great (r. -561), as Babylonian emperor.

594 BC Solon "the lawgiver" appointed sole *archon* (ruler) of Athens.

586 BC Fall of kingdom of Judah and city of Jerusalem to Babylonians.

551 BC Birth of Confucius, philosopher and founder of major Chinese religion.

550 BC Cyrus the Great unites with Medes and founds Persian empire.

547 BC Persians gain control of Asia Minor.

539 BC Cyrus the Great of Persia conquers Babylon and makes Judah and Phoenicia into Persian provinces.

525 BC Persia under Cambyses conquers Egypt; Egypt under Persian kings until 404 BC.

521 BC Darius emperor of Persia (r. -486); under him, imperial power is at greatest extent.

c. **511 BC** Chinese general Sun Tzu writes *The Art of War*, first known work of its kind.

c. **509 BC** Treaty between Rome and Carthage; first known Roman treaty.

509 BC Foundation of the Roman Republic.

c. **500 BC** Buddhism founded by Siddhartha, otherwise known as the Buddha.

A Greek warrior with a dove decorating his shield on a sixth- or fifth-century BC Greek vase.

The Emergence of Greece

The "wedded rocks" at Futamiguara, Ise Bay. According to tradition, they sheltered Izanagi and Izanami, the legendary creators of Japan.

The world that emerged in Greece after 1000 BC was centered on the *polis*: fiercely independent city states which experimented with many forms of government, most notably democracy. The founding of the Olympic Games in 776, to which every polis sent athletes, fostered a common Greek identity. So did the two great poems attributed to Homer—the *Illiad* and the *Odyssey*, with their heroic visions, written around the same time. Poets probably adopted the Phoenician alphabet to record these poems, so reviving literacy. Land hunger from growing populations required the founding of new cities, from Marseilles, France, in the west to Trebizond in eastern Turkey. But in Asia Greeks encountered a far superior power: Persia. Persia conquered the Greeks of Asia by 540 BC and slowly pressed into Europe, invading in force in 480 BC. Its defeat at Salamis saved Greek liberty and, arguably, European civilization.

5000	2000	1000	500	AD1	400	600

Redating Chavín de Huantar

The northern Andean mountain site of Chavín de Huantar was formerly dated about 1500 BC, but radiocarbon dating now suggests that Chavín may have been a modest settlement that developed about 800 BC, becoming influential after its expansion about 400 BC. Chavín's sophistication and influence on surrounding cultures was considered a turning-point in ancient Andean history, and the implications of this new data are still being absorbed into the study of ancient Andean peoples. Magnificent buildings, in any case, were constructed in South America as early as 1700 BC: many were U-shaped ceremonial centers. The complex at Sechín Alto, in the coastal lowlands north of Chavín, has been radiocarbon-dated at about 1290 BC, and is the largest complex of its age in the Western hemisphere. The rich necropolis of Paracas, further south, shows pre- and post-Chavín phases in its arts. Mummies in fetal positions, wrapped in beautifully woven and embroidered textiles, were buried in subterranean chambers. Many of the textiles use alpaca wool, providing evidence of contacts with highland cultures where alpacas are found. The skilful Paracas textile artists made full use of wool's ability to hold many more dye colors than cotton.

An embroidered band from Paracas shows the intriguing mythological "Oculate Being" with an elaborate headdress, serpentine tongue, and cat-like whiskers.

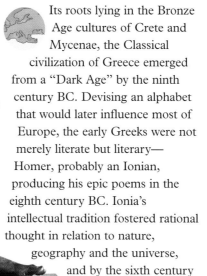

A magnificent bronze of a Greek javelin thrower. Individual champion athletes at the Olympic Games, which were initiated by the Greeks in 776 BC, were frequently honored in bronze and other art.

The Greeks

Its roots lying in the Bronze Age cultures of Crete and Mycenae, the Classical civilization of Greece emerged from a "Dark Age" by the ninth century BC. Devising an alphabet that would later influence most of Europe, the early Greeks were not merely literate but literary— Homer, probably an Ionian, producing his epic poems in the eighth century BC. Ionia's intellectual tradition fostered rational thought in relation to nature, geography and the universe, and by the sixth century BC had laid the foundations of Greek philosophy. The Greeks worshipped a pantheon of deities, including Zeus, Athena and Dionysus; the latter was honored by ritual choruses from which drama would develop, while athletic trials known as the Olympic Games glorified the gods believed to reside on Mount Olympus. Typical Greek cities such as Sparta and Athens had as a central feature an *acropolis* (citadel); that at Athens is dominated by the Parthenon temple. Below, the *agora* (market-place) extended, and the commerce of the Greeks gave rise to Europe's earliest coinage. The defeat of Persia in 480 BC initiated the "Golden Age" of Greece, during which sciences and the arts flourished.

800	1000	1200	1400	1600	1800	2000

Early Japan

The early history of Japan is characterized by its isolation from the increasingly dominant Chinese culture of mainland Asia. Japan's geographical position relative to the Asian continent is often compared with that of Great Britain relative to Europe; but whereas only about twenty miles of sea separate England from France, about 115 miles separate Japan from its nearest continental neighbor, Korea. The origins of the Japanese people are still mysterious. Archaeological discovery of Paleolithic artefacts suggests they share common ancestry with the earliest peoples of Asia, who may have crossed over a now-vanished land bridge in a remote geological age. Linguistic similarities between Japanese, Korean, and the Ural-Altaic languages of northern Asia seem to confirm this. However, Japan also shares cultural traditions with Polynesia and Southeast Asia; and the Ainu people who still live in northern Japan are of different ethnic origins from most of the Asian peoples. Neolithic culture may have begun as early as 10,000 BC and lasted until about 300 BC. This culture is called Jōmon (rope pattern) because of characteristic designs impressed on pottery. Whether the Ainu, undoubtedly of ancient origin, can be identified with the Jōmon people is uncertain.

The Jōmon people of early Japan made pottery of lively and various designs, as well as expressive, sometimes fantastical figurines, known as dōgu. This figurine is from a late period in Jōmon culture.

From Old to New Babylon

The most famous accomplishments of the Old Babylonian era, which began about 2000 BC, may be the innovative Code of Laws set down by the Armorite ruler Hammurabi (r. 1792-1750 BC), and the first written record of *Gilgamesh*, an epic inspired by the exploits of a Sumerian king who lived about 2600 BC. The Old Babylonians were also the most advanced mathematicians of antiquity. After the Hittites decimated Babylon in 1595 BC, the next powerful rulers in the region were the Assyrians, who arrived from the north in 1225 BC. Sennacherib (r. 705-681 BC) finished the Assyrian conquest of western Asia, and built a magnificent new capital, Nineveh. Sennacherib's

A colorful tile lion from the Babylon city gate constructed during the reign of Nebuchadnezzar II.

grandson Assurbanipal (r. 668-627 BC), completed the splendid library, containing the accumulated knowledge of Sumeria and Old Babylonia. In 612 BC, however, the Chaldeans and Medes combined forces to destroy Nineveh, leaving the Chaldeans to become the New Babylonians. Under Nebuchadnezzar II (r. 604-562 BC) Babylon became legendary, with one of the seven wonders of the ancient world: the famous "Hanging Gardens." New Babylonians were also skilled astronomers, who identified five planets with five gods in a system later adopted by the Greeks and Romans.

Connections with the Middle East

Egypt, having developed iron technology and achieved extensive conquests, suffered from internal difficulties after 1000 BC, becoming subject to kings from Libya and Ethiopia. About this time the peoples of Canaan emerge into history. The Phoenicians were maritime traders, mining lapis lazuli (used for Egyptian make-up) and manufacturing purple dye from murex shells, which they exported in exchange for precious metals and spices. Around 850 BC they founded Carthage, capital of the Classical province of *Africa* (modern Tunisia). Inland in Canaan, the intrusive Philistines had been dominant, but by *c.* 1000 BC Israelite kings had subjugated regional petty rulers. The monotheistic Jews believed in *Yahweh*, a just heavenly Father who had revealed Himself to His chosen people. Devising the Hebrew alphabet, they collected Yahweh's commands together in the Torah. The Israelite rulers are documented in the Old Testament Book of Kings. Internal dissension caused Israelite overkingship to disintegrate. The tributary transjordan kingdom of Moab reasserted its independence *c.* 830 BC. Its people worshipped a god called Chemosh. The northern Jewish kingdom of Israel fell to the Assyrians and Jerusalem was destroyed in 586 BC.

The stele of Mesha, king of Moab (Palestine's oldest written source c. 830 BC), commemorates his reversal of Jehoram, king of Israel.

THE AGE OF ALEXANDER

This I can confidently affirm: ... even if he had added Europe to Asia ... he would still have gone on seeking unknown lands beyond.

Arrian

The dramatic sweep of Alexander, king of Macedon, through Persia to the edge of the world then known to Europe, so captured the imagination of contemporaries and of later commentators alike that few would hesitate to style him "the Great." Later Classical writers including Plutarch, Arrian, and Curtius relate accounts of Alexander's deeds, admiring his victories and censuring his excesses. Alexander is popularly credited with having extended Greek conquest from the Adriatic to the Indus River, carving out the greatest empire the ancient world had known. The extent to which such views accurately reflect his achievement deserves some comment.

ALEXANDER'S INHERITANCE

Succeeding his father Philip in 336 BC, Alexander inherited a strong Macedonian kingdom and overlordship of various other Greek states. Macedonia had already expanded into neighboring Thrace, and a congress at Corinth in 338 had acknowledged Philip's dominance of Greece. Philip had also seized Byzantium and established a foothold in Asia Minor. A Hellenic presence already existed here, as several Ionian cities including Ephesus stood along the Aegean coast of Asia Minor once overshadowed by Troy. Although subject to the Persian empire, some of these cities might support a Hellenic initiative. In political terms, therefore, Alexander had a not inconsiderable foundation for his venture. He also inherited a formidable war machine. Philip had engaged in grand-scale military reform, creating a large, well-trained army with effective tactics. Developing an infantry formation known as the Macedonian phalanx, he also perfected the use of light cavalry.

Motivated, perhaps, by the history of conflict between Persia and the Greek states Alexander, having asserted his authority over Greece, moved against the empire of Darius. Although it included other Greek allies, the core of Alexander's army was made up of Macedonians and so, at least in the early campaigns, it was a relatively homogeneous unit. In contrast, the army of Darius was an unwieldly host, reflecting his wide realms with their diverse cultures. Alexander's initial victory at Granicus, on the shore of Marmara, in 334 was a body-blow for Darius. Some Ionian cities, including Ephesus, joined the Macedonian side but others, like Miletus, had to be coerced. The battle of Issus in southwest Asia Minor the following year was a more serious defeat for the Persians, prompting Darius to sue for peace. Alexander at this point turned south into Egypt where the Persian viceroy, not having the resources to resist, capitulated. Crossing back through Mesopotamia, the Macedonians completely shattered the Persians at Gaugamela, near Arbela, in 331 BC. The cities of Babylon, Susa and Persepolis rapidly fell to Alexander's advance and King Darius perished while fleeing for his life. Not content with this achievement, Alexander spent the next six years pursuing remnants of the Persian forces to the northern frontier of the empire, before turning southwards to the Indus Valley. Only in 324 BC did he return to Susa, dying the following year at Babylon, apparently of fever.

ALEXANDER AS OVERLORD

From the outset, Alexander had shown political astuteness by respecting local religious custom. Whether or not he offered sacrifice at the Temple of Jerusalem, as Josephus claims, there is reason to believe that Alexander participated in religious rites at Memphis and he is depicted on coins wearing the horns of the Egyptian god Amun. He subsequently restored the temple of Bel at Babylon. Presumably, this deference to local custom was aimed at winning the support of subject populations within the Persian empire. Certainly, various population groups rallied to the Macedonian cause, hastening Persia's collapse. There are, indeed, indications that Alexander envisaged a permanent conquest. Aside from receiving defectors into his forces, he levied troops within the Persian provinces. He also recruited Persian boys for military education according to Greek custom. In addition, he founded a string of cities across the former Persian realms and planted colonies—

The Battle of Issus, 333 BC. Detail showing Alexander, bareheaded, leading his troops against the army of Darius. The mosaic, from the Casa del Fauno in the Roman city of Pompeii, is based on an earlier Greek painting by Philoxenos.

mainly, it seems, made up of war-weary soldiers. Several of these cities bore his own name: there was Alexandretta in Asia Minor (Iskanderun), and Alexandria in Egypt. Other cities called Alexandria were founded in Aria and Arachosia (Afghanistan) and in Bactria (Uzbekistan).

LEGACY OF ALEXANDER

Clearly, Alexander had destroyed the Persian empire, but his achievement in the positive sense might understandably be questioned. Even before his return to Susa in 324 BC his army, now largely composed of foreign troops, was more preoccupied with plunder than with discipline. It seems clear that no stable Hellenic government had been created to replace that of Darius. The officer left in charge of the treasury had fled and there were widespread revolts against Alexander's overlordship. There was to be no Hellenic empire of Persia; Alexander, much given to carousing in his last years, had not even bothered to appoint an heir, decreeing instead that he should be succeeded by "the best." The Macedonian overlordship collapsed with his death, his generals fighting among themselves.

Many of the cities Alexander founded proved to be ephemeral, although the Macedonian episode was long remembered in Indus tradition. What did result was a number of Hellenized kingdoms, founded by Alexander's generals. Pergamum and Bithynia in western Asia Minor were within the former Ionian zone, Cappadocia and Pontus lay further east. Egypt became Hellenized under Ptolemy Soter, supposedly a half-brother of Alexander, founder of the Ptolemaic dynasty. Seleucus founded the Seleucid dynasty of Syria in 312 BC. Surely the most curious case, however, is the isolated Hellenized kingdom of Bactria, which survived for some time in distant Uzbekistan. Thus the "Age of Alexander" would bequeath a degree of European influence to the northeastern corner of Africa and parts of Asia.   *A.M*

From the Andes to the Arctic

Important cultures flourished throughout the Americas after 500 BC. In the central Andes, the cult at Chavín de Huantar spread along trade routes, uniting peoples of the North Coast and Casma Valley in an event called the Early Horizon. In Central America, villages large and small dotted the landscape; they became the basis of the Mayan civilization, which fluoresced several centuries later. And far to the north, along the arctic coasts of central and eastern Canada, the Dorset Inuit thrived. The Dorset were superior hunters who used the harpoon as well as the bow and arrow to spear land and sea mammals. In their battle with the elements, the Dorset people turned to powerful shamans, who acted as healers and seers with the help of the animal-spirits. The Dorset had only intermittent contact with other peoples—usually through trade—but they survived another millennium before the Thule Inuit displaced them.

A Dorset Inuit face mask, possibly used by a shaman in religious ritual.

Alexander the Great

The greatest conqueror of antiquity was the son of King Philip II of Macedon, a small kingdom in northern Greece. His father had conquered Thrace and controlled most of central Greece. Alexander swept into Asia Minor and then through Armenia, Palestine, Egypt, Persia and modern Afghanistan and Pakistan as far as the Indus valley. His empire touched the east coast of the Adriatic, the southwestern coast of the Black Sea, the south shore of the Caspian Sea, the northern coast of the Persian Gulf from the mouth of the Euphrates to that of the Indus, and the eastern Mediterranean on both the European and the African sides. He occupied Damascus and destroyed the Persian empire. And yet he was dead at thirty-three. Could he have maintained order in this vast empire? Probably not: communications were too difficult. But he spread Hellenistic culture far to the east, a legacy on which the Romans were to build.

Alexander the Great as the Greek god Hercules on a silver tetradrachme coin, c. 325 BC.

- 490 BC Battle of Marathon: Darius's Persians fail to push into Europe as Greeks triumph.

- 481-221 BC Warring States Period in China.

- 480 BC Greeks defeat Persians in naval battle of Salamis.

- 479 BC Greek victories on land at Plataea and at sea at Mycale end the Persian threat.

- c. 463 BC Pericles ascendant in Athens; encourages development of democracy.

- 460 BC Growing rivalry between Athens and Sparta leads to the First Peleponnesian War (-446).

- 446 BC Peace with Sparta leaves Pericles supreme in Athens.

- 431 BC Great Peleponnesian War (-404) in which Sparta finally defeats Athens.

- c. 400 Navigation advances among Pacific Islands.

- 390 BC Gauls sack Rome.

- 380 BC The XXXth dynasty, comprising three kings, last native rulers of Egypt (- 343).

- 359 BC Philip II regent and, three years later, king of Macedon.

- 338 BC Battle of Chaeronea, in which Philip of Macedon defeats Athenian alliance.

- 336 BC Assassination of Philip; succeeded by his son Alexander, "the Great" (-323).

- 332 BC All of Palestine, Egypt and Mesopotamia conquered by Alexander the Great.

- 331 BC Alexander destroys the Persian empire of Darius III, founds Alexandria.

- 326 BC Alexander the Great crosses the Indus but does not occupy India.

- 323 BC Death of Alexander at Babylon.

- 323 BC Ptolemy I, one of Alexander's generals, becomes the first of his line to rule Egypt (-283).

- 305 BC Seleucus I Nicator, one of Alexander's generals, establishes Seleucid empire from Asia Minor to the Indus valley.

- c. 300 BC Rise of Maya Late Pre-Classic period.

- c. 300 BC Rise of Hopewell Mound-Building culture in eastern North America.

- c. 273 BC Asoka's empire covers more than half the Indian sub-continent (- c. 232). He converts to Buddhism. One of India's greatest rulers.

- 264 BC First Punic War (-241): Rome wins, gaining western Sicily.

- 221 BC Rise of the Ch'in Dynasty in China (-207) from which China is named.

- 219 BC Second Punic War (-201), dominated by Carthaginian general Hannibal Barca.

- 218 BC Hannibal crosses the Alps in fifteen days, invades Italy.

- 216 BC Hannibal wins stunning victory at Cannae but fails to march on Rome.

- 207 BC Foundation of Han dynasty, which centralized and expanded the Chinese empire.

- 202 BC Hannibal defeated at decisive battle of Zama by Romans under Cornelius Scipio.

- 201 BC Capitulation of Carthage; Rome now the major Mediterranean power.

800	1000	1200	1400	1600	1800	2000

The Ptolemaic Dynasty

In 525 BC, Egypt fell to the Persians, who remained there for almost two centuries. But the forces of Alexander the Great swept the Persians aside in 332. Alexander appointed the Macedonian general Ptolemy I to govern Egypt. Ptolemy assumed the kingship in 323, founding a long-lived dynasty that at various times extended its realm into western Asia. The Ptolemies set up their capital at Alexandria, which became a center of commerce and culture during the Hellenistic period. They reduced the monarchy's role in affairs of state and depended on a large bureaucracy to maintain order. Ptolemaic kings even adopted the traditional customs and garb of ancient Egypt, but many Egyptians reviled government officials, who were usually either Greek or Macedonian. Despite frequent revolts, the Ptolemaic dynasty declined only after 200 BC with the encroachment of the Romans, and did not end until 30 BC, when Cleopatra committed suicide.

The double temple dedicated to the Egyptian gods Sebek and Haroeris.

Athenian Zenith

Athens emerged as the pre-eminent Greek *polis* (city state) after effectively heading resistance to the Persian invasion of 480-79 BC, although Sparta had been the nominal Greek leader. By then Athens was a full democracy where all citizens, rich and poor, voted directly on all political matters. Citizenship did not extend, however, to women, slaves or resident foreigners, nor, more importantly at the time, to Greeks of other cities enrolled in the alliance against Persia, the Delian League. The League soon became an Athenian empire, run by and for Athenians, a cause of fear among the Spartans and so of the long Peloponnesian War (431-404 BC) which half-ruined Greece. But for half a century, chiefly guided by Pericles, Athens enjoyed a genuine golden age in which art, literature and philosophy flourished. Athenian democracy recovered in the fourth century to be finally extinguished by the Macedonians in 322 BC.

Bust of Pericles, the brilliant Athenian politician of the fifth century BC.

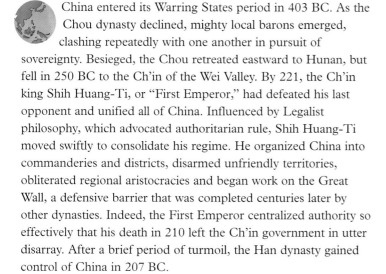

The Ch'in Dynasty

China entered its Warring States period in 403 BC. As the Chou dynasty declined, mighty local barons emerged, clashing repeatedly with one another in pursuit of sovereignty. Besieged, the Chou retreated eastward to Hunan, but fell in 250 BC to the Ch'in of the Wei Valley. By 221, the Ch'in king Shih Huang-Ti, or "First Emperor," had defeated his last opponent and unified all of China. Influenced by Legalist philosophy, which advocated authoritarian rule, Shih Huang-Ti moved swiftly to consolidate his regime. He organized China into commanderies and districts, disarmed unfriendly territories, obliterated regional aristocracies and began work on the Great Wall, a defensive barrier that was completed centuries later by other dynasties. Indeed, the First Emperor centralized authority so effectively that his death in 210 left the Ch'in government in utter disarray. After a brief period of turmoil, the Han dynasty gained control of China in 207 BC.

A section of the Great Wall. The emperor Shih Huang-Ti began to connect up a series of defensive walls in 214 BC.

The Parthenon, originally decorated by a magnificent naturalistic frieze depicting Greek warriors killed in battle. Known as the Elgin Marbles, the frieze is now in the British Museum.

Carthage and Nok

Having survived conquest by Alexander the Great, Egypt found itself under Greek Ptolemaic kings from 323 BC. These rulers, establishing their capital at Alexandria, initiated a new cultural phase encouraging art and learning (Euclid flourished during the reign of Ptolemy I) and building a great library. Parallel to this, the Phoenicians of Carthage extended their trading settlements along the coast of Numidia and Mauretania (modern Algeria and Morocco). Exporting metals, grain and slaves, Carthage accumulated fabulous wealth prior to its destruction by Rome in the second century BC. It is claimed that Carthaginians engaged in trans-Saharan trade, but evidence is slight. This merchant culture preserved Middle Eastern religion, venerating Baal Hammon, a deity with solar associations.

Meanwhile, agricultural development in the valley of the River Niger had, as elsewhere, facilitated cultural advancement. By *c.* 500 BC, the Nok culture had emerged at such centers as Taruga. Characterized by its art forms, which include decorated pottery and terra cotta figures, Nok is an early representative of an Upper Niger tradition which would have far-reaching influences.

A Nok terra-cotta human head, Nigeria (500 BC to AD 200).

The Greeks and Celts

By 400 BC Greek culture was reaching its apogee with the emergence of drama and philosophy. Aeschylus (d. 455 BC) developed tragedy, isolating speakers in the Dionysian chorus which facilitated dialogue. Comedy came later, as Aristophanes (d. 385 BC) satirized government and social manners. By the mid-fourth century BC, the academy of Plato flourished and his most distinguished student, Aristotle (d. 322 BC), pioneered logic and natural philosophy; his teachings would later influence Christian culture.

Emerging from *c.* 500 BC, La Tène Celtic culture ultimately extended from Asia Minor to Ireland. Essentially a linguistic term, "Celtic" has been extended to other aspects of culture including mythology, social organization and material heritage. The Celts are associated with two phases of material culture: the earlier Hallstat, named from an Austrian site, and La Tène which developed in Switzerland. Their art distinguished by curvilinear designs and triskele motifs, Marne chariot burials and insular epic tales reflect a Celtic warrior ethos. Artifacts were deposited in rivers as offerings to gods but some deities demanded human sacrifice.

The Hopewells were known for their fine artifacts. This raven or crow, with a pearl eye, is made from a sheet of copper. The metal may have been obtained through trade with people of the Great Lakes region.

East Asian Philosophy and Religion

The Chou (Zhou) period in China (1122 BC - c. 250 BC), initially marked by expansion through both conquest and trade, resulted in a system of territorial governance sometimes compared with medieval European feudalism. By the mid-fifth century, China was embroiled in the political turbulence of the Warring States period. Although strife-ridden, this was an age of accomplishments in literature and philosophy, the latter so prolific that this is known as the "Hundred Schools" period. One influential figure was K'ung Fu-tzu (Kongzi) or "Master Kung," also known by the Latin version of his name, Confucius (c. 551-479 BC). This alert thinker, inspiring teacher, and failed statesmen (coincidentally contemporary with the Buddha in India) articulated a philosophy that still provides a basis for Chinese identity. He emphasized reciprocity in family relationships, which should extend by degrees into the community. A different set of values provide a similar identity in Japanese culture. The Yayoi people who succeeded the Jōmon about 300 BC are associated with the development of Shintōism (only so designated much later, to distinguish it from Buddhism), a diffuse polytheistic religion characterized by a sympathetic appreciation of nature. The rich Shintō mythology contrasts with the socioethical concerns of Confucian philosophy, but has similarly enduring influence.

Mound-Building Societies

Massive earthen mounds in North America once gave rise to excited speculation about mysterious lost "European tribes." Although the origins and ultimate fate of the peoples who constructed these earthworks is still uncertain, research has established that they were indeed native Americans. The Adena culture, named after a site in present-day Ohio, dates back to about 1000 BC, and seems to end about 200 AD, overlapping with the later and more expansive Hopewell culture (300 BC-700 AD). Both are among the many peoples grouped together as Central and Eastern Woodland cultures. The rich terrain allowed them to live settled lives without extensive agriculture. Hopewell remains also testify to widespread trading, reaching as far north as Canada, west to the Rocky Mountains, and south to Florida. Adena mounds began as honored individual burials, and were later constructed over multiple burials, sometimes to a height of eighty feet. Symbolic effigy mounds were also constructed; one of the most famous is the Great Serpent Mound in Ohio, extending 1330 feet in the shape of a curving snake. The Hopewells were even more ambitious; a site in Newark, Ohio, once included four miles of embankments in various geometric shapes.

Buddhism and Jainism

Buddhism and Jainism emerged about the same time in India as "unorthodox" faiths: both rejected the centrality of the Hindu Vedas. Buddhism was founded by Siddhartha Gautama (c. 563-483 BC), whose followers called him the Buddha, or "Enlightened One." According to legend, the Buddha received enlightenment while resting under a tree. He taught that *nirvana*, or release from the painful cycle of death and rebirth, could be reached through meditation and following ethical precepts. Jainism, whose founding is attributed to a contemporary of the Buddha called Mahavira or "Great Hero" (c. 540-468 BC), extended Buddhist injunctions against violence into the doctrine of *ahimsa*, the command to do no harm to any living being. About 500 years after its founding, Buddhism split into two major branches. The stricter Hinayana cult is still dominant in Sri Lanka, Burma, Thailand, and Laos; the Mahayana cult fused more easily with local religions, and offered the ultimate possibility of Buddhahood to all, inducing the faith to become widespread throughout Asia. Unlike Buddhism, Jainism did not become a world religion, but it remained after Buddhism disappeared from the country of its origin, and today there are still about two million Jain followers in India.

Early Buddhist art did not represent the Buddha. This relief from the Buddhist temple at Amaravati shows the tree under which the Buddha received enlightenment.

An idealized portrait of the philosopher Confucius. After his death his doctrines were compiled under the title The Analects of Confucius.

東亮州郰曲阜縣人

5000	2000	1000	500	AD1	400	600

- c. 200 Rise of Nazca culture in southern Peru.

- 185-30 BC Shunga dynasty replaces Mauryan dynasty in India.

- 171 BC Mithridates I becomes Parthian king.

- 168 BC Revolt under Judas Maccabaeus leads to autonomy for Judea from the Seleucids.

- 146 BC Third Punic War ends with the total destruction of Carthage.

- 110 BC Chinese emperor Wu Ti pushes imperial boundaries south and west.

- 108 BC Manchuria and northern Korea incorporated into China.

- c. 100 BC Roman trading posts extend as far as southwest coast of India and southern edge of the Sahara Desert.

- c. 100 BC Rise of Hohokum culture in southwest North America.

- c. 100 BC Goods begin to be carried on the "Silk Road" between China and Europe.

- 88 BC First Mithridatic War: major Roman war against Mithridates of Pontus (northeast Asia Minor).

- 64 BC Final conquest of the Seleucid empire by Pompey.

- 63 BC Pompey annexes Judea as a Roman province.

- 60 BC Buddhism reaches China from central Asia and India.

- 60 BC First Triumvirate—Julius Caesar, Crassus and Pompey—in control of Rome.

- 58 BC Start of Caesar's conquest of Gaul, completed in 51 BC.

- 54 BC Roman invasion of Britain under Julius Caesar.

- 51 BC Hsiung-nu people of central Asia, antecedents of the later Huns, subjugated by Chinese.

- 49 BC Pompey, sole consul, commands Caesar to disband his army. Instead, Caesar crosses the Rubicon into Italy.

- 48 BC Pompey murdered in Egypt.

- 45 BC Caesar supreme in Rome, having defeated all his enemies.

- 44 BC Assassination of Caesar in Rome.

- 43 BC Second Triumvirate: Octavian, Mark Antony and Lepidus.

- 30 BC Suicide of Cleopatra, last Ptolemaic ruler of Egypt.

- 27 BC Octavian first Roman emperor, henceforth known as Caesar Augustus.

- 4 BC Birth of Jesus Christ, founder of Christianity.

The Moche and Nazca

The once thriving Chavín cult fell flat around 200 BC, and in its wake several highly developed societies took root in the central Andes, among them the Moche and Nazca. After two centuries of warfare, the principalities of the Moche valley united politically in about AD 1. Soon, the Moche dominated the entire north coast of Peru. Divine kings, supported by four levels of nobles and bureaucrats, ran the Moche state, while the Moche people were mostly farmers and fishermen. The Nazca, who lived in the arid valleys of Peru's south coast, built a major ceremonial center at Cahuachi as early as 200 BC. Cahuachi hosted fertility rites, burials, and possibly human sacrifice. The Nazca population lived in scattered farming villages and was apparently organized into a confederacy of clans without a central political regime. Both the Moche and Nazca peoples thrived until the sixth century AD.

Clay vessel in the form of a warrior, Nazca culture.

The Roman Republic

When the Second Punic War ended with Roman victory at Zama in 201 BC, the Roman republic became the dominant power in the central Mediterranean. It embraced all the Italian peninsula and the coast as far as Massilia (Marseilles) as well as the Carthaginian colonies in eastern Spain. Over the next two centuries, its control spread east along the Balkan coast and into Greece, then into Asia Minor and Armenia. Eventually Palestine and Egypt came under Roman rule. In the west, all of Spain except for Galicia and the Basque country became a Roman province and in the first century BC Julius Caesar invaded Gaul and Britain. The republican form of government once suitable for a city state could no longer contain the ambitions of the various warlords who had accomplished the great territorial conquests. After a series of civil wars, Caesar Augustus became the first emperor in 27 BC.

Roman funerary relief of a chariot race.

A reconstruction of Herod's temple as it appeared c. 20 BC.

Jerusalem

At the start of the second century BC, the Seleucids of Syria, a Macedonian dynasty, ruled most of Asia Minor, including Palestine. Seeking to Hellenize the kingdom, Antiochus IV Epiphanes plundered the Jewish Temple at Jerusalem in 168 BC and made it a site for Greek rites. Incensed, the Jews, led by Judas Maccabaeus, expelled the Seleucids in 164, an event remembered as Hanukah. Judas secured the victory by allying with Rome, and in 143, under Simon Maccabaeus, Palestine became an independent state. The Maccabee kings reigned as high priests, but their often lax observance of Judaism made them unpopular among many Jews. In 63 BC the Roman general Pompey deposed the Seleucids and swept into Jerusalem. The Roman senate installed Herod as king in 37 BC. To court the Jews' favor, Herod rebuilt the Temple according to Jewish scripture. Part of Herod's Temple still stands as the Wailing Wall.

Han Dynasty

The borders of the Chinese empire greatly expanded under the Han Dynasty (207 BC-AD 220). Wu Ti (141 BC-AD 87), the "Martial Emperor," captured the Tarim Basin, southern Manchuria and the southeastern coast, and subjected the Mekong Thai and Annam peoples. At its peak, the Han kingdom rivaled the Roman empire in size. Han emperors supervised this vast territory through an enormous bureaucracy. Although autocratic, the Han discarded the repressive tactics of the Ch'in. By the second century BC, Confucianism had become the state philosophy, and at its lower levels, the civil service consisted almost entirely of Confucian scholars trained at government expense. A peasants' revolt briefly interrupted Han rule, from AD 9 to 23. The Later Han dynasty was financially and administratively weaker. By 184, rebellion had broken out again, and in 220, the Han's own generals overthrew the exhausted dynasty.

The Ch'in "Terra-cotta Army", c. 220-210 BC of Shanxi province. The Ch'in were overthrown by the Han dynasty in 207 BC.

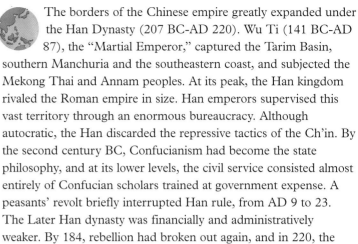

Nubia

Known as Kush in ancient times, Nubia had long had uneasy relations with its northern neighbor, Egypt. The Kushites worshipped Egyptian gods, used hieroglyphics and even built their own pyramids. But Kush also vied with Egypt for control of the upper Nile valley, and in the eighth century BC the Kushites dominated Egypt itself until the Assyrians ousted them. Around 270 BC, however, Nubia entered its Meroitic period, a time of renewal lasting until the fourth century AD. During this era, Nubian rulers (often Queen Mothers) expanded the Kushite pantheon to include new gods from sub-Saharan Africa, even naming the lion-headed Apedemak as the official state deity. The capital of Meroë, which gave this period its name, became a major center of industry, especially iron. Even as North Africa, including Egypt, fell under Roman rule in the first century BC, Nubia remained sovereign and declined only after AD 1.

A nineteenth-century photograph of Nubian warriors.

A superb second-century AD Chinese bronze horse from the Eastern (or Later) Han period.

The Ch'in and Han Dynasties in China

The Ch'in ruler known as Shih Huang Ti, or "First Emperor," first unified China in 221 BC. His harsh and magnificent reign is remembered in the foreign name for his country, "China." The Chinese themselves referred (and still refer) to their country as Chung-kuo, the "Central Country" (or "Middle Kingdom"), an oasis of civilization surrounded on four sides by barbarians. At his death, Shih Huang Ti was buried in an extraordinary mausoleum surrounded by an army of 8000 life-sized, individualized terra-cotta figures. Civic improvements undertaken by Shih Huang Ti, such as roadbuilding, were continued by his successors, the early Han rulers. During

this period Chinese silks began to travel the great trade route known as the Silk Road to eager buyers in India, western Asia, and, eventually, Rome. Han rulers also resurrected what remained of the philosophical schools persecuted by Shih Huang Ti. They were particularly interested in the principle of the "Mandate of Heaven," first articulated by the Confucian scholar Mencius, which upheld a ruler's right to rule only so long as the people were contented (which, conveniently, justified their usurpation). Interest in the arts, technology and sciences flourished during the Han dynasty, which lasted until 220 AD.

Roman North Africa

The destruction of Carthage (146 BC) gave the province of *Africa* to Rome. By the time of Octavian's conquest of Egypt in 30 BC, Roman power extended right across the Maghreb, the continent's Mediterranean coast. Colonies were established and Roman-style cities built, like Caesarea in Mauretania and Augila in Cyrenaica (modern Libya), complete with public buildings. Such centers, linked by a road network, mirrored the empire in Europe. Parallel to this, colonial cultural influences fostered a

Romano-Berber tradition. At several surviving villas, mosaics depict rural landscapes and farms. While production of wines and oils was suppressed to preserve Italian interests, grain cultivation was increased in North Africa—the region becoming the "breadbasket" of the Roman world. Industry flourished, specializing in distinctive orange-colored pottery, statuettes and lamps.

A stone head of Octavian, the Roman emperor Augustus, conqueror of Egypt. From Ephesus, first century AD.

Inuits and Aleuts

"Eskimo," meaning "raw meat-eater," was the name given by the Algonquins to the peoples who lived north of them. Among themselves the Eskimos prefer the name Inuit, which simply means "the people." Inuits are related culturally and ethnically to the Aleuts (named by later Russian fur traders; the meaning is forgotten), who also call themselves "the people," *unanqan.* Aleut population has declined since contact with outsiders and is now confined to the Alaskan islands that bear their name, but Inuit peoples still inhabit northern lands stretching from eastern Siberia to Greenland. Although the ancestors of the Inuits and Aleuts migrated from northern Asia, some scholars argue for North

American origins of their cultural traditions. The Arctic Small Tool culture (*c.* 5000-3500 BC) and Old Whaling culture (*c.* 1800 BC) are possible precursors of fully developed Inuit cultures such as the Okvik and Old Bering Sea cultures of Siberia and St. Lawrence Island, or the Dorset culture of central Canada, all of which date to approximately the early centuries AD. Living on inhospitable, frozen tundra, the Inuits became skillful hunters and fisherfolk. They made efficient use of the animals they hunted, not only for food, clothing and shelter, but also for tools and fuel and cooking oil. Inland Inuits hunted caribou using the bow and arrow, which may have been introduced from Asia by their ancestors.

800	1000	1200	1400	1600	1800	2000

Judaism in the Hellenistic World

In 168 BC, tension between Hellenism and Judaism erupted into conflict in Palestine, when the Syrian king Antiochus IV Epiphanes abolished Jewish ritual in the temple at Jerusalem and introduced the worship of Zeus. Under the leadership of the priest Mattathias, the Jews revolted. In 164 BC Mattathias' son Judas Maccabaeus reconquered Jerusalem and reconsecrated the temple, an event commemorated by the Hanukah festival. The Maccabee dynasty ruled Palestine until 63 BC, when Pompey conquered it for Rome, and the Jews once again became a subject people. Although the Jews achieved a precarious political independence under the Maccabees, the texts known as the Dead Sea scrolls, which are dated from the first century BC to the first fifty years AD, reflect a time of spiritual searching. Composed by members of a Jewish sect that is associated or identical with the Essenes, the Dead Sea scrolls show a likely influence of Persian Zoroastrianism in their stress on religious dualism (Satan opposing God), the anticipation of a judgement day, and expectations of a messiah. The last notion also suggests an association with early Christianity, and has led to the controversial proposal that the historical figures of Jesus and John the Baptist may have been members of the Essene sect.

Ancient scrolls found in 1947 and later in the Qumran caves (above) northwest of the Dead Sea sparked historical controversy over the Jewish religion and early Christianity.

Rise of Rome

Originating from Bronze Age Latin settlements along the Tiber, Rome had an established civilization long before it achieved dominance of the Italian peninsula (*c.* 275 BC) and of an empire which embraced most of Europe—besides North Africa and the Levant. The Romans created an extensive Latin literature with epics like the *Aeneid* of Virgil (d. 19 BC) and poetry such as that of Ovid (d. 17 AD), whose themes included legend and love. Although its tradition in learning did not rival that of the Greeks, Rome had an organized education system. Its larger cities, linked by extensive road networks, were well furnished with amenities including a forum (central market-place), public baths, libraries, restaurants, and arenas where great spectacles like chariot-racing were held. There were temples to such deities as Jupiter and Mars. Common folk lived in urban condominium dwellings, while the patrician class had sumptuously decorated villas in the suburbs or country estates. Slaves, generally foreign captives, provided the labor force.

The twin cities of Pompeii and Herculaneum, preserved in volcanic ash from an eruption of Mt Vesuvius, provide a detailed insight into Roman city life.

Decoration in a Roman villa at Boscoreale, dating to c. 50 BC.

| 5000 | 2000 | 1000 | 500 | AD1 | 400 | 600 |

SPLENDOR AND DECLINE

Hour by hour resolve firmly, like a Roman and a man, to do what comes to hand with correct and natural dignity, and with humanity, independence, and justice.

Marcus Aurelius, Roman emperor and Stoic

It is interesting to compare the two great empires that flourished and declined at approximately the same time at opposite ends of the Eurasian continent. Unlike the decline of the western Roman empire, which signaled profound political, religious and cultural changes in Europe, the decline of the Han empire was one of many cycles in Chinese history which left significant facets of Chinese culture intact, some of which have lasted until the present day. Ancient Chinese writing is still legible to modern Chinese readers; Chinese philosophies institutionalized in the Han period, such as Confucianism and Taoism, remain relevant to modern Chinese, and continue to claim new adherents. In contrast, although Latin script is still used in European languages, and Latin influence is perceptible, the Latin language itself is considered dead. Few people can define popular Roman philosophies such as Stoicism and Epicureanism, let alone claim seriously to practice them.

SIMILARITIES AND DIFFERENCES

These two distinctive empires had similarities in their political histories. A few years after the first Han ruler came to power in 207 BC, Rome defeated Carthage and extended its rule over Spain, southern France, and Greece. The Third Punic War (149-146 BC), in which Carthage was utterly destroyed and its lands strewn with corrosive salt by the Romans, established Rome as the greatest power west of China. A few years later, the Han ruler Wu Ti, or "Martial Emperor" (r. 167-141 BC) began his expansion of China's domain to almost its current size. Each realm suffered a period of upheaval about the same time. The Roman republic underwent a half-century

of civil wars, finally quelled with the advent of Augustus (r. 27 BC--14 AD), who initiated the early empire. Augustus re-established a peace that endured for almost 250 years with few interruptions, enlarged the empire, and created conditions under which distinctive Roman literature and arts flourished. As Augustus was stabilizing Rome, the throne of the declining early Han dynasty was usurped by the reformer Wang Mang, in 9 AD. He was killed and the Han capital of Ch'ang-an was sacked in a rebellion in 23 AD, causing the complete collapse of the government. Order was re-established two years later by Liu Hsiu (Kuang Wu Ti), who established a new capital at Loyang. His dynasty is called the Eastern or Later Han, and it lasted until 220 AD.

The character of each empire was, nonetheless, quite different. Although Romans could boast of the marvelous poetry of Virgil, Horace and Catullus, and also of the rhetorical techniques of Cicero, their true genius was in military arts, engineering and architecture. Romans invented concrete, which made the vaulting of wide spaces possible. Roman monuments, aqueducts and bridges still stand today. Of the Han capitals of Ch'ang-an and Loyang, little or nothing remains. They were built of wood, no doubt magnificent in their day, but not durable. On the other hand, Chinese scientific and technological skills far surpassed those of the Romans. Paper was invented by the Chinese during the Han period, and the earliest forms of porcelain, called "china" by the rest of the world. Already skillful astronomers—the earliest recorded sighting of Halley's comet was made in China in 613 BC—and mathematicians, these arts were stimulated in Han China by contact with India.

India, with its own rich civilizations, was the crossroads where the Roman and Han empires met. Chinese textiles, especially their superb silks, surpassed any in the world. Imported into India via the ancient trade route of the Silk Road, Chinese textiles traveled to Rome from Roman trading outposts in India. During the reign of Nero (54-68 AD), the flow of Roman money to India to pay for silks was sufficient to cause a financial crisis.

THE EFFECTS OF BUDDHISM AND CHRISTIANITY

China, and perhaps Rome, were affected by religious developments in India. The Indian emperor Ashoka (reigned c. 269-232 BC), began his rule as a mighty conqueror, but after his conversion to Buddhism he attempted to establish a Buddhist kingdom. His efforts included sending Buddhist missionaries abroad, reportedly as far as Rome. Ashoka's support of Buddhism was instrumental in its great success in Asia, and it became widespread in China in the early centuries AD. Buddhism proved to be a very adaptable religion, capable of coexisting with other religions, absorbing them, or transforming itself into sects that accommodated local cultures.

Buddhism, although suffering occasional conflicts with Confucianism and Taoism in China, was accepted by the emperor Ming Ti about 60 AD, and eventually became an important world religion. Christianity, which also became an important world religion, developed rather differently in the Roman world. Originally one of many minor sects which proliferated in Rome, and sometimes the persecuted scapegoat of imperial power, Christianity slowly gained powerful supporters, of whom the most important

Han Dynasty bronzes of horsemen (top) and a Roman bronze of a horse and rider, both dating from the first century AD.

was the emperor Constantine (r. 307-337). The paradox of Christianity is that while the early Church absorbed many Roman traditions and institutions, its ethical orientation —emphasis on otherworldly reward and submission to a single, absolute God—was in many ways contradictory to the ideal Roman values of strength, independence, and discipline, exercised in this world.

In the fourth and fifth centuries, both Han China and the Roman empire fell prey to nomadic invaders. China, however, eventually reconstituted itself according to ancient patterns, while the western Roman empire vanished forever. In the surviving eastern Roman empire, Greek rather than Latin was the predominant language; and eventually the Byzantine empire more closely resembled a luxurious Asian satrapy than the ideal Stoic world emphasized by Cicero and Marcus Aurelius. *S.I.*

5000	2000	1000	500	AD1	400	600

Kingdom of Aksum

In remote antiquity, Ethiopia was ruled by Egypt but independent kingdoms formed from about 1000 BC. Distance and the difficult mountainous terrain facilitated this local particularism. The kingdom of Aksum—the predecessor of all modern Ethiopian states—was first formed around AD 100. It flourished for about five hundred years and included most of modern Ethiopia and some of southern Sudan. In the fourth century, Coptic Christianity spread south from Egypt. The Copts denied that Christ was simultaneously human and divine, so when this view was declared heterodox by the Church in 451 Aksum found itself outside the mainstream Christian fold. At its height, Aksum was an important commercial power, with influence on both sides of the Red Sea and as far away as India. The decline of the kingdom was caused by the expansion of Islam in east Africa, although the Christian tradition persisted as it continues to do in modern Ethiopia.

A fragment of a ceremonial fan depicting Ethiopian Coptic saints.

Gandhara

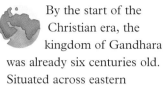

By the start of the Christian era, the kingdom of Gandhara was already six centuries old. Situated across eastern Afghanistan, northern Pakistan and northwest India, it controlled the Khyber Pass, the main entry route to India from the west. Its capital was Taxila (Islamabad). The population was of Scythian origin, having migrated from southern Russia. It was in turn a Persian province, one of Alexander the Great's conquests, and part of the north Indian Mauryan state whose capital was at Patna. In the first century AD, Gandhara was invaded by the Kushans, a tribe from Central Asia which established a Buddhist culture. Surprisingly, perhaps, they maintained strong links with the west, including the Roman empire. A trading crossroads, Gandhara absorbed many influences, not least the figurative art of the west which it adapted to eastern purposes in a uniquely eclectic style. The kingdom was shattered by the early Hun invasions.

Gandhara stucco relief from the fourth century. The mixture of western and Indian styles is evident from this piece.

■ *c.* 1-250 Maya Proto-Classic period.

■ 14 Death of Caesar Augustus, succeeded as Roman emperor by Tiberius.

■ 30 Crucifixion of Christ in Palestine.

■ 43 Chinese conquest of Tonkin and Annam (Vietnam).

■ 43 Roman invasion of Britain.

■ 64 Great fire destroys much of Rome during Nero's reign as emperor.

■ 65 First mention of Buddhism in China; introduced by missionaries from India.

■ 105 Invention of paper in China.

■ 107 Romans conquer the Dacians and reach the Carpathian mountains in central Europe.

■ 122 Hadrian's Wall near Anglo-Scottish border the northern frontier of the Roman empire.

■ *c.* 166 Chinese receive ambassador from Roman emperor Marcus Aurelius; probably an imposter.

■ 192 Chinese military dictator Tung Cho assassinated; civil war.

■ 220-265 Three rival kingdoms in China all claim imperial status.

■ 227 Sassanid neo-Persian empire pressurizes eastern boundaries of the Roman empire.

■ *c.* 250-600 Maya Early Classic period.

■ 265 China reunited under Western Chin dynasty.

■ 286 Diocletian creates eastern and western spheres of Roman empire, divided on the Adriatic.

■ *c.* 300-900 Classic period in Middle America: highly developed civilizations. Mayan civilization dominant in Central America.

■ 313 Following civil wars, Constantine is emperor of the Western empire.

■ 313 Edict of Milan grants full toleration to Christianity throughout the Roman empire.

■ 313 Korea splits into three kingdoms.

■ 320 Gupta dynasty, ruling from Patna, unites northern India after five centuries of division.

■ 323 Constantine reunites Roman empire; moves capital to Byzantium (renamed Constantinople).

■ 324 Christianity state religion of Roman empire.

■ 377 Peace between Rome and Sassanids, leaving Persians in control of Christian Armenia.

■ 379 Reign of Theodosius (-95) last of the great emperors of the united Roman empire.

■ 386 Northern Wei dynasty established in northern China (-534).

■ 395 On death of Theodosius Roman empire again divided, this time permanently.

■ 397 Rebellion by Gildo, Roman-appointed Berber chief of the province of *Africa*, crushed by Rome.

| | 1000 | 1200 | 1400 | 1600 | 1800 | 2000 |

The Roman Empire

By defeating Mark Antony at Actium in 31 BC, Octavian, called Augustus and Imperator (from which comes the word emperor), reunited the Roman world, ending its civil war. He also ended the Roman republic. The senate retained minor duties but Augustus had real power, especially over the army. He used this to extend the empire, annexing the Balkans, northern Spain and Egypt, building roads and cities which spread Roman civilization across Europe. His successors continued his policies, Claudius conquering Britain in AD 43. Under Trajan (AD 98-117), the empire reached the Persian Gulf but his successor Hadrian pulled back. Recurrent civil wars in the third century allowed invading "barbarians" almost to destroy the empire. Constantine (306-337) refounded Byzantium as a new capital, Constantinople (Istanbul), and converted to Christianity, dividing the empire at his death. The eastern (Byzantine) half survived fifth-century German invasions but the west collapsed by 476.

Battle scenes on the Great Lodovisi Sarcophagus of third-century Rome.

Korea: decline of Chinese rule

The Korean peninsula had remained free of Chinese influence until the first century BC, when a Chinese colonial state was established in the northwest. It did not succeed in establishing itself throughout the peninsula, however, and native Korean kingdoms coexisted with the Chinese. In 313 the country was divided between three kingdoms, with the Chinese position weakened. Later on, more native Korean kingdoms rose and fell but the failure of Chinese influence from the fourth century onwards, despite a presence of over 400 years, was decisive. Korea was destined not to be a Chinese province. By 668, it was united under native (Silla) rule and, despite many later vicissitudes, it never lost its own identity. Although under nominal Chinese rule from 1392 to 1910, it remained autonomous and regained full independence in the latter year.

This lacquered basketwork is from the Chinese colony of Lelang in north Korea.

The Rise of the Maya

The Mayan civilization of Mesoamerica passed through several distinct periods: the Preclassic (*c.* 2500 BC-AD 250), the Classic (AD 250-900), and the Late, or Post-Classic (AD 900-1500). Mayans lived in small villages through much of their early history, but in the late Pre-Classic they built large complexes and developed an aristocratic elite. By AD 250, the Maya had fully flowered. Large cities—such as Tikal, Uxmal, Palenque and Coba—anchored independent kingdoms spread across the Yucatán, central Mexico, Guatemala, Honduras, and Belize. Within each city-state, a religiously sanctioned nobility ruled tens of thousands of peasants. Mayan kings were warriors and demi-gods, and they sometimes practiced rites of bloodletting to incur divine favor. Awesome palaces and pyramidal temples served as a visible reminder of their power. The Classic Mayans enjoyed a brilliant florescence, but rampant population growth, feuding elites and prolonged drought triggered their collapse around AD 900.

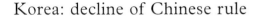

A terra-cotta Mayan incense burner of the early Classic period representing a priest with ear and nose plugs, arm rings, and headgear.

5000	2000	1000	500	AD1	400	600

Emperor Constantine transfers the symbols of imperial power to Pope Sylvester.

Christianity

Christianity began as a dissenting Jewish sect. It was spread through parts of the Near East by a series of brilliant missionaries of whom the most famous was St. Paul. Gradually, non-Jews began to outnumber Jews. In time, the doctrines of Christianity—based on the Four Gospels and most of all on the formulations contained in the Epistles of St. Paul—gave rise to theological disputes and heresies. The dual nature of Christ and the doctrine of the Trinity were much debated before becoming settled Christian belief. Early philosopher-theologians such as St. Augustine furnished the intellectual bedrock of the faith in these early centuries and influenced all who came later. Often Roman emperors attempted persecution, supplying the early Church with many martyrs. Still it grew until, in 324, the Roman emperor himself—Constantine the Great—converted and made Christianity the official religion of the empire. From that moment, it became the single most potent influence on later European culture.

The New Persian Empire

In 224, the Sassanid king Ardashir I defeated the last Parthian king, Artabanas V. With this victory, he inherited the Parthian hegemony, reaching from modern Afghanistan to Syria. The Parthians (originally from the Caspian steppes) had ruled for some 500 years. They were famed archers (remembered in the phrase "a Parthian shot"), but their control of the region had often been challenged. The Sassanids (from Persia) also inherited Parthian problems, including territorial disputes with the Roman empire, and religious challenges by emerging cults, such as Christianity and Manichaeism, to the traditional Persian religion of Zoroastrianism. Ardashir I's son, Shapur I, however, is remembered for his expansion of the empire, and for the overthrow of three Roman emperors, Gordian III, Philip I, and Valerian. The last was captured and carried away to Persia. Although the Sassanids, like the Parthians, maintained a capital at Ctesiphon in Babylonia, they also lavished artistic attention on their homeland, founding new cities such as Gur (Firuzabad) and producing notable rock carvings. They are most renowned for their magnificent silverwork, including ornamented plates, flasks, and sculptures. The Sassanid dynasty lasted for over four centuries, until it was ended by the Arab invasion in 637.

A plate of gold, rock crystal, and garnet depicts the Sassanid Persian king Khosru I (r. 531-579), a powerful military leader and patron of arts and letters. During his reign Greek and Sanskrit texts were translated into Persian.

Teotihuacán

Although the Maya became dominant, there were many highly developed civilizations in the Classic period of Mesoamerica (*c.* 300-900 AD). Mesoamerica's first true city, Teotihuacán, was built by an unidentified people who flourished between 300 and 700 in the Valley of Mexico. Teotihuacán covered nearly eight square miles, with a population estimated between 125,000 and 200,000. The city's neighborhoods were planned according to status and occupation. Two massive temple pyramids (larger than those of Egypt), dedicated to the sun and moon, anchored each end of a three-mile-long central axis, the Avenue of the Dead. Many buildings were decorated with sculpture and beautiful frescoes. Teotihuacáns also used hieroglyphic writing and developed a calendar, worshipped Quetzalcoatl (the Plumed Serpent) and Tlaloc (the rain god), and practiced human sacrifice. Teotihuacán artistic and cultural influences traveled to other centers, including those of the Maya. Their architectural influence is evident at Monte Alban in Oaxaca, where Classic-

A Teotihuacán wall painting probably depicts the paradise of the rain god Tlaloc, where the souls of those who pleased him are in bliss.

period Zapotecs leveled the mountain-top site of a shrine dating back to 500 BC, and constructed temples, ball courts, and palaces around a central plaza. El Tajin in Veracruz, famous for its calendar-inspired pyramid with four sides and 365 niches, may have been built by the Teotihuacáns.

A sacred bronze drum from the island of Bali, called the "Moon of Pejeng." It is the largest known drum of the type produced by the ancient Dong-Son culture.

Early Southeast Asia

Southeast Asia forms a tapestry of cultures with distinctive indigenous features and various adaptations to Chinese, Indian and, later, European influences. Vietnam provides one interesting example of these tangled histories. The oldest surviving artifacts in Southeast Asia come from the Dong-Son site in Vietnam. The Dong-Son culture, which can be dated to 2000 BC, produced figurines and, most typically, bronze drums that were used in sacred ceremonies. The culture was also dispersed through some of the Southeast Asian islands and survived there into the early centuries AD. Yet the Vietnamese language is distinct from the Austronesian languages spoken in these islands; it is sometimes included in the Sinitic languages to which Chinese also belongs, but it may be related to a third linguistic group, the Cambodian Khmer. Culturally, Vietnam is closer to China than any other Southeast Asian country. It was annexed by the Han emperor Wu Ti in 111 BC, and North Vietnam remained a part of China until 939 AD. Southern Vietnam, however, was home to the state of Champas, linguistically tied to Indonesia and culturally bound to India, which extended its regional influence via sea routes during the second and third centuries AD.

Aksumite Culture

Beyond the sphere of Rome, Ethiopia had developed, in the centuries before Christ, a culture with south Arabian influences. This Aksumite culture was not unrelated to that of Saba; inscriptions survive in a Sabaean dialect. The Aksumite kingdom, emerging into history from the first century AD, is discussed by the Greek scholars Pliny and Ptolemy. Its kings, among whom were Kaleb and Ezana, built cities like Adulis and Aksum itself. Architecture was distinctive with public buildings of stone, generally rectangular in layout, elevated on tiered bases and reached by steps. Palaces, such as Enda-Semon, comprise residences thirty-five yards square surrounded by great courtyards. Ordinary citizens lived in two- or three-room houses. With kings issuing coinage, industry and commerce flourished. Aksumites produced terra cotta pottery, mostly utilitarian with checkered or zigzag decoration, and hunted for ivory which was exported to the Mediterranean. An impressive temple stood at Yeha, northeast of Aksum, but the only pagan deity recorded is Astar. King Ezana, contemporary with the Roman Emperor Constantine, accepted Christianity.

A stele (commemorative stone) at Aksum from the fourth or fifth century.

5000	2000	1000	500	AD1	400	600

- *c.* 400 Kingdom of Ghana in West Africa founded, with capital at Kumbi.

- 407 The first Mongol empire, founded by the Avars (until 553).

- 410 Alaric the Visigoth sacks Rome.

- 429 Vandals establish a kingdom in North Africa.

- 433 Attila, ruler of the Huns (453).

- 440 Leo I, the Great (-461) establishes primacy of papal power as western empire declines.

- 450 Chinese begin to push into Sinkiang.

- 452 Attila and his Huns (descendants of the Hsiung-nu people of central Asia) invade Italy.

- 455 Vandals sack Rome, as western empire crumbles.

- 465 White Huns dominate northern India.

- 465 Gupta empire of northern India breaks apart.

- 476 Romulus Augustus, the last emperor, overthrown by Odoacer; end of the western Roman empire.

- 477 Reign begins of Budhagupta, last important Gupta emperor in northern India (-495).

- 493 Theodoric the Great defeats Odoacer and establishes Ostrogothic kingdom of Italy.

- 496 Clovis, king of the Franks, converts to Christianity.

- *c.* 500-1000 Rise of the Srivijayan empire of Malaysia and Indonesia. Lasts until the fourteenth century.

- 507 Weak Visigothic kingdom established in Spain.

- 520 Rise of Huns in northern India as Gupta empire declines.

- 527 Accession of Justinian as Byzantine emperor (-565).

- 529-33 Emperor Justinian codifies Roman Law throughout the Byzantine empire.

- 535 Destruction of Vandals' North African kingdom by Byzantine general Belisarius.

- 547 Vietnamese under Li-bon revolt against Chinese rule; rebellion crushed.

- 552 First evidence of Buddhism in Japan.

- 553 Turks establish a brief empire in central Asia (-582).

- 554 Emperor Justinian completes the imperial reconquest of Italy.

- 589 Following nearly 400 years of discord, China reunited under Sui dynasty.

- 590 Accession of Gregory the Great, one of the outstanding popes (-604).

- 600 Early Intermediate period in Andean culture. Important century for Bolivia's Tiahuanaco culture.

Tiahuanaco

One of the most influential cultures of the central Andes was centered at Tiahuanaco, which stood some 12,500 feet above sea level on the southeastern shore of Lake Titicaca. Founded perhaps as early as 200 BC, Tiahuanaco enjoyed its greatest prominence in the five centuries following AD 500. Kinship units dominated the city early on, but administrators and bureaucrats appeared as Tiahuanaco grew into a state-level polity. These elites lived and worked in buildings that sat atop great stone platforms. The masses, mostly farmers, inhabited humbler dwellings dispersed throughout the surrounding countryside. Tiahuanaco's great temple complexes suggest a society grounded in religious ritual. Most scholars also believe that Tiahuanaco was imperial, subordinating nearby towns through diplomacy and warfare. Ecological disaster—probably flooding—led to Tiahuanaco's demise around AD 1000. Nevertheless, alongside the Moche and Nazca, Tiahuanaco provided an important antecedent for the later and more spectacular Inca civilization of Peru.

A Tiahuanaco incense burner.

Ghana

The first trans-Saharan state of which we know anything with reasonable certainty is the ancient kingdom of Ghana, situated not in the modern African country that bears its name, but to the north of the River Niger in southeast Mauretania and southwest Mali. This is part of the so-called Sahel corridor, a belt of fertile grassland running horizontally across the continent just south of the Sahara. The kingdom of Ghana was first discovered by Berber traders pushing south. What drew them was gold, for Ghana controlled the Bambuk goldfield which soon became the principal source of the precious metal in the entire Islamic world. The ruling people of Ghana were the Soninke, although there were also subordinate groups within the kingdom. The capital was at Kumbi, to the west of Timbuktu. Eventually the kingdom was destroyed by Berber pressure from the north in the eleventh century.

The Sahara Desert, the northern boundary of the kingdom of Ghana.

The oldest (c. 450) Buddhist rock carvings in China, at Yungang, Shanxi province. Buddhism flourished during the Northern Wei dynasty.

The Northern Wei, China

After the Han dynasty's demise in 220, China entered a period of disunity and division. Non-Chinese peoples invaded the rich plains of the north and established themselves there. Of these, the most successful were the Wei, who by 420 ruled a united kingdom across the entire North China Plain, while a succession of native Chinese dynasties controlled the south. Although non-Chinese in origin, the Wei pursued a policy of energetic Sinification, which led to resistance from other non-Chinese groups in the north and eventually to the Wei's overthrow in 534. The work of the Northern Wei endured in the longer term, however, and facilitated the final reunification of China under the Sui dynasty in 589. This was followed less than thirty years later by the T'ang dynasty which ruled a united country for almost three centuries, one of the most brilliant periods in Chinese history.

Byzantium

The eastern half of the Roman empire, called Byzantine after its capital Byzantium (today Istanbul), survived fifth-century invasions almost unharmed. Emperor Justinian (527-565) even reconquered half the west (Italy, North Africa, southern Spain). Byzantium, by 600 Greek in language and culture, was the greatest city in Europe, wealthy and civilized when the west was chaotically barbarous. Although Arab invasions after 632 stripped the empire of outlying provinces and twice threatened to destroy it, Byzantium recovered to dazzle "barbarians" from visiting Vikings to neighboring Slavs, some of whom (Serbs, Bulgars) adopted Greek Orthodox Christianity. The powerful Russians of Kiev, stunned by Byzantine splendor, also became Orthodox in 996, not Roman Catholic. In 1054 Pope Leo IX, angered by the Orthodox Church's rejection of papal supremacy, excommunicated it, starting the "Great Schism" between eastern and western Churches, which underlies still existing divisions between eastern and western Europe.

The Emperor Justinian built grandiosely, notably the cathedral Hagia Sophia.

The Gupta Kingdom, India

Originally founded in the fourth century, this kingdom managed to reunite most of the subcontinental mainland. The collapse of the Maurya kingdom after six centuries had resulted in regional division and discord. The Gupta kingdom ended this chaos. It was consolidated under Chandragupta II, who reigned from about 375 to 413. It embraced all of modern India and Pakistan, except for the extreme south. The dynasty ruled India for almost two centuries until the incursions of the so-called White Huns from the north around 500, which eventually undid the work of unification. In the seventh century, a king called Harsha briefly recreated a united Hindu kingdom in India. But it broke up on his death and the subcontinent was plunged into centuries of division. The Gupta had been the last united Hindu kingdom of India.

Hindu temple, Khajurajo. Indian Hindus were unable to form a centralized Hindu state after the fall of the Gupta kingdom.

5000	2000	1000	500	AD1	400	600

Byzantines and Vandals

Under the late Roman and early Byzantine empires, Christianity became established in the northern reaches of the African continent. Harassed by desert nomads, early Christian communities constructed fortified churches like that at Jebel Musa, Sinai. Gaining in confidence, the early Church included Alexandria and Carthage among its major centers. Pachomius (fl. 320) pioneered monasticism in Egypt, while Augustine of Hippo (d. 430) emerged as one of the greatest early theologians. As imperial power elsewhere succumbed to "barbarian" onslaught, the Byzantine historian Procopius documented how Germanic Vandals swept across Tunisia in the 430s before settling. Vandal wealth from the grain trade is reflected in Germanic-style jewelry, examples of which have been found from Carthage and Mactar. Restoring Byzantine dominance over the region, the Emperor Justinian (r. 527-65) encouraged building and urban development and strove to revive the Christian faith. Elaborate churches like those at Sabratha and Kelibia date to Justinian's reign, which witnessed a great revival of Byzantine mosaic and epigraphy. Meanwhile, by the sixth century, Iron Age cultures were already established in the Zambezi Valley, where iron fabrication included agricultural tools and trade was conducted in pottery and copper.

Japanese Tomb Culture

The fourth and fifth centuries in Japan are characterized by the development of huge tomb mounds for aristocratic burial. Some resemble those on the mainland, suggesting Korean influence, but the earliest are in a "keyhole" shape unique to Japan. Tomb sculptures, known as *haniwa*, accompanied burials. Originally simple cylinders, soon figurative haniwa became common. During the period of the tomb culture, haniwa represented warriors and horses for the first time, leading some historians to speculate about an invasion of mounted warriors, perhaps from Korea. Japan and Korea already had intertwined histories; Korean emigrants helped populate the island of Kyushu, and Japan invaded Korea in 369 to interfere in the wars between the three kingdoms then seeking to gain control of Korea. Chinese influences often entered Japan through Korea, such as the introduction, about 405, of the Chinese writing system. The Japanese had no written language, and since Chinese and Japanese are from different linguistic families, it required a heroic effort for the Japanese to develop literacy using these foreign characters. Another lasting Chinese influence (originally from India) was Buddhism, which arrived via Korea *c.* 552.

Haniwa are traditional Japanese sculptures intended to accompany burials. This haniwa from about 500 AD represents a warrior.

A Moche fisherman paddles his little reed boat in this stirrup-spouted effigy vase. The Moche were a maritime people.

From the Río Moche to Tiahuanaco

Many different cultures flourished along the desert coast, mountains, and highland plateaus of western South America. The Moche (Mochica) of northern coastal Peru, who thrived during approximately the first seven centuries AD, built a splendid metropolis at Cerro Blanco. Little remains except for the ruins of the Huaca del Sol (Sacred Place of the Sun); their capital was destroyed shortly before 600, apparently by climatic disaster. The Moche practiced ritual human sacrifice, and also produced fine jewelry and gold artifacts. Many examples of distinctive Moche effigy pottery survive. These "stirrup-spouted vases" are fashioned in a variety of ways: as detailed human portraits, skeletal musicians, realistic and fantastical animals, boats, and houses, to name only a few. The Nazca of southern Peru produced their own distinctive painted pottery, and are known for intriguing geoglyphs, or large drawings, made upon the desert floor in geometric and animal forms. Still further south, on the high inland shores of Lake Titicaca, some 13,000 feet above sea level, are the extraordinary ruins of the great ceremonial center of Tiahuanaco. Archaeologists have identified six temple complexes, the most important of which includes the famous Gateway of the Sun.

The important Hindu god Krishna has many playful aspects as well as awesome ones. In this eighteenth-century illustration, he is shown playing his flute to please the gopi, or daughters of cowherds.

Sanskrit Literature and Drama

Under the Gupta dynasty (*c.* 320-*c.* 540), the great Hindu texts were given their definitive forms. Although the Sanskrit language was already ancient, in this period it became, as Latin did in Europe, the *lingua franca* of literature and scholarship, and reached expressive heights in both old and new works. The ancient *Puranas*, histories of the origins of the gods, were set down. The epic *Mahabharata* was shaped by Hindu Brahmans to emphasize important themes. Religious reform cults in both Buddhism and Hinduism, called *bhakti*, stressed devotion to a personal god; in Hinduism the complementary strains of Vaishnavism (worship of Vishnu) and Shaivism (worship of Shiva) were the most significant. Vishnu is celebrated in the religious poem the *Bhagavad Gita* ("Celestial Song"), which had become attached to the popular *Mahabharata*. The *Gita* is a dialogue between the noble warrior Arjuna and his charioteer Krishna (an incarnation of Vishnu) explaining the importance of practicing *dharma*, or the ideal life associated with each caste. Theater, which involved dance, music, and gesture, as well as recitation, also flourished in this period. The greatest Sanskrit playwright was the fifth-century poet Kalidasa, who drew upon the *Mahabharata* for the plot of his masterpiece, *Shakuntala*.

"Barbarians" and Christians

Partitioned by Emperor Constantine who made Constantinople his capital, the Roman world became permanently divided from AD 395. While the Eastern Byzantine empire would survive into the next millennium, the west succumbed in the fifth century to "barbarian" incursions. Replacing Western Europe's Roman inheritance was a new order, neither literate nor Christian. From the western extremities, particularly from Ireland, a new cultural and religious impetus would emerge from the sixth century. Retaining Celtic language and customs, this region was characterized by political fragmentation and a poor material culture. Bypassed by Roman urban development, Ireland's ruling classes lived in earthen enclosures or in *crannógs*, island dwellings which differed little from Bronze Age lake settlements. Yet an insular Christianity already established there would facilitate the emerging Anglo-Saxon Church. Ireland's *peregrinatio* (religious exile) tradition, pioneered by Columbanus (d. 615) and his disciple Gall, introduced to France, Italy and Switzerland a form of monasticism that placed spiritual devotion over physical sacrifice. As illustrated by the grammarian Asperius (fl. 600), Irish scholars were already adept at Latin; in the following century they would increasingly diverge from monastic scholarship into literature, developing a Latinity that would significantly influence Continental writing.

Head reliquary of St. Oswald (d. 642), Anglo-Saxon king of Northumbria, who had been baptized by Irish missionaries. The twelfth-century casket is plated with gilded silver.

49

THE RISE OF ISLAM

There is no god but God, and Muhammad is His Prophet.
Opening of the Muslim daily prayer

The faith of Islam, which means submission (to the will of God), became established in Arabia in the early seventh century of the Christian era, following the emergence of Muhammad as a prophet bearing witness to monotheism. The very extent of the region and the dispersal of its population, separated by mountain and desert, was perhaps a factor in the accumulation of religious influences that were to be found there. Like other Semitic peoples, the Arabs were heirs to a Judaistic tradition, while certain Coptic Christian teachings had been assimilated through trade contact with Ethiopia. It was still the case, however, that pagan beliefs and practices remained strong. Rejecting pagan survivals, Muhammad would combine elements of the two major theistic faiths in the formulation of his message.

THE PROPHET'S MESSAGE

Born *c.* 570, the Prophet of Mecca belonged to the Koreish lineage, hereditary keepers of the shrine of Kaaba. His grandfather had been keeper, but Muhammad was orphaned at a young age and reared by his uncle Abu Talib. Tradition represents Muhammad as virtuous from his youth, a man whose integrity, sensitivity, and simple habits would mark him out as a future religious leader. His earliest inspiration may well have come from his experience as a merchant, visiting the great fairs of Syria where he encountered a wide range of cultural and religious influences. Subsequently, having married a wealthy widow named Khadija, he was able to devote himself to contemplation.

Around 609 to 612 he began preaching in Mecca following a period of prayer and fasting during which, Muslims believe, he had been commanded by Allah (God the Father) to deliver His message. The teaching which took shape accorded due reverence to Moses and the Jewish prophets, and to Jesus Christ, as earlier messengers of God. The ultimate revelation, however, requiring submission to the will of God as Creator and Heavenly Father of mankind, was that communicated to Muhammad himself. The message delivered has a great deal in common with the other theistic faiths. It stresses prayer and penance, brotherly love and almsgiving.

EVENTUAL ACCEPTANCE

The preaching of Muhammad took on a greater urgency as the Sassanids of Persia conquered Syria in 613, sweeping southwards into Egypt and northwest into Asia Minor. It certainly appeared for a time that the Byzantine empire was collapsing, that the "Old Order" of the Middle East was changing. His efforts, however, won few converts: only the protection of prominent Koreish members, including his uncle Abu Talib and cousin Ali and a prominent Mecca citizen named Abu Bekr, saved him from expulsion. Eventually, his uncle having died, it seemed opportune for the city fathers to drive him out in 622. Muhammad's subsequent *Hejira*, or migration, to Medina would later furnish Islam with a basis for chronology. Coincidentally, that same year the Byzantine emperor Heraclius launched a major offensive against Persia that would end five years later in defeat for the Sassanid kingdom. Meanwhile, Medina received Muhammad not only as teacher but as effective ruler of the city. His followers grew in number; in 630 they marched to Mecca which submitted at once. Muhammad called upon all rulers to embrace Islam. That same year, a skirmish took place with Byzantine forces near the Dead Sea. Non-compliant Arab communities were soon overpowered, and by Muhammad's death in 632 all Arabia was Muslim, that is "had submitted."

THE EXPANSION OF ISLAM

After his death, the teachings of the Prophet were incorporated into the Koran, which Muslims believe to be the holy word of God dictated to the Prophet by the Archangel Gabriel. Essentially a book of revelation, the Koran would also furnish a code of civil and criminal law. The Islam of these years was a militant creed. For many converts, while doctrines of brotherly love may have had limited appeal, the sense of patriotism inspired by a new-found religious unity provided a driving force. Responsibility for furthering the progress of Islam fell to the caliph, or successor of the Prophet. This office, as Muhammad had left no sons, was filled by four of his close associates in succession. The last of these was Ali, a cousin of Muhammad who had married his daughter Fatima. Ali was murdered in 661 and replaced by Umayyad caliphs, who would introduce dynastic rule quite different in character to that of the Prophet's early successors. In the interim, Islam as a political entity expanded rapidly at the expense of the neighboring Persian and Byzantine empires. Both of these powers had been weakened by years of mutual conflict. In addition, many subject peoples, to whom the Sassanids or Byzantines were oppressors, were only too willing to change masters. Persia had collapsed completely before Islam by 641 and the Byzantines sustained a series of defeats, with Emperor Heraclius seemingly powerless to stem the Muslim advance. Jerusalem had fallen in 637, Syria soon fell and Alexandria in Egypt had been taken by 642. The way was open for Islam—a faith less than fifty years old— to expand across North Africa. *A.M*

The Hejira, *or migration, of Muhammad in 622 brought him to Medina. This city would become, next to Mecca, the second most important center of Islam. The tile illustrated here (of sixteenth century date) shows a schematic view of Medina.*

5000	2000	1000	500	AD1	400	600

- *c.* 600 Middle Horizon period in the Andean region begins (-900).

- 606 Harsha, king of Thanesar, establishes an empire across north India (-647).

- 618 T'ang dynasty (-907) established in China, one of the greatest periods in China's history until *c.* 755 the country begins to split into different states.

- 622 *Hegira* (migration) of Muhammad from Mecca to Medina.

- 626 Siege of Constantinople, jointly conducted by Balkan Avars and Sassanians.

- 630 Muhammad enters Mecca.

- 632 Death of Muhammad and establishment of orthodox caliphate; Abu Bakr first caliph.

- 633 Arab invasion of Iraq introduces Islam to the Fertile Crescent.

- 635 Arabs take Damascus.

- 637 Jerusalem surrenders to the Arabs.

- 639 Arabs overrun Mesopotamia.

- 642 Battle of Nehawand: Arabs defeat Persians who become part of the Islamic world.

- 643 Harsha receives ambassadors from Chinese emperor T'ang T'ai-tsung.

- 661 Umayyad caliphate at Damascus, now the center of the Islamic world.

- 668 Silla, Buddhist kingdom of south-east Korea, unites the peninsula (-935).

- 681 Establishment of first Bulgarian empire in Balkans (-1018).

- 697-8 Arabs enter Carthage; new city of Tunis built nearby.

- *c.* 700 Rise of Mississippian (Temple Mound Building) culture in Mississippi basin and south-east North America.

- *c.* 700 Rise of Kanem-Bornu in modern Nigeria, which controlled trans-Saharan trade.

- 711 Arrival of first Muslims under Tariq in Spain at Gibraltar (Jabal Tariq = Tariq's Rock).

- 711 Umayyad forces reach the Indus valley.

- 712 Arabs establish a state in Sind, in modern Pakistan.

- 717 Leo III, Byzantine emperor, founds the Isarian dynasty.

- 732 Battles of Tours and Poitiers arrest the advance of Islam in western Europe.

- *c.* 750 Gurjara-Prathihara dynasty controls northern India (-1036), resists Islamic incursions.

- 750 Umayyads overthrown in Damascus by the Abbasids (-1258).

- 751 Arabs defeat the Chinese at Samarkand.

- 756 Pepin the Frank defeats Lombards; grants Lombard lands to the papacy, thus beginning the Papal States.

- 756 Establishment of the Umayyad dynasty in Muslim Spain, based in Cordoba (-1031).

- 763 Baghdad founded by al-Mansur, strongman of the early Abbasids.

- 768 Charlemagne king of the Franks (-814).

- 786 Harun al-Rashid caliph of Baghdad (-809).

- 787 First Viking raids in Britain.

- 788 Franks complete conquest of Saxony and Bavaria.

The Spread of Islam

The third of the great monotheistic religions of the Middle East, Islam, was founded by a merchant, Muhammad, born in Mecca *c.* 570. In 622, as a widower with a small following, he traveled from Mecca to Medina. Known as the *Hegira*, this journey is the foundation event of Islam. From there he soon converted Mecca and by 630 controlled the Arabian peninsula. Although Muhammad died in 632, his message spread with a speed unmatched in history. Islam's growth is arguably the single most important event of the seventh century. In barely a hundred years from the Hegira, it reached North Africa, Persia and almost India, where it did arrive a few centuries later. By the early eighth century it had crossed as far east as south-central Asia and as far west as Spain. In 758 Islamic traders in China were sufficiently numerous and confident to sack Canton.

A pilgrim caravan en route to Mecca. All Muslims must visit Mecca once in their lives.

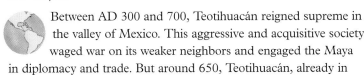

El Tajin

Between AD 300 and 700, Teotihuacán reigned supreme in the valley of Mexico. This aggressive and acquisitive society waged war on its weaker neighbors and engaged the Maya in diplomacy and trade. But around 650, Teotihuacán, already in decline, was burned to the ground and never recovered. A new regional power soon emerged: the Classic Veracruz, centered at El Tajin. This state spread southwards along the Gulf coast and prospered for 500 years. El Tajin displays the influence of both Teotihuacán and the Maya. A giant niched pyramid, possibly dedicated to the sun, stood at the city's center. The sculptures covering its temples, palaces and ball courts—in which a game called *tlachtli* was played—convey gruesome images of warfare and human sacrifice. There is also reference to a skilled leader named 13 Rabbit, although his achievements remain unknown. After 800, the Classic Veracruz existed alongside a rising Toltec civilization.

The Pyramid of the Niches at El Tajin.

Kanem-Bornu

The second African state of consequence, after the kingdom of Ghana, is the empire of Kanem-Bornu, which began its long rise to eminence in the eighth century. It was based near Lake Chad. The state was founded by the Kanuri, a Nilo-Saharan people; the capital was Njimi. Kanem existed as a vehicle for trans-Saharan trade. The Sanhaja Berbers had introduced camels from Asia and mastered the art of domesticating them. These provided the means to make vast desert journeys. Kanem's position on the route from Ghana—and later from Songhai and Mali—to the Red Sea lands gave it a crucial strategic importance. In time, it covered the region from the Niger river in the west to what is now western Sudan. Kanem played an important role for centuries, remaining independent until the nineteenth.

Chenla: Early Khmer state

The earliest state in the region that is now Cambodia of which we have knowledge is Funan. In the early seventh century, however, the area called Chenla—occupying what is now northern Cambodia and southern Laos—established its independence from Funan. Its king, Isanavarman I (r. *c.* 611- 635), expanded his kingdom westwards to embrace much of modern Cambodia and a small portion of eastern Thailand. One of his successors, Jayavarman I, who is thought to have reigned for forty years in the second half of the seventh century, conquered central Laos. But that was the limit of Chenla's success. Internal dissension weakened the kingdom in the eighth century and the area came under Sumatran rule for a while. But the successor state to Chenla, that of the Angkor kings, controlled southeast Asia for over five centuries, from 802, presiding over one of the most brilliant civilizations of its time.

The Khmer horse-headed god called Jajimukha, represented in this piece of polished limestone c. 600-650.

The Saxons and Vikings

By 600 the Anglo-Saxons, who had invaded Britain *c.* 400, had pushed the Britons (Welsh) into the west, confirming Saxon supremacy over what became England. At first England comprised seven kingdoms, the "Heptarchy." These soon became Christian, for St. Augustine, arriving in 597 from Rome, began converting them. Offa, king of Mercia 757-96, imposed unity over other English states, but his power died with him. The Vikings— raiders from Denmark and Norway—invaded after 800, overrunning England until Alfred king of Wessex (871-99) checked them in 878. Alfred founded the English navy and started a cultural revival. Later Wessex kings reconquered much of England, but the Vikings settled firmly in the north. The Christianized Dane Cnut seized the English throne in 1016, ruling an empire including Norway and Denmark, but this fell apart at his death in 1035. By then Vikings and Saxons were beginning to merge.

The Gokstad Viking Ship, c. 900, from Bygdoy, Norway.

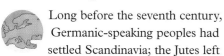
The Vikings

Long before the seventh century, Germanic-speaking peoples had settled Scandinavia; the Jutes left their name on Jutland, the Danes occupied the adjacent islands and the south of modern Sweden, while Swedish and Norwegian tribes lived further north and west. Farming was central to the economy, especially sheep-raising for wool production; however, like many maritime peoples, fishing and seal-hunting were of great importance. Northwards along the Norwegian coast, population density was low with settlement largely confined to fjords. Scandinavian religion was polytheistic, their deities including Odin, the war god, and Thor, god of thunder. During the Vendal period (seventh century), the funeral rite for nobility involved cremation, with burial in a ship-grave. The art of this period, displayed on brooches, horse-trappings and ceremonial helmets, featured abstract human faces and animal heads. In the later Urnes phase, art would be characterized by interlaced animal designs. By the eighth century, the Scandinavians had perfected streamlined clinker-built ships, capable of crossing the high seas. From this time, population pressure and centralized kingship prompted young aristocrats to pursue their fortune in raiding and colonizing overseas—thus inaugurating the Viking Age.

An eighth-century funerary stone from Gotland, Sweden, featuring a Viking ship framed in interlace pattern.

Islam's Arrival

Following the death in 632 of Muhammad, the Prophet of Islam, his teachings rapidly diffused via the intercontinental crossroads of Palestine into Africa. Interpretation of the spread of Islam in terms of conquest, Islamic historians argue, fails to differentiate between religious growth and political expansion where the general aim was not conversion.

Many seventh-century Egyptian Copts apparently welcomed the monotheistic Muslims. The Copts considered that the human nature of Christ had been elevated to the divine, a belief for which they had been persecuted by the Byzantines. Now Muslim teaching, while venerating Christ as an important prophet, stressed that divinity was confined to God alone; this, it was asserted, was the message confided to Muhammad. Islam rapidly advanced into the province of *Africa*, converting native populations and achieving regional dominance by the early eighth century. Along with the Muslim faith, Arabic language and culture spread across northern Africa. This is reflected in the architecture of early mosques, like Kairouan. Meanwhile, in sub-Saharan Africa, the Iron Age Sanga culture of the Upper Zaire Valley had established trade links from the Atlantic to the Indian Ocean.

The mosque at Kairouan, Tunisia, dating from c. 670.

The World of *The Arabian Nights*

The sumptuous and cruel world depicted in the tales of The Arabian Nights immortalized the reign of the Caliph Harun al-Rashid (786-809). His splendor and severity epitomizes a triumphant period in Islamic history, the reign of the Abbasid caliphs. Arab expansion in the seventh century was motivated by the quest for wealth as well as Islamic missionary zeal. In less than a century the Arabs had conquered ancient Persia as well as much of the former Roman world. In Persia, Islam replaced Zoroastrianism, which today survives only with the Parsees of India, descendants of Sassanid Persian refugees. The Islamic title "Caliph," which is both religious and secular, means "Successor of the Prophet." An early and lasting schism in Islam

800	1000	1200	1400	1600	1800	2000

followed quarrels about the succession to Muhammad. The Shi'ite minority unsuccessfully maintained that only descendants of Muhammad's daughter Fatima were eligible for the caliphate; the majority Sunnites supported the custom of rule by elected caliphs which began with the Umayyad dynasty in 661. Under the Umayyad successors, the Abbasids, whose rule began in 750, the caliphate adopted a more Persian character, shifting the center of power east to the new capital of Baghdad.

A modern painting showing the mosque that contains the tomb of Muhammad's grandson Hussein, killed by Umayyad troops in 680 at Kerbala, Iraq. The mosque is a pilgrimage site for Shi'ite Muslims.

Korean Kingdoms

Chinese influence is apparent in the legendary early history of Korea, which traces the founding of the Chosŏn state to a scion of the Shang dynasty. The Han ruler Wu Ti ("Martial Emperor") conquered Chosŏn about 109 BC. As early Chinese rule waned, especially following the collapse of the Han Empire, native kingdoms emerged in Korea. The oldest was Koguryŏ in the north, followed by Paekche in the southwest, and Silla in the southeast. Cultural developments in China continued to influence the three kingdoms competing for control of the Korean peninsula. Buddhism, already established in China, was introduced in Koguryŏ in 372, and spread throughout Korea. The Chinese writing system was also adopted, although, as in Japan, it was foreign to the native language and difficult to use. China, reunified under the Sui and T'ang dynasties, attempted to invade Korea in the early seventh century, but was successfully repulsed by the three kingdoms. The powerful T'ang dynasty nonetheless provided political and artistic models for Korea. Silla emerged as the leader of a unified Korea in 668, and many beautiful Buddhist monuments were built before the final extinguishing of the Silla kingdom in 935.

A sixth-century silver crown, once covered with semi-precious stones, from the Korean kingdom of Silla. Similar "curved jewels" have been found in Japanese tombs, another indication of the intertwined cultures of these two countries.

The Maya Classic Period

The Maya achieved unrivaled intellectual and artistic dominance in Mesoamerica in the Classic period (c. AD 300-900). Over 100 Maya sites are known in Mexico and northern Central America. Their accomplishments lay in the elaborate refinement of the arts and sciences of earlier peoples, in particular the Olmecs and the Teotihuacáns. The great Maya pyramids at Tikal and elsewhere are all the more remarkable for being constructed without the use of wheeled transport or beasts of burden; like other Americans, the Maya did not have the wheel, nor any domesticated animals other than dogs and fowls. The Maya were sophisticated sculptors, fresco artists and weavers

as well as advanced mathematicians and astronomers. They developed the most complex writing system of Mesoamerica, with ideographic and pictographic symbols, and, apparently, phonetic symbols as well. It remains only partially translated; most of the Mayan codices, or books, were destroyed by the Spanish. The Maya were fascinated with time, and developed systems for coordinating astronomical events with terrestrial history, recorded with precise arithmetical notation that included the concept of zero. The Mayan calendar was more accurate than any in Europe before 1582, and also contained a wealth of ritual and historical information.

Towards the end of the Maya Classic period, regional architectural styles began to develop in different Maya centers. The Great Palace at Sayil on the Yucatán peninsula is an example of the elegant Puuc style.

5000	2000	1000	500	AD1	400	600

- *c.* 800 Conquest of territory of modern Zimbabwe by Bantu people.

- 800 Charlemagne crowned emperor of the west (Holy Roman Emperor) in Rome by pope.

- 802 Capital of Khmer empire in Southeast Asia established at Angkor Thom.

- 808 Establishment of a powerful Bulgarian kingdom under Krum.

- 813 Reign of al-Mam'un the Great, Abbasid caliph (-833); moves capital to Baghdad.

- 814 Death of Charlemagne, followed by gradual disintegration of his empire.

- 817 Beginning of division of the empire among Charlemagne's grandsons.

- 831 Muslims complete conquest of Sicily.

- 841 Vikings establish kingdom in the lower Seine valley, later the duchy of Normandy.

- 843 Carolingian lands divided into kingdoms of west and east Franks, later France and Germany.

- 867 Basil I (r. -886), inaugurates an era of Byzantine glory.

- 868 The first printed book, *The Diamond Sutra,* is made in China using wood blocks for printing.

- 868 Ahmad ibn-Tulun establishes Tulunid dynasty in Egypt.

- 882 Kiev capital of new state of Kievan Rus, later basis of medieval Russia.

- *c.* 900 Magyar people invade and occupy the Great Hungarian Plain.

- *c.* 900-1500 Post-Classic period in Middle America.

- 907 End of T'ang dynasty in China is followed by civil war until 960.

- 912 Abd ar-Rahman III caliph of Cordoba in Muslim Spain (-961), apogee of Umayyad power.

- 935 Silla yields dominance in Korea to newly formed kingdom of Koryŏ (-1392).

- 939 First in a series of civil wars breaks out in Japan.

- 944 Kiev-Constantinople treaty opens the way for Christian influence in central Russia.

- *c.* 950-1050 Igbo-Ukwu culture thrives in eastern Nigeria.

- *c.* 950 Apogee of the kingdom of Ghana, stretching almost from Atlantic to Timbuktu.

- 950 Kupe, great Maori (Polynesian) navigator discovers New Zealand on canoe voyage.

- 960 Song dynasty in China (-1279) responsible for modernization of state.

- 965 Baptism of Prince Miesko I; foundation date of Polish Christianity.

- 968 Establishment of Fatimid dynasty in Egypt (-1171).

- 978 Chinese begin compiling an encyclopedia of 1000 volumes.

- 982 Eric the Red discovers Greenland.

- 988 Prince Vladimir of Kiev founds Russian Orthodox Church.

- 998 Mahmud, Turkish ruler of Ghazni (r. 1030), founds empire in northern India and eastern Afghanistan.

- *c.* 1000 Hohokum people of Arizona develop acid etching of shells.

Tribes in Transition

The last centuries of the first millennium AD marked a time of transition for many North American peoples. Around 750, the Anasazi of the southwest shifted from their "Basketmaker" period to their "Pueblo" period by moving into adobe dwellings in the desert. In about 800, the Thule Inuit of Alaska migrated across Arctic Canada, settling Greenland and absorbing the older Dorset culture. In the Plains region, agricultural towns cropped up along the Missouri River around 850, though they remained vulnerable to the frequent raids executed by their nomadic neighbors. In the river valleys of the Midwest, the Mississippian culture supplanted the Hopewell. Like their predecessors, the Mississippians practiced a mortuary ceremonialism that involved building large earthen mounds for their honored dead. And in the Eastern Woodlands, beginning about AD 1000, chronic warfare among the Owasco peoples initiated a process of agglomeration that eventually gave rise to the Iroquois tribes.

Pottery effigy-head vessel with sealed eyelids, stitched mouth, and facial decorations: Mississippian culture, c. 1000.

Ghaznavid Kingdom in Afghanistan

The incredible spread of Islam in the first two centuries of its existence brought it to the borders of India. In the fullness of time, it would make a profound impact on the life and history of the subcontinent. But in these early years, it remained merely at the gates. One of the most easterly of the Islamic states in the tenth and eleventh centuries was that of the Ghaznavids, originally from Turkey but by then the rulers of Afghanistan and the Punjab. For over 200 years from the founding of the state around 950, the Ghaznavids controlled this important region, launching punitive raids into the plains of north India and greatly enriching both themselves and their kingdom. The capital was eventually moved from the original mountain fastness of Ghazni to Lahore, and the kingdom was overthrown in the late twelfth century.

800	1000	1200	1400	1600	1800	2000

Charlemagne and the Carolingian Empire

The Franks, who gave their name to France, were the chief successors to the Romans in the west but they were chaotic, if Christian. When the Arabs crossed the Pyrenees, France seemed powerless until Charles Martel checked them at Poitiers (732). Charles was only "mayor of the palace" (prime minister) to decadent Merovingian kings but his son, Pepin, made himself king with the pope's blessing in 754. Pepin's son Charlemagne conquered much of Europe, including Italy and Germany, being crowned emperor in Rome in 800. He built an imperial palace at Aachen, Germany, surrounded himself with

scholars and issued edicts on everything from wine-making to religion. But the Carolingian empire lacked cohesion, depending totally on its ruler. Louis the Pious, succeeding Charlemagne in 814, was weak. Viking raids and civil wars between Louis' sons hastened the disintegration of the empire which, after repeated sub-divisions, effectively collapsed in 899.

Emperor Charlemagne

The T'ang Dynasty in China

For almost three centuries until 907, the T'ang dynasty ruled a united China. It raised the country to heights never before achieved. China was united; its territories were vast, ranging from Manchuria to Vietnam, although not embracing Sinkiang and Tibet. Its capital at Chang'an was reckoned to be the richest and most populous city on earth. The T'ang encouraged foreign trade: under them the Silk Road to western Asia and Europe was developed and maintained. They encouraged scholarship, especially Confucianism which they employed as an instrument for the creation of a unified national culture. They also attempted to strengthen central government at the expense of local warlords and succeeded in this for a while. But the last years of the dynasty were plagued by rebellion and destruction. Nonetheless, the T'ang legacy passed to the next powerful dynasty, the Song, who re-established Chinese unity after 960.

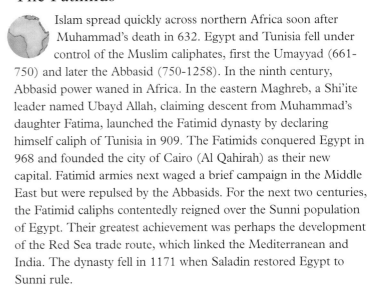

View of Fatimid Cairo from the Great Friday Mosque. Cairo gained its most significant features during its Fatimid period.

The Fatimids

Islam spread quickly across northern Africa soon after Muhammad's death in 632. Egypt and Tunisia fell under control of the Muslim caliphates, first the Umayyad (661-750) and later the Abbasid (750-1258). In the ninth century, Abbasid power waned in Africa. In the eastern Maghreb, a Shi'ite leader named Ubayd Allah, claiming descent from Muhammad's daughter Fatima, launched the Fatimid dynasty by declaring himself caliph of Tunisia in 909. The Fatimids conquered Egypt in 968 and founded the city of Cairo (Al Qahirah) as their new capital. Fatimid armies next waged a brief campaign in the Middle East but were repulsed by the Abbasids. For the next two centuries, the Fatimid caliphs contentedly reigned over the Sunni population of Egypt. Their greatest achievement was perhaps the development of the Red Sea trade route, which linked the Mediterranean and India. The dynasty fell in 1171 when Saladin restored Egypt to Sunni rule.

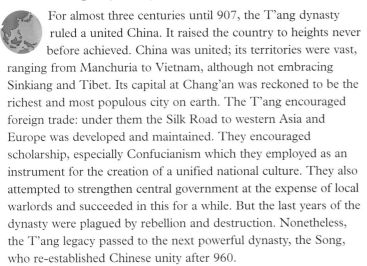

An authentic reconstuction of the T'ang fort at Dunhuang on the Great Silk Road.

5000	2000	1000	500	AD1	400	600

Igbo

Bronze pendant from Igbo-Ukwu, representing an Eze Nri.

The Igbo people of the east Niger delta had developed an advanced Iron Age culture by the ninth century AD, based on centers like Ezira and Igbo-Ukwu, which was probably a royal site. Engaging in manufacture and commerce, the Igbo exploited local ores to fabricate swords and other iron implements. Bronze ornaments, some representing human images, were fashioned using imported copper and occasionally decorated with gold filigree. The Igbo also imported glass and carnelian, exporting ivory and slaves. There are some indications of trans-Saharan contact. Agriculture was much focused on yam production. Igbo political organization was centralized and closely bound to religion. The supreme ruler (Eze Nri) was essentially a priest-king whose authority, which extended to a hegemony over several neighboring states, was religious rather than military in character. It may be that the Igbo did not perceive the need for extensive military organization; defensive earthworks, quite common west of the Niger, are rare within their realms. Members of the nobility were buried around Igbo-Ukwu in wooden lined chambers, with grave goods including highly decorated pottery and bronze ornaments.

Urban Development in Non-Roman Europe

One outcome of the Viking period, most often remembered for violent raids, was colonization with the foundation from the ninth century of commercial towns in non-Roman Europe. Arguably based on models in their homeland, such as Hedeby in Denmark, these Nordic colonists built settlements which grew into towns like York in England or Dublin in Ireland. Seats of kingship and foci of population, these centers had many urban characteristics. Patterned streets of wooden houses made up quarters of craft-industry. More importantly, they traded with the Continental mainland and with the Middle East, duly popularizing the notion of weights and measures and coinage. Parallel to these developments, a renaissance of learning gathered pace patronized by Frankish emperor Charlemagne (d. 814), who had united much of Western Europe under his rule. To facilitate copying of texts, a standardized writing known as Carolingian miniscule was developed. The emperor's successors promoted scholarship in various disciplines. Their protégés included historian Einhard (d. 840), author of the *Life of Charlemagne*, theologian Hincmar (d. 877), and Irish thinker Eriugena (d. 877), whose *Periphyseon* has been placed among the worthiest Western philosophical productions.

A tenth-century Irish-Scandinavian silver penny issued by King Sitric of Dublin.

The Srivijayan Empire

During the eighth and ninth centuries, the Malay-Indonesian empire of Srivijaya was probably the predominant center of Buddhist art in the world. The *stupa*, or temple, at Borobudur on the island of Java is a superb example of the Buddhist tradition of rock carving. Actually a hill encased in stone, it has nine terraces and 1500 carved stone panels in its four galleries. The wealth of the Srivijayan empire, especially powerful between the fifth and tenth centuries but lasting until the fourteenth, came from the seafaring abilities of its people and their control of maritime trade in the western Indonesian Archipelago. This control extended as far as southern China. Influenced by India, as was most of Southeast Asia by the ninth century (only northern Vietnam, which came under Chinese influence, and the Philippines, which were geographically distant, were unaffected), the Srivijayan empire provides one example of how distinctive indigenous cultures were blended with Indian traditions. Artistic and religious models were modified according to regional tastes, sometimes with significant differences. Although Hinduism as well as Buddhism traveled to the mainland and islands of Southeast Asia, for example, the caste system was never adopted there.

The Buddhist stupa, Borobudur, Java. Each niche holds a Buddha figure, representing the many facets of the single Buddha-nature.

The Toltecs

The Toltecs, nomadic warriors of the Chichimec ("Sons of the Dog") peoples, began arriving in Mesoamerica from the north in the eighth century. Absorbing cultural influences from the collapsed civilizations of the Teotihuacáns and the lowland Maya of the Valley of Mexico, the Toltecs established a capital at Tollan (Tula) by about 987. From there they established trade networks as far south as Guatemala and east into the Yucatán peninsula, where they blended with the remaining Maya to produce the last great phase of Maya civilization, often referred to as "Maya-Toltec." The splendid ceremonial centers of Chichén Itzá and Mayapan, powerful in the eleventh and twelfth centuries, resulted from this mixture of cultures. The Toltecs also elaborated a mythology for the ancient deity Quetzalcoatl, then worshipped throughout Mesoamerica. Their legends intertwined stories of the god with one of their historical leaders as a bringer of civilization. One legend stated that this leader-deity fell from power when he tried to ban human sacrifice; another that, when he burnt to death, his flaming heart became the planet Venus. Even after their civilization's fall in the twelfth century, the Toltecs remained a respected warrior elite, much admired by the later Aztecs.

Chacmool figure at the Temple of the Warriors, Chichén Itzá. These reclining figures, often featured in Maya-Toltec art, could represent a rain god or perhaps captives.

The T'ang Dynasty in China

The cultural achievements of the T'ang dynasty (618-907) provided a model for the world surrounding them, as well as for later Chinese periods. Buddhism, introduced into China from India about 65 BC and widely disseminated by the beginning of the T'ang period, inspired architecture and sculpture, and introduced new forms of music and musical instruments. Buddhism also stimulated native thought, as it was transformed into various new sects adapted to Chinese life. One which became popular in the ninth century was the Ch'an or Meditation sect, better known by its Japanese name, Zen. The Ch'an sect was influenced by Chinese Taoist philosophy, attributed to Confucius's contemporary, Lao-tzu. Taoism was formalized into a religion in the T'ang period, shaped partly through antagonism to Buddhism, and partly through borrowing from its rival. Confucianism also underwent a revival in the late T'ang period. Literature flourished, especially poetry; over 49,000 poems remain from this period. New technologies emerged. The first book, printed using the woodblock technique, appeared in 868. Paper, invented during the Han period, was improved, as were porcelain techniques. Other innovations were the wheelbarrow and gunpowder for fireworks.

Painting was an important art in the T'ang period, and painters were treated with respect. In this work, ladies of the T'ang imperial court enjoy a concert and banquet.

5000	2000	1000	500	AD1	400	600

NORSEMEN IN NORTH AMERICA

Karlsefni and his men had realized by now that … they could never live there in safety … because of the native inhabitants.

Saga of Erik the Red

Stories of Leif Eriksson's "Discovery of America" *c.* 1000 AD had an understandable appeal, especially to Americans of Scandinavian descent. However, a medieval Scandinavian presence in America appeared to be in doubt by the 1950s as, one by one, "runic inscriptions" and "Viking weapons" from various parts of the United States were shown to be forgeries or misinterpretations. Then, from the 1960s, the identification of settlement remains and of Scandinavian artifacts on Canada's east coast and in the High Arctic made it possible to re-examine medieval accounts in a new light. In part, the difficulties had been caused by glibly equating the Vinland of Leif and his companions with "America," rather than with the Labrador/St. Lawrence coasts. Identification of the region described by these Scandinavian pioneers has opened enquiry into such issues as settlement and interaction with native peoples.

SETTLEMENT OF GREENLAND

Nordic settlement of Greenland is well attested, although it postdates the Viking period proper which saw Scandinavian migration not only to western and southern Europe but also to Russia. While Danish navigator Gunnbjørn Ulfsson has been credited with the first sighting of Greenland around 930 AD, the early twelfth-century *Islendingabók* (*Book of the Icelanders*) attributes the first Greenland settlement to Erik the Red. This took place fourteen or fifteen winters before Christianity came to Iceland, an event which is conventionally placed about 1000 AD. The archaeological record suggests that Greenland was uninhabited when the Scandinavian settlers arrived,

although traces of a earlier Paleo-Eskimo occupation have come to light. Two principal colonies, *Østerbygd* and *Vesterbygd* (Eastern and Western Settlement), developed on this fringe of the Scandinavian world. The colonists were self-sufficient fishermen-farmers; the most prosperous kept cattle, others sheep and goats only. Hunting seal, walrus and reindeer was crucial to their economy. They could make a viable living by exporting sealskin and buckskin, furs and walrus ivory, importing timber and iron.

DISCOVERY OF VINLAND

Expeditions further afield were undertaken from around 1000 AD, the role of the Greenlanders being charted in the early thirteenth-century *Graenlendinga Saga* and *Eiriks saga rauða*. Doubtless, curiosity was a factor in sailing further west; but shortage of raw materials, including timber, in the colonies was perhaps a more pressing consideration. Sailing west and south, new territories were found including *Helluland* (a place of slabs), *Markland* (a forest region) and *Vinland* (a grape-growing district): these have been equated with Baffin Island and the coasts of Labrador and St. Lawrence, respectively. The first sighting of a forested coast, probably part of Canada, is credited to Iceland's Bjarni Herjólfsson, but the sagas emphasize the role of Leif, son of Erik, his brothers Thorvald and Thorstein, and the Icelander Thorfinn Karlsefni. It was Leif who first traveled, perhaps in 1001, to Vinland. He established a base camp for exploration and discovered various unexpected wonders including crops of wild grapes.

SETTLEMENT IN VINLAND

Several expeditions followed, and attempts at settlement were made. Leif's brother Thorvald and some others were slain on the wooded coast of Markland in an encounter, which the Greenlanders seemingly provoked, with a party of native people whom the sagas refer to as "Skraellings." This is, in effect, a generic term for "dark foreigners" and there is some uncertainty as to whether the people concerned were Inuit or American Indian. The tracing of population movements in prehistoric Canada has prompted some consensus that these particular "Skraellings" were Amero-Indian, probably of Algonquian stock. A more ambitious effort at establishing a permanent colony in Vinland was made by Thorfinn Karlsefni. According to the *Graenlendinga Saga*, he brought a large party of 160 men,

A nineteenth-century depiction of Norse ships off the coast of Greenland.

at least a few women, and some livestock. Their settlement lasted for a few years; Thorfinn's son Snorri was born during this time. It may be noted that a complex site at L'Anse aux Meadows in northern Newfoundland, excavated in the 1960s and '70s, has produced conclusive evidence of Scandinavian settlement. It consists of eight buildings, three of which are multi-roomed halls. There is ample evidence of craftwork at the site, including iron smelting and boat repair, along with cloth manufacture pointing to the presence of women. The settlement is sufficiently large to have accommodated about a hundred people. Notwithstanding the fact that no evidence for farming has come to light, some case might be made for viewing L'Anse aux

Meadows as the colony of Thorfinn, rather than as the base camp of Leif Eriksson. As to the fate of the colony, the saga mentions at least two encounters with the "Skraellings." At first it seems that they traded, exchanging cloth for pelts. But relationships apparently deteriorated and Thorfinn decided to withdraw the colony for fear of it being annihilated. His men were not Viking warriors, but medieval Scandinavian farmers. The landscape favored the natives and, being so far from any Greenland settlement, they had little expectation of help or support. Although attempts at colonization were abandoned, the Scandinavians continued to visit the region primarily to obtain timber. A Runic stone from *c.* 1050 AD found in Ringerike,

Norway, was understood to have commemorated a certain Finn Fegin, drowned on a voyage to Vinland. Later, Erik Gnupsson, bishop of Greenland, set off for Vinland *c.* 1121, perhaps with the intention of converting the natives. In any case, he was recalled by his superiors in Norway. Later still, Scandinavians would explore the High Arctic, trading with the Inuits of that region. Some Greenlanders would settle in Arctic Canada. However, the significance of the early eleventh-century explorations and settlement on the Canadian coast is clear: Europeans, having crossed the Atlantic, had encountered American Indians who had migrated across a continent. For the first time, west and east had met.

A.M.

61

5000	2000	1000	500	AD1	400	600

- *c.* 1000 Fujiwara clan, hereditary civil dictators in Japan.

- *c.* 1000 Colonization of Polynesian islands under way.

- 1000 Venice eliminates the Dalmatian pirates to assume unchallenged control of the Adriatic.

- 1000-1250 Maya Early Post-Classic period.

- *c.* 1000 Vikings sight North American coast.

- *c.* 1000 Rise of Japanese warrior class, the Samurai.

- 1018 Battle of Carham. King Malcolm II of Scotland defeats Anglo-Saxons; unites lowlands.

- 1018 Mahmud of Ghazni pillages the sacred city of Muttra in India.

- 1019 Accession of Yaroslav the Wise, greatest ruler of Kievan Rus (-1054).

- 1024 Conrad II first Holy Roman Emperor in the Salian line.

- 1025 Boleslaw Chrobry crowned first king of Poland.

- 1028 Cnut adds kingdoms of Denmark and Norway to that of England.

- 1030 Start of the Islamic incursions into India.

- 1037 Foundation stone laid for cathedral of St Sophia in Kiev.

- 1039 Accession of Henry III, greatest Holy Roman Emperor of the Salian line (d. 1056).

- 1044 Union of Arakan and Lower Burma in a single Burmese kingdom.

- 1046 Almoravid dynasty establishes itself in Al-Andalus (Muslim Spain).

- *c.* 1050 Mossi kingdoms resist spread of Islam in modern Burkina Faso.

- *c.* 1050 Culture of the Yoruba of Ife flourishes in West Africa.

- 1054 Abdullah ben Yassim begins the Muslim conquest of West Africa.

- 1055 Seljuk Turks capture Baghdad, later conquer Palestine and Syria (1075).

- 1056 The Almoravids, a Berber dynasty, begin conquest of Morocco and part of Algeria.

- 1066 Battle of Hastings. William, Duke of Normandy, defeats Anglo-Saxon King Harold, captures English throne.

- 1069 Radical reform program in China under Wang an-Shih.

- 1071 Battle of Manzikert: Seljuk Turks rout Byzantines in Asia Minor; remote cause of the First Crusade.

- 1073 Pope Gregory VII (Hildebrand) elected pope; reformer who asserts papal authority.

- 1075 Investiture Controversy in Christian Church: struggle between papacy and empire.

- 1076 Almoravids overrun Ghana and introduce Islam to West Africa.

- 1077 Emperor Henry IV does penance at Canossa.

- 1084 Completion of Ssu-ma Kuang's *History of pre-Song China*.

- 1086 Domesday survey, a remarkably thorough survey of land ownership in England by conquering Normans.

- 1088 Foundation of University of Bologna, the oldest in Europe.

- 1093 Establishment of the commune of Asti, first prototype for the Italian city states.

- 1095 Proclamation of the First Christian Crusade against Islam.

- 1096 Coinciding with the First Crusade, virulent persecutions of Jews in Europe (-1215).

- 1099 Crusaders capture Jerusalem.

- *c.* 1100 Ghana empire in West Africa declines.

The Normans and their Conquests

The Vikings or Northmen (known as Normans) settled in northern France by 911. They adopted French language, religion and culture, while retaining their aggressive Viking energy. In the eleventh century Normans under Robert Guiscard carved out principalities in Italy and Sicily, creating the Kingdom of Sicily where Arabs, Greeks and Italians cohabited. Other Normans, Bohemond and Tancred, ventured even farther, founding the principality of Antioch, north Syria, *c.* 1100. But the greatest Norman conquest was England. Weakened by Danish invasions, England tempted Duke William to invade in 1066. Good generalship and luck (the Danes had just attacked northern England) led to his victory over King Harold at Hastings. William installed Frenchmen in all posts, completely reorganizing Church and State, suppressing native risings ruthlessly. The Domesday Book of 1086, listing every mill or farm, reveals the thoroughness of royal power. From then on, England was linked to France, not Scandinavia.

Harold, the last Anglo-Saxon king, from the Bayeux Tapestry, Norman embroidery showing the progress of the invasion of England.

A Pueblo cotton shirt from Arizona. Unlike later Navaho weaving, Pueblo weaving was done by men.

The Pueblo Anasazi

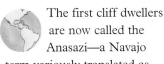

The first cliff dwellers are now called the Anasazi—a Navajo term variously translated as "Ancient Ones" or "Ancient Enemies". During their "Basketmaker" period (1 BC-AD 750), the Anasazi inhabited caves, but they entered their "Pueblo" period, constructing above-ground, adobe stone houses in the eighth century AD. In the "Classic Pueblo" period (1050-1300), the Anasazi clustered into villages of terraced, multi-storied pueblos built into the desert cliffs. The ruins of one such complex still stand at Mesa Verde in present-day Colorado. The Pueblo Anasazi never cohered as a single state, but existed as a series of independent towns linked by trade and a common culture. Life within these agricultural societies was communal and egalitarian, and religious rituals performed in underground rooms called *kivas* may have reinforced social bonds. Although drought or invasion displaced them in the thirteenth century, the Anasazi parented numerous other Pueblo peoples, including the Hopi and the Zuni.

The Empire of Pagan, Burma

In 1044, the semi-legendary King Anawratha united what is now officially called Myanmar and better known as Burma. He conquered and subdued a number of previously independent kingdoms, most particularly those of Pegu and Thaton. From his capital at Pagan in Upper Burma he then conquered the important coastal kingdom of Arakan, which ran along the Bay of Bengal littoral of modern Burma and Bangladesh. Both he and his son Kyanzittha (r. 1084-1112) repulsed a number of Chinese invasions on their eastern borders. In 1106, the emperor of China received an ambassador from Pagan, thus acknowledging its claim to independence. The Pagan empire lasted until 1278 when it was overrun by the Mongols under Kublai Khan.

A calligraphic tile wall at the Haayon Buddhist monastery, Datong, China. The monastery was built during the Liao dynasty in 1038.

The Liao, China

While the Song dynasty restored Chinese unity, this process was neither absolute nor unchallenged. In the early eleventh century, the northern Song fought and lost a series of battles with the Liao, a people whose lands lay in the vital border region with Mongolia. In 1004, the Song concluded a treaty with the Liao acknowledging their full local autonomy and even paying them a tribute in return for policing the border. Nor were the Liao the only such people who had to be appeased. Eventually only an alliance between the Chin of Manchuria and the Song defeated the Liao, but even then the Chin turned on the Song. This increasingly confused situation persisted until the Mongol invasion of the thirteenth century.

The Almoravids

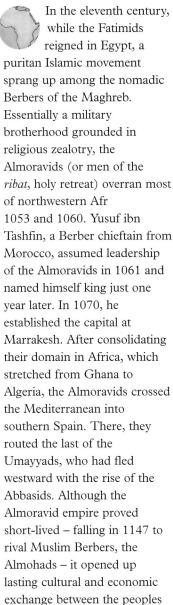

In the eleventh century, while the Fatimids reigned in Egypt, a puritan Islamic movement sprang up among the nomadic Berbers of the Maghreb. Essentially a military brotherhood grounded in religious zealotry, the Almoravids (or men of the *ribat*, holy retreat) overran most of northwestern Afr 1053 and 1060. Yusuf ibn Tashfin, a Berber chieftain from Morocco, assumed leadership of the Almoravids in 1061 and named himself king just one year later. In 1070, he established the capital at Marrakesh. After consolidating their domain in Africa, which stretched from Ghana to Algeria, the Almoravids crossed the Mediterranean into southern Spain. There, they routed the last of the Umayyads, who had fled westward with the rise of the Abbasids. Although the Almoravid empire proved short-lived – falling in 1147 to rival Muslim Berbers, the Almohads – it opened up lasting cultural and economic exchange between the peoples of northern Africa and Spain.

The entrance to the Qarawiyin Mosque at Fez, Morocco. The mosque was completely reconstructed by the Almoravids in 1135.

5000	2000	1000	500	AD1	400	600

Henry II, German king and Holy Roman Emperor who presided over an age of significant church reform in Europe.

Church Reform

The power of the Franks having declined in the late ninth century, Europe in general lacked centralized authority. The revival of a "Holy Roman Empire" from the late tenth century, in which Henry II (d. 1024), son of Henry, Duke of Bavaria, figured prominently, resulted in a league of German-speaking principalities across Central Europe. This was also an age of significant development in the Christian Church. Hildebrand, who became pope in 1073 as Gregory VII, epitomized the reform movement of the time, stressing adherence to discipline for clergy and faithful alike. The eleventh century saw a great revival of piety. This was clearly evidenced in France, where new orders of monks emerged to lead lives of prayer and contemplation under strict rules. St Bruno established the first Carthusian community at Chartreuse in 1084 and St Robert founded the Cistercians at Citeaux in 1098. On a more popular level, there was a surge in cathedral building across Europe as Romanesque architecture, with its square bell-towers and rounded arches, gained favor.

Africa: Ife

In the eleventh century, as the Ghana empire collapsed under pressure from new Islamic lordships further north, the Ife culture of Nigeria was reaching its apogee. Having perhaps evolved from the earlier Nok culture, Ife society included Yoruba and Edo speakers. Over time, centralized political and religious institutions had developed. Sovereignty was vested in the Oni who, like the Igbo ruler, was a priest-king but had a military role. Greater emphasis on militarism is indicated by the extensive earthworks throughout the Ife realm. Royal power was based on towns like Ife itself and Oyo, where upper-class houses, fronted by an atrium or forecourt, featured pavements of stone and potsherd. The architecture embodied Roman and Arab influences from North Africa. Ife craftsmen produced pottery decorated with paint and rouletting, along with terra cotta figures and bronzes. Their merchants exported ivory, kola nuts and slaves in exchange for horses, swords and iron tools. Religion centered on sacred groves, with deities worshipped including Obatala the creator of mankind, Ogun the god of war and iron, and Olukun the sea god.

Ife bronze head perhaps representing an Oni, or the sea god Olukun.

A sculpture from the late Fujiwara period of the priest Hoshi shows the face of a deity emerging from his. Hoshi was believed to be the earthly incarnation of the deity.

The Fujiwara Period in Japan

The Fujiwara period (c. 868-1160) is named after one of the powerful aristocratic families who were the true manipulators of political power in Japan. The emperor held a sacrosanct position, but was usually content to reign rather than to rule. Japan, like Korea in the Silla period, had earlier aspired to the glories of Chinese T'ang culture, adopting Buddhism and making efforts to centralize the government. Gradually such borrowings were transformed into wholly Japanese traditions. The art and literature of the Fujiwara period is uniquely Japanese, and, at its best, of rare beauty and sensitivity. A distinctive form of painting evolved, with flowing lines and flat colors, often used to tell stories in scroll form. The earliest surviving example illustrates a contemporary literary classic, *The Tale of Genji* by the noblewoman Murasaki Shikibu. Poetry was highly prized, and was now composed in Japanese. A phonetic script developed, better suited to the Japanese language than the ideographic Chinese script. Calligraphy was a valued art, and many women earned distinction with Japanese script while their husbands continued to use Chinese in an elitist but uninspired fashion. The Fujiwara period was brought to a close by civil war among the nobility, culminating in conquest by the first shogun, Minamoto Yoritomo.

800	1000	1200	1400	1600	1800	2000

Developments in Mogollon and Hohokum Cultures

Artistic innovations characterize the Mogollon and Hohokum cultures of the North American Southwest in the tenth and eleventh centuries. Like their neighbors the Anasazi, the Hohokum and Mogollon peoples probably arose from the Archaic Cochise Desert culture about 100 BC. The Mogollon, or "Mountain People," produced the first known ceramics in the Southwest. They may have been the first Southwestern people to adopt settled agriculture; but they also continued to hunt, using the bow after about 500 AD. The Mimbres, a Mogollon people, began to produce black-on-white painted pottery about 900 AD, which shows Anasazi influence but is nonetheless unique. The Hohokum, or "Vanished Ones" in the language of their probable descendants, the Pima, adopted settled agriculture about the same time as the Mogollons, using extensive irrigation to farm the desert. About 1000 AD, the Hohokums were perhaps the first people in the world to successfully employ etching, using the fermented juice of cactus fruit to incise designs in shells. Copper bells among Hohokum artifacts suggest that metallurgy had traveled north from Mesoamerica; indeed, other remains, including ball courts and rubber balls, suggest extensive contact. Influence traveled in both directions: the bow came into use in Mesoamerica about 1000 AD.

This Mimbres bowl was intended as a burial offering. The hole is from the ritual "killing" of the bowl at the time of burial in order to release its spirit into the next world.

Religion and Dance in India

Dance and music are intricately interwoven with religious celebration in Indian religions. Perhaps the most familiar image is that of the Dancing Shiva of Hinduism, but dance is also associated with Buddhism and Jainism as well. The purposes of dance are varied in religious expression: to delight the gods, to express divine happiness, and to seek escape from the cycles of death and rebirth (not unlike the dances of some Islamic Sufi mystics). Shiva's dance of cosmic destruction is represented in its most classical form in the bronze sculptures of southern India. As early as the tenth century, this Shiva Nataraja was adopted by the rulers of the Chola kingdom as their patron deity. It became customary for *devadasi*, or "maids of the god," to dance for his divine pleasure every evening. This later degenerated into temple prostitution, and the British finally ended the practice; but originally it was an expression of worship, and it is still usual for practitioners of the dance-drama called *bharata-natyam* to begin by invoking Shiva as Lord of the Dance. Religious music and dance might also express simple or even teasing joyfulness. Sculptures of Shiva's son, the elephant-headed Ganesha, often show him in childish imitation of his father; and

Krishna is sometimes represented in the triumphant little dance he executes after he has stolen butter from his mother's larder. An older Krishna is often shown playing his flute and dancing with the daughters of cowherds in a romantic analogue of divine love.

A bronze sculpture of Shiva as Lord of the Dance from southern India.

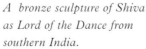

65

The ruins of Gedi, an important center of the East African slave trade. Founded around 1105, it was destroyed in 1630.

Medieval East Africa

Muslim traders arrived on the eastern shores of Africa at the beginning of the second millennium AD. There, they encountered the Swahili, Bantu-speaking peoples who had migrated from the African interior to the coastal region at least seven centuries before. The Swahili lived in towns and had long engaged in a brisk maritime trade with ports in India, Arabia, and the Persian Gulf. Women in these societies had substantial property rights, and they often ruled as queens. The coming of Islam changed the Swahili in important ways. Islamic law fused with customary law to produce a distinct cultural identity among the Swahili. They built stone towns, such as Kilwa in the south, with large palace complexes and great mosques. These communities grew rich by trading in ivory, iron ore, gold, textiles, and slaves. Women retained a relatively high status, though it appears that they often preferred the ancient customs to Islam.

The Seljuks

The Seljuks were a Turkish dynasty originally from central Asia who converted to Islam in the tenth century and settled in northern Iran. From this base they rose to be masters of both Iran and Iraq by 1055. In the second half of the tenth century they spread to Syria, Palestine, and Anatolia. For all of the eleventh century, the Seljuk empire was the dominant power in the Near East and a constant threat to the eastern borders of Byzantium. The capital was at Isfahan in Iran. The Seljuks were champions of orthodox Sunni Islam and therefore bitterly opposed by the Fatimids of Egypt, the principal Shi'ite state in the Islamic world.

Countryside near Nazareth in Palestine. In the tenth and eleventh centuries, this was in the heart of the Seljuk empire.

The First Shogun

By 1160, the Fujiwara family had dominated Japanese government for three centuries. In that year, however, the Taira—a warrior clan based in the southwest of the country—overthrew them, having also defeated the Minamoto clan from the east. But in Minamoto Yoritomo, the latter had a leader of genius. He rebelled against the Taira in 1180 and in the sea battle of Dannoura in 1185 he routed them and made himself master of Japan. He did not attempt to overthrow the emperor, satisfying himself with the title of *shogun* or military dictator. He established his capital at Kamakura near Tokyo. Although the Minamoto family rule only lasted until 1219, he established the pattern of Japanese government that persisted until the nineteenth century.

Minamoto Yoritomo.

The Toltecs

The Toltecs were a Native American people who established themselves in the rich central Mexican valley in the tenth century. From this base they spread south and east, abandoning their former capital of Tula some time after 1000. They overran the Maya and established themselves at the Mayan town of Chichen Itza in north Yucatán which they developed into a great ritual and religious center. They were at their zenith in the eleventh and twelfth centuries before being reconquered by the Maya, who then enjoyed a final brief efflorescence before their own disappearance from history.

Toltec ruins at Chichen Itza, formerly a great religious center.

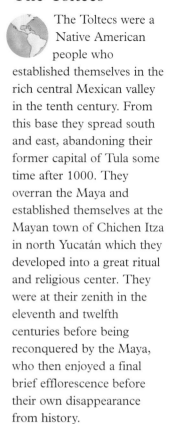

800	1000	1200	1400	1600	1800	2000

- *c.* 1100 Powerful state of Kanem-Bornu at its apogee in the Lake Chad region.

- 1102 Dynastic union with Hungary draws Croatia towards Latin rather than Slav world.

- 1106 China receives ambassador from Burma, a recognition of Burmese independence.

- 1108 Accession of Louis VI, the Fat, to the throne of France north of the Loire (-1137).

- 1125 Conquest of northern China by Chin dynasty who rule from Peking.

- 1130 Count Roger II of Sicily unites Sicily, Apulia and Calabria in new kingdom.

- 1138 Conrad III first Hohenstaufen ruler of the Holy Roman Empire.

- 1139 Alfonso Henriques first king of independent Portugal.

- 1143 Manuel I Comnenus emperor of Byzantium (-1180); apogee of Byzantine splendor.

- 1147 Second Crusade (-1149) achieved nothing.

- 1147 Almohads, Berber Muslims, capture Marrakech and go on to take Muslim Spain from the Almoravids.

- 1152 Accession of Frederick Barbarossa (Redbeard) as Holy Roman Emperor (-1190).

- 1154 Plantagenet dynasty in England (-1399); wider empire included all of western France.

- 1150s Zagwe dynasty rules in Ethiopia.

- 1156 Civil war in Japan between rival emperors.

- 1160 Rabbi Benjamin of Tudela (Navarre) begins thirteen-year journey to China via Persia.

- 1161 First known use of high explosive by Chinese general Yu Yun-wen in battle near Nanking.

- 1167 Stevan Nemanja grand zupan of Serbia; established autonomous Serbian state.

- 1171 Saladin, commander in the Egyptian army, overthrows Fatimid dynasty.

- *c.* 1180 The Buddhist state of Srivijaya controls the Straits of Malacca and dominates region.

- 1181-1219 King Jayavarman VII erects Neak Pean shrine at Angkor.

- 1183 Beginning of the Kamakura period of Japanese history (-1333).

- 1185 Establishment of second Bulgarian empire, free of Byzantine control (-1389).

- 1187 Saladin recovers Jerusalem for Islam, lost in the First Crusade.

- *c.* 1190 Temujin (Genghis Khan) oversees creation of new Mongol empire in central Asia.

- 1192 Battle of Tararori: Mohammed of Ghur defeats Hindus, establishes Islam in northern India.

Conflict between Popes and Emperors

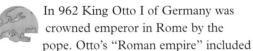 In 962 King Otto I of Germany was crowned emperor in Rome by the pope. Otto's "Roman empire" included Italy and Germany but not France, partly reviving Charlemagne's, not Augustus's, empire. Subsequent emperors controlled both Church and State: the papacy was the plaything of local aristocrats. But a reforming spirit, originating in French monasteries, encouraged the Church under Pope Leo IX (1049-54) to reject imperial control. As emperors used bishops to rule, this led to conflict. When Pope Gregory VII excommunicated Emperor Henry IV for meddling with Church affairs in 1075, civil war became endemic. North Italian cities later formed the Lombard League against Emperor Frederick "Barbarossa" (Redbeard), defeating him at Legnano in 1176. Frederick's compromise peace did not survive his death in 1190. His grandson Frederick II (r. 1215-50) spent his reign fighting papally-supported opponents. The reality, though not title, of empire died with him.

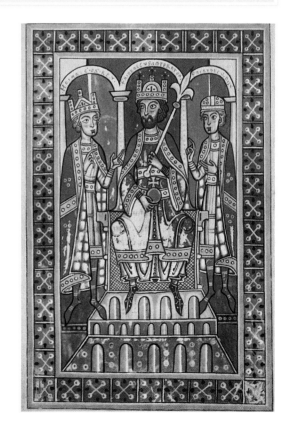

Frederick I, flanked by his sons, King Henry VI, emperor 1191-97, and Duke Frederick V. Book miniature c. 1180.

5000	2000	1000	500	AD1	400	600

A twelfth-century Swiss manuscript depiction of a church school, the master and pupil relationship delineated by their relative sizes.

Castles and Universities

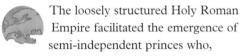

The loosely structured Holy Roman Empire facilitated the emergence of semi-independent princes who, while ruling from great fortresses or castles, were often willing to patronize the building of monasteries and cathedrals. It was against this background that an intellectual movement was generated in the twelfth century that would lead to the development of the discipline of scholasticism. Its pioneers including Anselm (d. 1109) of Canterbury and Abelard (d. 1142) of Paris, scholasticism sought, through focusing on the works of Plato and Aristotle, to adopt a philosophical approach to theology. A growing interest in intellectual activity contributed to the emergence of early universities such as that of Salerno in Italy which, founded in 1150, incorporated an even earlier medical school. Oxford in England existed as a university by the 1160s, while that of Paris would be established in 1210. Some of the earliest universities evolved from private academic societies, developing into corporations. Typically, they taught grammar, logic, and rhetoric as foundation studies. Students then proceeded to specialize, usually in law, medicine or theology.

Islamic Arts and Sciences

Political disintegration of the caliphate between 945 and the invasion of the Mongols in 1258 had little effect on the flourishing Islamic culture. The inherited traditions of Byzantium and Persia, united under Islam, sparked creativity in science, arts, and literature, in contrast with Europe in the same period. Religious mystics called Sufis inspired diverse cults, including the dervishes, and also beautiful poetry, such as Farid ud-Din Attar's *Conference of the Birds*. Another famous poet, Omar Khayyam, was also a mathematician. Greek philosophy was translated by *faylasufs* (from Greek *philosophia*) such as Averroës (Ibn Rushd), renowned for his commentaries on Aristotle, or Avicenna, whose medical canon was accepted as authoritative in Europe until the seventeenth century. Other Islamic achievements included discoveries in optics and chemistry, and further study of Greek geometry and the mathematics of the ancient Hindus (the first to describe the concept of zero and the actual inventors of so-called "Arabic numerals"), resulting in advances in spherical trigonometry and algebra (an Arabic word). Islamic preservation and expansion of philosophical and scientific works, in particular the works of Aristotle, was essential to the European revival of learning in the early modern period.

An illustration from an Arabic edition (1224) of De Materia Medica, *by the Greek physician Dioscorides (c. AD 20-70), shows a pharmacist preparing his drugs. Dioscorides' five-volume pharmacological treatise was used until about the seventeenth century.*

The Changlang Ting (Surging Wave) Pavilion Garden, founded by the Song poet Su Tzu-mei in 1044, provided a place for scholars, poets, and philosophers to construct their musings on nature.

The Song Dynasty in China

The Song dynasty (960-1279), which succeeded the T'ang dynasty in China after a brief period of unrest, is associated with increasing urbanization and with the improvement and even perfection of certain arts and technologies. The craft and elegance of Song dynasty ceramics would be difficult to surpass in any era. Chinese potters applied highly sophisticated glazing techniques to simple shapes, creating fine pottery that set the standard for what is called, not coincidentally, "china" in English. The Song empire was smaller than the T'ang empire, eroded by conquests along its northern borders, and in 1138 the capital was moved south to Lin-an (Hangchow). Long after the fall of the Song dynasty, Marco Polo still described this city as "beyond dispute the finest and noblest" in the world. The Song period also saw significant improvements in agriculture, the use of the abacus, and the adaptation of gunpowder for use in weapons. Printing became widespread. The woodblock method was best suited for the Chinese language, but movable type had also developed as early as 1030. The Song period might be called the "golden age" of Chinese landscape painting, and poetry also flourished. Changing status for women was manifested in the growth of concubinage and footbinding.

The Anasazi

The civilization of the Anasazi, or "Ancient Ones," as the Navajo later called them, reached its height in the twelfth and thirteenth centuries. Probably developing from the Archaic Cochise Desert culture about the same time (*c.* 100 BC) as the Mogollon and Hohokum peoples, the original center of the Anasazi was in the "Four Corners" region where the present-day states of Utah, Colorado, New Mexico, and Arizona meet. The initial "Basketmaker" period of the Anasazi lasted until about AD 750, gradually succeeded by the "Pueblo" period, whose name comes from the Spanish for "town." The pueblo was an architectural innovation. Originally a single-storeyed adobe building, gradually it became a multi-storeyed complex with shared walls, where one family's rooftop became another's terrace, the whole structure connected by ladders. As the Anasazi's culture flowered, they abandoned many of their *mesa* (mountain "tabletop") pueblos in favour of communities built in high recesses in canyon walls. Although the Anasazi also made beautiful turquoise jewelry, mosaics, and skilfully painted pottery, it is for these dwellings that they are best remembered. After 1300, perhaps because of drought, perhaps because of raids by Athapascan Navajos and Apaches, the Anasazi abandoned these homes and moved southwards.

One of the largest Anasazi cliff communities was at Mesa Verde in Colorado. The round structures are ceremonial centres called kivas.

A Berber stronghold, or kasbah, *in the Atlas Mountains, Morocco.*

The Berbers

The Almohad rulers, one of whose principal centers was Marakesh, endeavoured from the mid-twelfth century to unify the Maghreb. Up to this time, as is clear from the later writings of historian Ibn Khaldun, Berber culture continued to flourish throughout the region. Speaking Hamito-Semitic languages, the Berbers were a desert people whose principal settlement type was the fortified *kasbah*, surrounded by palms and cultivation plots where they grew wheat, nuts, and olives. Indigenous Berber religion involved worship of the forces of nature. These peoples would be largely drawn into the sphere of Islam and of Arabic culture with the advent of the Moroccan Marínid dynasty from the thirteenth century. The gap would widen between the sedentary Baranis and the nomadic tent-dwelling Butr, who herded goats and left domestic industry, including weaving and pottery, to the womenfolk. Meanwhile, the collapse of the Ghana empire towards the end of the eleventh century had facilitated the extension of the Muslim faith south-westwards. The Keita ruling dynasty of the Mali empire which rose to power from the early thirteenth century believed themselves to be descended from a servant of the Prophet Muhammad named Bilali Bunama.

5000	2000	1000	500	AD1	400	600

THE MONGOL CENTURIES

We should ourselves practice the arts of war,

so as to be able to kill those who do not submit to us.

A general of the Hsien-pi (Xianbi) nomads, fourth century AD

For a brief time, the Mongols ruled one of the largest empires in history. One of the many different nomadic peoples who inhabited the vast northern steppes beyond the Great Wall of China, the nomadic life of the Mongols was governed by migrations between summer and winter pasture lands. They were fierce warriors and exceptionally skillful horsemen, whose mounts were stronger and swifter than the farm horses used by the Chinese. The nomads were a persistent challenge to successive Chinese empires, but not until various tribes were united by the ruthless and brilliant strategic abilities of a warrior named Temüjin did the Mongols begin their conquest of Asia.

GENGHIS KHAN

Born about 1167, Temüjin was the son of a Mongol chieftain. His father was murdered while Temüjin was still a boy, and he then entered the service of Toghril Khan, the most powerful Mongol leader of the time. Eventually rebelling against his overlord, he subjugated one tribe after another, until, in 1206, he was proclaimed Genghis Khan (also spelled Jenghiz, Chinggis, etc.), or "Universal Ruler." The following year he began a series of devastating invasions. He defeated the Chin empire in northern China (founded in 1122 by the Tungusic-speaking Jurchen people, also originally from the northern steppes), and occupied Beijing in 1215. He proceeded to subdue the lands of the Russian steppes and raided Persia and eastern Europe. Eventually the Mongol empire of Genghis Khan stretched east and west from the Black Sea to the Pacific, and north and south from Siberia to Tibet. He efficiently reorganized the states he

conquered, and though illiterate, left behind an innovative code of laws.

After his death in 1227, the lands taken by Genghis Khan were divided among his four sons into the Hulagu khanate in Persia; the Jagatai khanate in Turkistan; the Kipchak khanate in southern Russia, and, perhaps the most famous, the East Asian khanate, where Genghis Khan's grandson Kublai Khan completed the conquest of China and founded the Yüan dynasty that ruled China until 1368.

KUBLAI KHAN

Kublai Khan, or "Great Ruler," extended the Mongol empire to its largest size. By 1279 he had beaten the last Chinese army of the Song dynasty. The defeated commanding general is said to have leapt into the sea, clutching the baby prince of the Song. Kublai Khan then invaded much of Southeast Asia, and, using Song vessels, attempted to invade Japan. A ferocious typhoon destroyed most of the Mongol fleet, and the Japanese remained unconquered.

Kublai Khan established a lavish court at Beijing. Educated by Confucian scholars, he later converted to the Lamaist Buddhism that had originated in Tibet. Under Kublai Khan's patronage, this religion spread rapidly throughout his realm, and remained influential among the Mongols for centuries.

New Chinese literary forms emerged under his reign, in part because Chinese scholars found few opportunities in the official service of the Mongol regime. Some of these would-be bureaucrats and court officials turned their talents to writing plays instead, which flourished in the Yüan period (1280-1368).

Kublai Khan's court was visited by a number of Europeans, of whom the most famous was the son of a Venetian merchant. Marco Polo arrived with his father and uncle at the summer court of the Khan in Shando (Shan-tu) in 1275, and remained in China for seventeen years. A favorite of the Khan, Marco Polo traveled widely as a diplomat in his service. His detailed memoirs of east Asia were the only European accounts of the region until the visit of the Jesuit priest Matteo Ricci in 1582. Europeans found Marco Polo's descriptions of the wondrous magnificence of the east unbelievable until other travelers confirmed them. The

800	1000	1200	1400	1600	1800	2000

A fanciful depiction of Marco Polo at the harvest of black pepper plants, from a French edition of his travel writings, 1375.

memoirs remained influential in Europe until the nineteenth century.

THE WESTERN MONGOLS AND THE NEXT GREAT CONQUEROR

Although true Mongol states had disappeared by the end of the fourteenth century, each khanate left lasting traces in its region. The conquest of the Kipchak khanate, also known as the khanate of the Golden Horde, was completed by another grandson of Genghis Kahn, Batu Khan. The name "Golden Horde" refers to the colorful tents of the Mongol camps. Batu Khan overran most of Russia, Poland and Hungary. His devastation of the Russian state of Kiev in 1240 is considered to be the principal factor in Russia's decline from an advanced European state to a backward one over the subsequent centuries. The Mongols of the Golden Horde merged with the Cumans (Kipchaks), Tatars and other Turkic peoples, eventually adopting their language and their Islamic religion. Conflicts between the Blue (eastern) and White (western) hordes led to their being conquered between 1389-1395 by the Turkish ruler Tamerlane, who claimed descent from Genghis Khan. Tamerlane captured the Persian and Turkistan khanates as well, and was on his way to conquer China when he died in 1405. Although probably not descended from Genghis Khan, Tamerlane earned the allegiance of many of the peoples who had followed his predecessor, and seemed capable of building a similar empire with even more ruthless and devastating military skill.

S.I.

5000	2000	1000	500	AD1	400	600

The Late Maya

Around AD 1000, the Toltecs of central Mexico descended on the Yucatán peninsula, merging with the remnants of Classic Maya civilization. The Toltecs were brutal—they performed human sacrifice and waged religious warfare—but their influence in the region quickly ebbed. Between 1250 and 1446, the Late, or Post-Classic, Maya reasserted themselves as an independent state. The ruling families resided at Mayapán and supervised the surrounding provinces through stewards. Mayapán was less impressive than earlier Mayan cities: its temples and palaces were smaller, and it had no ball court. Perhaps to compensate, Mayapán kings ordered the construction of twenty-five carved and painted stelae. Like the Classic Maya, the Late Maya fell victim to warring elites. A later king hired foreign mercenaries for protection: the aristocracy replied by demolishing Mayapán. When the Spanish arrived in the sixteenth century, the once-great Maya civilization consisted of scattered regional states.

The buildings of the Nuns' Square at Uxmal in Yucatán.

- **1200** Hunac Ceel revolts against the Maya of Chichén Itza and sets up new capital at Mayapán.

- **1200-1465** Chimú civilization in Andean region.

- **1200-1500** Aztec civilization dominant in Mexico.

- **1204** Fourth Crusade degenerates into a successful Venetian assault on Constantinople.

- **1206** Establishment of sultanate of Delhi (-1526) consolidates Muslim rule in northern India.

- **1208** Albigensian Crusade (-1213): northern French destroy brilliant Provençal culture.

- **1212** Battle of Las Navas de Tolosa breaks unitary power of Muslim Spain.

- **1214** Battle of Bouvines establishes France as a significant European power.

- **1215** Magna Carta: remote origin of English constitutional government.

- **1215** Genghis Khan overruns northern China.

- **1219** Hōjō shogunate supplants that of Minamoto in Japan (-1333).

- **1221** Foundation of Nizhni Novgorod (Gorki).

- **1223** First appearance of the Genghis Khan's Mongol hordes in Europe.

- **1224** Soso people under King Sumanguru conquer Mali.

- **1227** Death of Genghis Khan, having conquered land from the Black Sea to Korea.

- **1231** Mongols complete conquest of northern China and Korea.

- **1236** King Ferdinand III of Castile recaptures Córdoba from the Muslims.

- **1239** Mongols seize Tibet.

- *c.* **1240** Russia overrun by "Golden Horde," western arm of the Mongol empire (-1480).

- **1248** Castilians recapture Seville, former capital of Muslim Spain.

- **1250-1440** Maya Late Post-Classic period.

- **1250** Mamlukes from central Asia seize power in Egypt and found a military state.

- **1256** Ilkhan dynasty, Mongol descendants of Genghis Khan, in power in Persia (-1349).

- **1257** Mongols take Tonkin, including Hanoi.

- **1258** Mongols sack Baghdad and execute the caliph.

- **1260** Victory of the Mamelukes over the Mongols at Ain Jalut saves Egypt.

- **1272** Edward I English king (-1307); conquers Wales, fails in similar Scottish enterprise.

- **1273** Rudolf of Hapsburg Holy Roman Emperor, the first of his line to be so.

- **1274** First unsuccessful Mongol invasion of Japan.

- **1279** Song empire (central and southern China) conquered by Kublai Khan, founder of Yüan dynasty.

- **1281** Second Mongol invasion failure in Japan.

- **1282** Sicilian Vespers: massacre of the Norman-French garrison.

- **1287** Mongols overrun Burma but are repulsed in Annam.

- **1290** Turkish leader Firuz founds the Khalji Dynasty in Delhi (-1320).

- **1291** Union of Three Cantons—Uri, Schwyz, Unterwalden—remote origin of Swiss independence.

- **1292** Union of much of southern India under Hoysala ruler Viraballala III.

- **1292** Completion of the restoration of China's grand canal from Hangchow to Peking.

- **1294** Death of Kublai Khan, ruler of unified Mongol empire from China to eastern Europe.

600	1000	1200	1400	1600	1800	2000

The Sultanate of Delhi

In 1175, Mohammed of Ghur—a powerful Muslim kingdom in what is now Afghanistan—invaded northern India. He took Multan and Uch; by 1186 he held Lahore; by 1193 he had advanced to Delhi and Benares. In 1199 one of his generals, Bakhtiyar, captured Bengal and expelled its last Hindu ruler. The entire northern plain of India was now in Muslim hands. Mohammed did not settle in India, preferring to rule through his viceroy and slave, Qutb-ud-Din. On Mohammed's death in 1206, Qutb-ud-Din proclaimed himself sultan of Delhi and founded what became known as the Slave dynasty. Under this and later dynasties, the sultanate spread Islam to the Deccan and Gujarat, but its constituent provinces had begun to assert their independence from Delhi long before Timur's devastating invasion in 1398. Muslim India was not reunited until the founding of the Mughal empire in 1526.

The Rise of Venice

By the thirteenth century, Venice was the richest and most beautiful city in Europe. It was a republic. Almost alone in Italy, it was subject to a constitution, with checks and balances. The *arengo* or general meeting of citizens remained an important feature of government until the fourteenth century. Real power was exercised by a small number of aristocratic families through the Great Council of over 1,500 members, but never despotically. The senate of about 150 people discharged day-to-day business. As the arengo faded, a cabinet-style Council of Ten rose to prominence: the Venetian system effectively traded participation for efficiency as the state grew more complex. At the apex was the doge, usually a senior figure long experienced in government. The Venetians made their naval power indispensable to the defense of Christendom against Islam. For three centuries they were the leading Christian power in the eastern Mediterranean.

The interior of St Mark's Cathedral shows the strong Byzantine influences which underlay the entire Venetian experience.

The Mongol Empire

By 1206 Genghis Khan was undisputed king of Mongolia. He then crossed the Great Wall of China and conquered the Chin Tartars in the north, later to sweep across central Asia to the Black Sea. In 1279 his grandson, Kublai Khan, defeated the southern Song, uniting China and founding the Yüan dynasty. He also exercised personal control over the rest of the far-flung empire which Genghis Khan's other descendants had carved out. At its zenith, the Mongol empire embraced China, Korea, Burma, Annam (Vietnam), Tibet and all of central Asia, the Indus valley, Afghanistan, Iran, Iraq (the Mongols sacked Baghdad and executed the caliph), Armenia, Ukraine and Russia. Through the sultanate of Delhi, it effectively ruled much of north India. Imperial unity gradually dissolved after Kublai Khan's death. The Yüan were overthrown in China in 1368; but the Golden Horde, the most westerly Mongol force, controlled Russia until 1480.

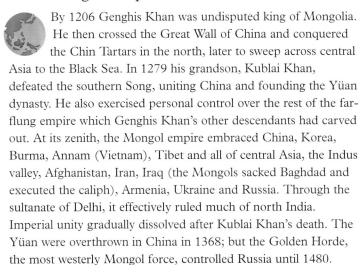

Marco Polo at the court of Kublai Khan.

The Guinea States

From the thirteenth century on, a number of new states began to form in West Africa south of the territories of the Songhai or the Kanem-Bornu empires. The Akan and Yoruba people established states along the coast of the Gulf of Guinea in the valleys of the lower Volta and the lower Niger. Although primarily agricultural areas, most people lived in towns and villages rather than in dispersed homesteads. The most celebrated of the early kingdoms was that of Benin, an Edo state which was well established three hundred years before the Portuguese first reached this part of West Africa. Its capital, Benin City (now in western Nigeria), was already flourishing in the thirteenth century. Urban life in Ife, also in Nigeria, is even older. The sophistication of Ife culture is manifest in the brilliance of its naturalistic sculpture.

A disc-shaped Akan terra-cotta head used in royal funerary memorials, a stylized representation of great beauty in the Akan culture.

5000	2000	1000	500	AD1	400	600

Chimor

Chimor began its rise in the eleventh century. At its height (*c.* 1200-1470) the domain of the Chimú people covered about two-thirds of the Pacific coast, stretching from the southern border of modern Ecuador to just north of modern Lima. They established a magnificent coastal capital, Chan-Chan, which covered nine square miles. There were nine distinct compounds within the city, with high surrounding walls and plazas. Some of the interior walls have lattice-work designs, perhaps inspired by textiles; the Chimú were also skillful weavers, sometimes adorning their ponchos with feathers or metal plaques. Design motifs at Chan-Chan, in both architecture and textiles, are often inspired by the sea, including stylized depictions of fish, seabirds, and waves. The Chimú also fashioned gold and silver jewelry and artefacts, including discs with intricate embossing, mummy masks of flattened gold with insets of copper, and ceremonial knives with handles representing winged human-like figures

wearing headdresses and earrings, often set with stones. These may have represented deified nobles. The Chimú long resisted the attempts of their southern neighbors, the Incas, to absorb them, but ultimately the second-largest South American domain fell to the largest one, in about 1470.

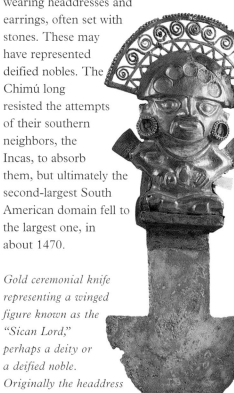

Gold ceremonial knife representing a winged figure known as the "Sican Lord," perhaps a deity or a deified noble. Originally the headdress and earrings were set with precious stones.

Southern India

India has a complex multi-faceted identity, even without cultural influences from other parts of Asia. The Sanskrit language, for example, may be distantly related to the Indo-European languages which also comprise many of Europe's tongues; but the Dravidian languages of southern India appear to be unrelated to any others in the world. Traditions of northern India were modified by peoples of southern India: religious reform movements there profoundly shaped Hinduism. Southern India was also less subject to the various invasions that plagued the north, simply because of distance. The Arabs established a Muslim state in Sind in northwest India early in the eighth century, but Arab contacts with southern coastal India were peacefully commercial. In the tenth century, the Cholas of the Indian southeast coast gained ascendance in the south. They

Arab Commerce

Arab adventurers explored and settled the coast of East Africa, paving the way for trading centers such as Gedi (in modern Kenya) and Kilwa (in modern Tanzania) which, at least from the thirteenth century onwards, had begun to take on the character of urban settlements. Kilwa had an impressive mosque, fine courtyards, a public bathing pool, and washing facilities. It was defended by a fortress which overlooked the sea approach. The Arabs traded local raw materials such as ivory, but the mainstay of their commerce was the slave market. Caravans were dispatched inland to purchase strong young laborers from local rulers of the Swahili, Masai, Yao, and other peoples. These captives were brought to the ports, from where many were shipped to the Islamic states of North Africa. Slavery in the Muslim world was regulated by law and slaves even had certain rights. In time, an even more lucrative market in India would be opened and Kilwa, the glories of which were described by the fourteenth-century scholar Ibn Battuta, would be sacked (in 1505) by the Portuguese.

The great mosque of Kilwa, founded in the thirteenth century.

constructed beautiful Hindu temples, and were especially noted for their exquisite bronze sculptures. In the twelfth century, however, their power was weakened by the Hoysalas of the Mysore plateau, and in the thirteenth the Pandyas of the southern tip became the dominant power in the south, with a fabulously wealthy empire admired by Marco Polo when he visited as the Chinese emissary in 1288 and 1293.

Ganesha, the elephant-headed Hindu god of wisdom. The son of Shiva and Parvati, Ganesha is worshipped as the remover of obstacles.

The Crusades and Byzantium

The socio-cultural impact of the Crusades upon western Europe was manifest by the thirteenth century, even if the original ideals of these "holy wars" had long faded. Western nobility adopted the custom of crests and armorial bearings, initially devised to distinguish crusading contingents, and embraced Middle Eastern architectural ideas including the so-called "keepless castle." Changes in lifestyle arose from contact with the Arab world; wealthy Europeans acquired a taste for spices, and for eastern fabrics including silks and carpets. There was also renewed interest in the Greek heritage, and the Dominican Aquinas (d. 1274), through study of Aristotle, sought to reconcile Christian faith with human reason. Following a period of Latin dominance at Constantinople, Palaeologian emperor Michael VIII from 1261 presided over a late—if limited— flourishing of Byzantine culture, the Greek character of which is reflected in its art. Perhaps it was a sense of insecurity, from a past of iconoclastic controversy and a

present Islamic threat, that underlay the preoccupation of Byzantine art with religious expression. Typically, its frescos and mosaics illustrate an elaborate liturgy and a hierarchical view of the universe.

Aquinas: scholar, saint, and philosopher.

The Angkorian Empire

In 1296, the Chinese envoy Chou Ta-kuan reported that Angkor was the richest city in Southeast Asia. The wealth of the Khmer people of Cambodia came from efficient hydraulic engineering and a large pool of available labor. Harnessing the seasonal rains in a system of reservoirs and irrigation, the Khmer were able to produce three rice crops per year— enough to feed a population of over one million. The Angkorian empire encompassed areas of modern Thailand, Laos, and Vietnam as well as modern Cambodia. A complex of extraordinary temples still remains as a reminder of Angkor's greatness. Perhaps the most impressive of these is the huge temple-mountain of Angkor Wat, built by Suryavarman II in the early twelfth century. Constructed of stone with carved reliefs, with many towers, and surrounded by a wide moat, it is probably the largest religious monument ever built. Another shrine, the Bayon, which is Buddhist rather than Hindu in inspiration, was built to rival Ankgor Wat by Suryavarman II's son, Jayavarman VII. (Buddhism and Hinduism often coexist and even intermingle in Asia.) Many smaller shrines erected between the tenth and the fourteenth centuries testify to the magnificence of the Khmer empire before the ultimate abandonment of Angkor Wat in the fifteenth century.

The carved relief frontispiece of the beautiful small temple of Banteay Srei, built by a Brahmin priest and dedicated in 967. The demons Sunda and Upasunda are fighting over the aspara (celestial nymph) Tilottma.

5000	2000	1000	500	AD1	400	600

c. 1300-1500 Mississippian Southern or Death Cult flourishes.

1300 Mongols removed permanently from Burma.

1307 Rise of Mali under Mansa Musa, based at Timbuktu.

1309 Removal of the papal court from Rome to Avignon (-1378).

1314 Victory of Robert the Bruce over English at Bannockburn ensures Scottish independence.

1315 Swiss defeat imperial forces at Morgarten to confirm independence.

1316 Reign of Gedymin (-1341), founder of Lithuanian state.

1324 Emperor Musa of Mali makes pilgrimage to Mecca.

1325 Aztecs establish an impregnable capital at Tenochtitlan; dominate central and southern Mexico.

1326 First Polish War between Teutonic Knights and Poles (-1333); victory to the Knights.

1326 Ottoman Turks sweep through Anatolia to the Sea of Marmara.

1328 Philip VI first Valois king of France (-1350).

1328 Ethiopians conquer Ifat, small Muslim Red Sea state, to protect Coptic Christians.

1330 Delhi sultanate at greatest extent, controls northern and central India.

1331 Apogee of Serbian power under Steven Urosh IV (-1355).

1333 Casimir III, powerful Polish king and founder of University of Cracow.

1333 Fall of the Hōjō in Japan; brief restoration of direct imperial rule under Daigo II.

1336 Ashikaga shogunate (-1568), but deposed emperor Daigo foments long civil war.

1337 Outbreak of the Hundred Years' War between France and England.

1338 Bengal independent of sultanate of Delhi (-1539).

1340 Hindu kingdom of Vijayanagar in southern India blocks Muslim advance (-1565).

1340 English victory over the French fleet in the Battle of Sluys.

1341 Civil war in the Byzantine empire (-1347).

1342 Louis the Great of Hungary (-1382) establishes Hungarian power in southeast Europe.

1344 First written use of term Hanseatic League: mercantile alliance of north German cities.

1345 Ottoman Turks in Balkans for the first time, ironically as allies of the Byzantine emperor.

1346 Stunning English victory over the French at Crécy.

1347 Bahmani kingdom (-1527) Muslim buffer between Delhi sultanate and Hindu south.

1347 Revolution of Cola di Rienzi in Rome, abortive attempt at Italian unity.

1348 First appearance of the Black Death in Europe and Egypt.

1349 Majapahit empire based in Java dominates trade in Malay region.

Clement V who moved the papal court to Avignon in 1309.

The Papacy at Avignon

From about 1300, new royal kingdoms and city-states claimed independence from both the pope and the Holy Roman Emperor. France under Philip IV (r. 1285-1314), was the best example. He asserted a fuller claim to sovereignty than ever before, telling Pope Boniface VIII (r. 1294-1303) that "in temporalities we are subject to none." Philip invaded Italy and briefly captured the pope. Boniface died soon after and was succeeded by two French-controlled popes, the second of whom—Clement V (r. 1305-14)—moved the papal court to Avignon in 1309, effectively placing the papacy under French secular protection. His successor Benedict XII (r. 1334-42) built the massive papal palace there. This "Babylonish Captivity" of the papacy lasted until 1377. It marked the arrival on the European scene of a powerful new force: the kingdom of France.

King Philip IV of France

Aztec Empire Established

In 1325 the Aztecs of central Mexico founded the city of Tenochtitlan, now Mexico City. They occupied most of central and southern Mexico and a bit of the northwest coast of Guatemala. The empire was governed by an aristocratic caste, including warriors and priests, responsible to the emperor. Below the nobility were free commoners and slaves. A series of military alliances with outlying city-states like Texcoco evolved into outright colonization. By the reign of the last emperor, Montezuma II, there were thirty-eight such provinces. Aztec religion had many gods, of whom Uitzilopochtli— the sun god— and Quetzalcoatl—the plumed serpent who controlled fertility and learning—were two of the more important. Human sacrifice to the sun god, often but not exclusively of captured prisoners, accounted for up to 20,000 lives a year. This remarkable civilization never had an alphabet and never discovered the wheel.

Aztec mosaic head; the teeth are made from mussels.

Rise of the Ottoman Turks

The Ottoman dynasty was founded by Osman I (1259-1326). Originally from central Asia, they were vassals of the Seljuks. In the early fourteenth century they swept through Anatolia. In 1326 they captured the key town of Brusa after a nine-year siege. It took them just over a century to capture the Balkans and finally Constantinople itself. From there they would create an empire embracing the Islamic Near East and Mediterranean. The empire evolved a system of government based on the administrative devolution of power. There were four principal institutions of state: the imperial, controlling palace affairs; the scribal, which oversaw revenue collection; the cultural, which looked after religious matters, education and the legal system; and the military. Outside these areas of direct imperial concern, power was devolved to local religious communities. While the state was Sunni Muslim it tolerated Jews and Christians, many of whom rose to positions of eminence.

Osman I, the eponymous founder of the Ottoman dynasty, attended by his bodyguards.

Japan: Emperor versus Shogun

Shoguns were Japanese military strongmen. Since 1185, a succession of shoguns effectively ruled the country from Kamakura near Tokyo. The imperial court was reduced to a ceremonial role. Until 1219 the Minamoto clan controlled the shogunate; thereafter the Hojo displaced them. In 1274 and 1281, the Mongols invaded Japan. In repulsing them, the shoguns used resources which restricted their subsequent capacity for patronage. This, plus the succession of an ambitious emperor, Go-Daigo II, led to the imperial coup of 1333 which ousted the Hojo. Kamakura was captured by the emperor's troops. But Daigo had to rely on the loyalty of his generals, one of whom, Ashikaga, saw the chance to establish himself as the new shogun. This he did in 1336, driving Go-Daigo from Kyoto. There followed over half a century of civil war between Go-Daigo and his successors and the Ashikaga shogunate, which resulted in victory for the latter in 1392.

Himeji Castle, first constructed by the Akamatsu warrior family in the fourteenth century.

Mali

Mali rose as Ghana declined. Sundiata Keita (r. 1230-55), king of Kangaba, built a coalition of smaller kingdoms. He and his successors spread their rule east and west of their capital Timbuktu and converted to Islam. Thus they connected the empire to the extensive trading networks of Islamic North Africa. Mali touched the Atlantic between the mouths of the Senegal and Gambia rivers; in the east it reached the border of Kanem-Bornu. But its heartland was near the big bend in the Niger, where the floodplains yielded rich harvests. Its wealth was built on a royal monopoly of trade, especially gold which was abundant. Its greatest ruler was Mansa Musa. His empire comprised three autonomous provinces and twelve military districts. When he made the pilgrimage to Mecca in 1324, he brought a caravan of over a hundred camels, laden with gold. Mali eventually yielded to the rising power of the Songhai.

Mask of a type called Tankagle, from the Dan-Ngale tribal complex of West Africa.

5000	2000	1000	500	AD1	400	600

The Marínids and the Mali

The Marínid dynasty under Abú Yúsuf Ya'kúb emerged as rulers of Morocco in the later thirteenth century, developing Fez as a new capital. The Marínids encouraged urban renewal, and public buildings of this era include the impressive Koranic school of Bou Inania Madrasa at Fez. Andalusian settlers were attracted to Morocco in the fourteenth century, influencing the art and architecture of the region. Abú 'l-Hasan, perhaps the greatest of the Marínids

(r. 1331-48), completed the great Chellah Necropolis near Rabat, where features of the mosques suggest Andalusian inspiration. Parallel to this, Arab immigration also influenced Morocco in cultural terms, as Berber languages adopted Arabic characteristics and script. Meanwhile, the Islamic Mali empire, which had succeeded Ghana as the leading power of West Africa, reached its apogee under Emperor Musa I (r. 1307-32). The emperor, remembered for bestowing

fabulous gifts while visiting Cairo, patronized the building of an impressive mosque and palace at Timbuktu. Mali merchants became wealthy through trade in cloth and copper; the capital Niani had many substantial clay houses with cupola-shaped roofs of wood and reeds, as described by the scholar Ibn Battuta, who visited the city in 1353.

The Aztecs

The Aztecs, like the Toltecs before them, were nomadic Chichimecs who migrated southward. According to legend, the Aztec city of Tenochtitlán was founded in 1325 on the site where an eagle with a rattlesnake in its mouth perched on a cactus. Today this eagle appears on the Mexican flag. On this marshy site, the Aztecs built artificial islands for farming and constructed canals as thoroughfares. Tenochtitlán became a populous city with fine architecture. The foundation of its central temple pyramid serves today as the main square of Mexico City. Aggressive warriors, the Aztecs brought various Mesoamerican peoples under their hegemony: many of their finest gold objects were made by Mixtec craftsmen, for example. Aztec artifacts

reflect a complex pantheon of gods, for they often adopted the deities of subject peoples in addition to their own. Quetzalcoatl, the plumed serpent god, continued to be worshipped, as did another pre-Aztec deity, Xipe-Totec, the flayed god of regeneration. Coyolxauhqui was the moon goddess, slain by the bloodthirsty patron deity of the Aztecs, the sun god Huitzilopochtli. The intellectually and aesthetically sophisticated Aztecs also practiced ritual human sacrifice on a larger and more efficient scale than any of their predecessors.

This gold pendant representing the flayed god Xipe-Totec was made by a Mixtec artist.

Islamic religious art, focusing on abstract designs and calligraphy, contrasts strongly with Indian figurative religious art. This Islamic pulpit tile bears the inscription "There is no god but God, and Muhammad is his prophet."

Islam in India

The founding of the Tughluk dynasty in 1320 ensured the presence of Islam in India. Islamic Turkish Afghans had already seized the Delhi sultanate (1193) and sounded the death knell of Indian Buddhism with the destruction of the great center at Nalanda in 1199. Henceforth the Buddha would linger in India as only one of the avatars of the Hindu god Vishnu. Hinduism proved impossible for Islam to uproot, however, and the two religions have a complex history of coexistence and opposition in India. The fifteenth-century founders of the Sikh religious order intended to encourage fellowship between Muslims and Hindus, and peaceful coexistence was also

promoted by intermarriage. Some Hindus also found Islamic Sufi mysticism appealing. Originally a radical sect, Sufism was partially reconciled with orthodox Islam by the eleventh-century Persian theologian al-Ghazali, and Sufi warriors and missionaries were among the Islamic conquerors of India. Sufi literature, written in the vernacular, reached a wide audience, and Sufi mystical practices resembled those of some Hindu yogis. The Sufi emphasis on personal devotion to God was also not unlike some of the Hindu bhakti cults. These points of similarity allowed some Hindus to accept and even convert to Islam.

| 800 | 1000 | 1200 | 1400 | 1600 | 1800 | 2000 |

Japan was plunged into civil war in the fourteenth century. This scroll fragment from the early fourteenth century depicts a chaotic battle scene.

Koryŏ in Korea and Kamakura Japan

Although both Japan and Korea adopted bureaucratic political systems inspired by T'ang China, their traditional cultures re-emerged over time. The Koryŏ state (from which the name Korea is derived), which arose after the downfall of Silla, unified the country into almost its present form by the eleventh century. During this time, Buddhism reached its height in Korea, and beautiful celadon porcelains, inspired by but unlike Chinese Song pottery, were created. Even before the Mongol conquest of Korea in the thirteenth century, however, Koryŏ was suffering from quarrels among military leaders that more closely paralleled current events in Japan than in China. Medieval Japan, first unified by the Kamakura shogun Yoritomo in 1185, also experienced the widespread acceptance of Buddhism. The melancholy poetry of Saigyo, a warrior who became a Buddhist priest, delicately but powerfully evokes both loneliness and resignation, and marked a new tradition of travel poetry that rejected urban life. In other arts, realistic portraiture developed for the first time in the Kamakura period; one of the best known is the portrait of Yoritomo by Fujiwara Takanobu. The typhoon (*kamikaze,* or "divine wind") that frustrated the attempted Mongol conquest of Japan did not, however, prevent the collapse of the Kamakura shogunate and resultant civil wars of the fourteenth century.

Europe's Medieval World View and Humanism

Early fourteenth-century Europe was still very much part of the medieval world. The nobility pursued a colorful social life centered on the castle, which assumed a residential role. Their enjoyment of tournaments, with knights engaging in jousts or mock-battle contests, banquets, hawking, and hunting contrasted with the harsh lives of ordinary people, who lived in poor wooden dwellings and tilled the land around manor villages. The medieval world view, however, believed in a fixed order of things and was theocratic; the *status quo* was ordained by God. Perhaps the greatest literary work of this period was *The Divine Comedy* by Dante Alighieri (d. 1321) of Florence. A powerful allegory, it draws inspiration from Christian revelation, but Dante's work also reflects concerns about arbitrary rule versus just government. The next generation of writers included Petrarch (d. 1374) and Boccaccio (d. 1375) whose rediscovery of classical learning led to the development of Humanism, an approach that focuses on human effort rather than religion.

Below Franceso Petrarch, the fourteenth-century Italian poet, Humanist and philologist.

Above Dante Alighieri, whose work The Divine Comedy *tells of a soul's journey through hell and purgatory to heaven.*

BYZANTIUM AND OTTOMAN TURKEY

Fear them not; there is no concord among them. Everyone takes care of himself only;
no one thinks of the common interest .... Obedience to their superiors and discipline
they have none, and yet everything depends on that.
On the Europeans, attributed to Sultan Murat II

In the fourteenth century the Byzantine empire was struggling for its very survival. Heir to Imperial Rome in the east this empire, centered on Constantinople, was distinguished by Greek culture and by its Eastern Orthodox Christianity, the Church of Constantinople having formally separated from Rome in 1054. However, religious divisions remained within it, faced as it was with several external threats. Perhaps a sense of insecurity underlay the preoccupation of Byzantine art with religious expression. Typical are the frescos and mosaics which illustrate an elaborate liturgy and, more significantly, a hierarchical view of the universe. In political terms the empire declined dramatically with Islamic expansion in the Middle East and Asia Minor. Even before 1300, the Byzantine realms were reduced to an arc of territory from Thrace to Thessaly with only the easternmost fringe of Anatolia for which tributes had been paid to Muslim magnates.

THE LATE BYZANTINE EMPIRE

Nonetheless, this period witnessed what was arguably the last flourishing of Byzantine art under the earlier Palaeologian emperors. Following a period of Latin domination at Constantinople, during which rival Greek emperors held court at Nicaea, the Palaeologi had gained power under Michael VII in 1261. The years that followed saw fine examples of late Byzantine art adorn Constantinople's basilica of Hagia Sophia (Divine Wisdom), still considered to be the greatest church in Christendom. It is probable that Emperor Michael himself commissioned the mosaic of Christ in the south gallery after taking possession of the city. The magnificent Deesis mosaic close by is early fourteenth century, corresponding to the reign of Andronicus II (dep. 1328). Belonging to the same period are the mosaics and murals of the Church of the Holy Savior in Chora. This late cultural flowering, if such it was, would be short-lived. By the time the Turks finally conquered Constantinople, they would find an impoverished and depopulated city, shrunken within its walls, with many ruined buildings and sites overgrown with grass.

EMERGENCE OF THE OTTOMAN DYNASTY

Having emerged only a few decades earlier, the Osmani or Ottoman dynasty in 1326 captured the Byzantine city of Prusa, a wealthy silk center which had already changed hands more than once. Here would be the Ottoman city of Bursa, the first capital of an empire in the making. Osman the dynastic founder would be buried there, along with his successor Orhan. Later, in 1391, the Sultan Beyazit would place a mosque there. Meanwhile, the Turks defeated the Byzantines at Pelekanon, and subsequently captured Nicaea (Iznik) in 1331. A church, Hagia Sophia, less distinguished than that in Constantinople, was immediately converted to a mosque; a portent of things to come. The fall of Nicomedia (Izmit) six years later effectively isolated the few remaining Byzantine possessions in Anatolia. In or around this time, the Ottomans established a professional army comprising Yeni Çeri, or Janissaries. Infantrymen armed with bows and scimitars, these "new levies" were slaves (often Christian captives) trained from boyhood in military routine. Accommodated in barracks, fed and rewarded with payments, the Janissaries (at least in this early period) were unswervingly loyal to the sultan. A cavalry force, known as the Spahis, was also raised. Such full-time soldiery gave the Ottomans a marked advantage at a time when most medieval armies were made up of farmers called up for seasonal military service. Relationships between Turk and Byzantine were not always hostile. Common dynastic interests led the Sultan Orhan to marry Theodora, daughter of Co-emperor John Cantacuzene. Turkish soldiers served as mercenaries in the Byzantine army, while Christian troops of various origins served the sultan for payment.

CLOSING IN ON CONSTANTINOPLE

Its remaining territories gradually eroded, factional conflict within the Palaeologian dynasty only served to accelerate the demise of Constantinople. Refortification of Anadolu east of the Bosphorus in 1350 could not prevent Ottoman forces from taking Gallipoli in 1358, holding it until Savoians dislodged them eight years later. Murat I, succeeding to the sultanate in 1361, crossed the Hellespont and overran northern Thrace. Adrianople (Edirne) fell in 1363 and shortly afterwards was chosen as a new capital for the growing Ottoman empire. Its location made it eminently suitable as a base for future Turkish conquests in the Balkans. Sultan Beyazit almost delivered the fatal blow to Byzantium at the close of the fourteenth century. Having taken Salonica and

The basilica of Hagia Sophia, Constantinople, originally dating to the fourth century, was further adorned with mosaics by late Byzantine emperors of the thirteenth and fourteenth centuries. The basilica became a mosque after the Ottoman conquest of the city in 1453.

Larissa in Thessaly, he closed in on Constantinople and laid siege to the city in 1395. A crusading Hungarian army which sought to intervene was defeated at Nicopolis. The "second city of Christendom" might well have fallen then, had Beyazit not been distracted by more pressing concerns elsewhere. The Tartars, under their king Tamerlane, were pushing towards Asia Minor. In the battle of Ankara 1402, Beyazit was defeated and taken prisoner by Tamerlane. The ensuing internecine strife within the Ottoman dynasty enabled Constantinople, though wracked by internal disputes, to survive for fifty years more Nevertheless the Turks were established in Europe, effectively replacing the Byzantines as *the* power of the east Mediterranean. *A.M*

5000	2000	1000	500	AD1	400	600

Divisions in the Holy Roman Empire

By the second half of the fourteenth century, the Holy Roman Empire was little more than a nominal presence. The German lands were a patchwork of statelets and provinces in which local magnate power was supreme. The empire was unable to provide a central authority for Germany, as the French kings were doing beyond the Rhine. The emperor was a powerful figure only in his own domain. As an elected emperor, he could not ensure the succession in his own family. The Golden Bull of 1356, which laid down procedures for the imperial election, also confirmed the political independence of the princely electors, whose domains stretched from the Rhineland to Bohemia. The failure to create a central imperial German state left the German lands vulnerable to the ambitions of their increasingly cohesive neighbors. It also created a constant tension between imperial ambition and local particularism.

- c 1350 Maoris flourish in North Island, New Zealand.

- 1352 Arab traveler Ibn Batuta crosses the Sahara, leaving an account of the Mandingo empire.

- 1354 Turks take Gallipoli, their first permanent conquest in Europe.

- 1356 Golden Bull defines the rights of the German princes and severely limits the power of the Holy Roman Emperor.

- 1357 Apogee of Marinid leader Faris I who conquers Algeria and Tunisia.

- 1358 The *jacquerie*, peasant uprising in northern France, defeated by nobles and Parisians.

- 1359 Civil war in the khanate of the Golden Horde (-1379) begins its decline.

- 1364 Accession of Charles V, the Wise, to the French throne.

- 1365 The Ottomans overrun Thrace, establish capital at Adrianople.

- 1368 Chu Yüan-chang ends Mongol domination in China; founds Ming dynasty (-1644).

- 1370 Hindu state of Vijayanagar conquers far south of India to complete its regional dominance.

- 1372 Ottomans complete the conquest of Macedonia and Bulgaria.

- 1376 Ottomans reduce the Byzantine empire to Constantinople, Thessalonika, and Morea.

- c. 1380s Foundation of Kongo kingdom, Zaire, Central Africa.

- 1380 French victories on land and sea reverse English gains in Hundred Years' War.

- 1381 English Peasants' Revolt crushed with great severity.

- 1381 War of Chioggia: Venice finally defeats long-standing rival Genoa.

- 1382 Chinese conquer Yunan to complete national unity.

- 1385 Portuguese defeat Castilians at Aljubarrota to confirm their independence.

- 1385 Union of Poland and Lithuania blocks eastward expansion of Teutonic Knights.

- 1388 Ming Chinese invade Mongolia and loot the capital, Karakorum.

- 1389 Battle of Kosovo: Serb-Bulgar coalition crushed by Ottoman Turks; Serbia and Bulgaria henceforth part of Turkish empire.

- 1392 End of long civil war in Japan.

- 1392 Yi dynasty comes to power in Korea (-1910) under loose Chinese suzerainty.

- 1395 Turkish sultan Bayazid begins first Ottoman siege of Constantinople.

- 1396 Crusade of Nicipolis, led by Sigismund of Hungary against the Turks, ends in disaster.

- 1398 Apogee of Timur (Tamerlane), Tartar warrior-king of Samarkand.

- c. 1400 Kingdom of Great Zimbabwe in southern Africa flourishes.

The Madrasa of Ulugh Beg, the oldest of three Islamic colleges that surround the market square in Samarkand, Timur's capital.

Timur in Northwest India

Timur the Lame (1336-1405), better known as Tamerlane, was a prince of Samarkand. He was of Mongol stock, although he was unrelated to Genghis Khan, as he claimed. In the 1390s, he smashed his way to power in Iran, Mesopotamia, Armenia and Georgia. He launched himself against northern India in 1398, captured Delhi and butchered its inhabitants in a spectacular act of mass slaughter. The Delhi Muslims were Sunnis. Timur was a Shi'ite and regarded them as little better than Hindus, whom he killed or enslaved. He looted Delhi of its wealth, further weakening the enfeebled sultanate, and also carried off skilled craftsmen to build a mosque in Samarkand. His later career took him to Anatolia where he captured the Ottoman sultan in 1402. When he died three years later, he was preparing an attack on Ming China. He was the greatest military conqueror in Asia since Genghis Khan.

| 00 | 1000 | 1200 | 1400 | 1600 | 1800 | 2000 |

The Chimú in Peru

The last major kingdom in Peru prior to the meteoric rise of the Incas was that of the Chimú. They dominated much of the coastal area of northern Peru during the fourteenth and most of the fifteenth centuries. Their walled capital, Chan Chan—whose important ruins are near the modern city of Trujillo—covered an area of more than fifteen square kilometers. Their agricultural production was facilitated by a complex irrigation system: the Chimú had advanced engineering skills. They bequeathed their infrastructure as well as their artistic traditions to their Inca conquerors, who defeated them in the late fifteenth century.

A gold mummy mask of the Chimu, probably dating from the fourteenth century.

Ming Dynasty in China

With the expulsion of the Mongols in 1368, China was again in the hands of a native dynasty, the Ming. They held power for almost three centuries until displaced by the Manchu, another non-Chinese group. They were therefore the last ethnic Chinese imperial dynasty. Their first emperor, Zhu Yuan-zhang, presided over bloody political purges and encouraged smallholders at the expense of the large estates. The empire was divided into fifteen provinces, administered by royal officials responsible for revenue, military affairs and the law. The dynasty stood for stability above all else: the country prospered and the population grew. Voyages of discovery were encouraged: in the early fifteenth century Chinese ships reached East Africa. But from the 1430s onwards, the Chinese turned away from the sea to concentrate on developments at home. The Ming period marks the start of the long Chinese isolation, which lasted until the Opium Wars and beyond.

A porcelain bowl dating from the Ming dynasty. Porcelain art was highly refined under the Ming.

Tripartite division of the Maghreb

From the 1230s onwards, the power of the Almohads—who had succeeded the Almoravids in North Africa—faded. The Maghreb divided into three areas roughly corresponding to Morocco, Algeria and Tunisia today, reflecting the natural topographical boundaries of the region. The Marinids took control of Morocco; the Ziyanids in Algeria; and the Hafsids in Tunisia. A brief Marinid expansion under King Faris I united the region. In the 1350s, Faris pushed east all the way to the Gulf of Tunis but was eventually beaten back by a Ziyanid-Hafsid coalition. Political unity in the Maghreb was not compatible with the independence of its peoples. However, the need for protection against aggression from Christian Spain—whose seamen attempted to occupy ports like Algiers—eventually drew the Maghreb into the Ottoman empire. It alone could guarantee the security of the region against Christian expansion in the western Mediterranean.

The Madrasa of al-'Attarin, an example of sophisticated Marinid architecture in Fez, Morocco.

Songhai Structure

Songhai, lying west of the central Niger, having been conquered by the Mali empire, re-emerged in the latter part of the fourteenth century. Its rulers having converted to Islam some 300 years earlier, resurgent Songhai had its capital at Gao (in modern Mali). On the surface, the political structure was not unlike that of other medieval empires: the sovereign had regional viceroys within the Songhai heartland and exercised indirect rule over several surrounding states. One of these was the Sultanate of Agades (in modern Niger), its capital a town of mud buildings dominated by a curious mosque.

What distinguished the Songhai empire was its complex administrative organization. There were ministries of finance, forests, waters, sanitation—and a Ministry for Whites was responsible for foreign visitors or residents within the realm. Songhai possessed a standing army and a developed system of agriculture and trade. The nobility had estates worked by slaves which produced cotton, kola nuts and spices. These products were exported along with gold, ivory and slaves, while imports from across the Sahara consisted mainly of cloths and salt.

Moorish Nasrid Period

Before the fourteenth century opened, the Moorish realms in Iberia (long in decline as the Christian kingdoms of Castile, Aragon and Portugal gained supremacy) had been reduced to the southern region of Andalucia, centered on Granada. Nonetheless, with the Christian kings distracted by conquests in the Mediterranean and by wars against each other, Islamic culture survived in this region for another two centuries. In addition to mosaic and ornamental pottery work, later Moorish art includes vivid frescos, such as those at the Palace of

Aguilar, sixty miles northwest of Granada, which depict the conquest of the Balearic Islands by Aragon forces. The Nasrid Period of the fourteenth century witnessed the construction of the magnificent Alhambra palace for the sultans of Granada. Surrounded by beautiful gardens with pools and fountains, the palace features decorative ceramic tiles with foliage designs while its multi-columned "Court of the Lions" exhibits impressive stucco work. The last Moorish ruler of Granada, Abu Abd Boabdil, known to the Spanish as El Chico, was deposed only in 1492.

Timur, Patron of the Arts

Although the terrible "Earth-Shaker" Timur-i-Lang (Tamerlane) had thoroughly devastated Delhi in 1398, he was careful to preserve the lives of stonemasons and other skilled artisans to employ them in his homeland. Timur was responsible for splendid palaces, mosques and tombs in Samarkand. Inscriptional panels, in tile mosaic of turquoise, manganese and cobalt, suggest the former beauty of the earthquake-damaged Bibi Khanum mosque (named after Timur's favorite wife). Miniatures also preserve the more ephemeral charms of gardens and tented camps on the outskirts of Samarkand, with embroidered tent hangings, carpets

The small but exquisite "Court of the Lions," so named for the nine statues of lions around the base of its central fountain, serves as an oasis amid the heat of a Spanish summer. It was built by Mohammed V as an addition to his Alhambra palace in Granada, in the fourteenth century.

800	1000	1200	1400	1600	1800	2000

The Timurids were known as patrons of the arts of bookmaking as well as architecture. This manuscript illumination depicts a scene from a Persian poem "Khamza from Nizami" when Khusrau is watching Shirin bathing. Her horse, richly adorned, has spotted the intruder and neighs a greeting to Khusrau's mount. Shirin, however, washing her long hair, remains serenely unaware that she is being observed.

and canopies supported by bird finials. The high-domed Gur Emir was constructed for Timur's son Muhammad Sultan (d. 1403), but became Timur's own tomb at his death in 1405. His grandson Ulugh Beg later provided a dark-green jade catafalque which is the largest known block of this stone. Ulugh Beg was also responsible for the madrasa, or Islamic college, whose tiled façade faces the city square, for the Registan with its twin minarets and for a famous observatory. Other Timurid accomplishments in the arts and architecture are remembered in the memoirs of a descendant, Babur, the founder of the Mughal dynasty of India.

Temple Mound Builders

 The different centers of the vast Mississippian culture, which extended over most of southeast North America, west to present-day Oklahoma and north as far as Wisconsin, were linked by a shared religion known as the Southern Cult or Death Cult. This cult seems to have been strongest between about 1300 and 1500 and opinions differ about whether this religion developed from indigenous regional traditions or whether it traveled north from Mesoamerica. Artifacts associated with the cult appear after about 1200 and reveal a preoccupation with death: pottery and sculptures depicting human sacrifice and stylized representations of skulls and weeping eyes. Contact with Mesoamerica is also suggested by a similarity of farming techniques. The Mississippians, whose culture originated about 700, share obvious similarities with their predecessors the Adena and Hopewell peoples. Like them, the Mississippians built burial mounds, but they also built large rectangular flat-topped mounds as platforms for temples and other important buildings. Thus, this culture is also known as the Temple Mound Builders. The most extensive site, at Cahokia near St Louis, contained eighty-five temple and burial mounds, the largest of which stood over one hundred feet high.

The Pacific Islands Before "Discovery"

 The inhabitable islands of the Pacific were probably settled by about 1000 AD. The Polynesian cultures which spread through much of the Pacific originated in Samoa and the Marquesas; adventurous sailors voyaged from these islands to Tahiti, Easter Island, the Australs, Hawaii, the Cook Islands and New Zealand. The Hawaiians became the most populous group as well as the most socially complex one. Their nobility wore magnificent feather cloaks, they devised massive irrigation systems and seawalls and concocted intoxicating liquors. The Maoris of New Zealand were the second most populous group, but were dispersed over a much larger territory. The fertile plains of the Tahitians supported a diverse society which gathered in large village assembly houses, or *marae*. The Tongans developed an influential culture on one of the least populated groups of islands; their society was highly stratified and ruthless, but they lived in almost complete peace with their neighbors between about 1200 and 1800. The Fijians were ingenious craftsmen, and also the most enthusiastic for cannibalism and human sacrifice, widespread in the Pacific. The mysterious Easter Islanders produced enormous stone sculptures between 1300 and 1700, and the only written script in the Pacific, still untranslated.

Huge stone figures on Easter Island have been the subject of much speculation.

Jeanne d'Arc, a contemporary portrait on parchment.

Jeanne d'Arc

The Hundred Years' War between England and France was in fact a series of wars stretching from 1337 to 1453. The essential issue was the claim of the kings of England upon the throne of France. By the 1420s, the English were winning. It was the visionary Jeanne d'Arc, an illiterate daughter of a farm worker, who helped to turn the tide. She convinced the dauphin and his court of her bone fides and was allowed to take up arms. She raised the siege of Orléans in 1429 and drove the English back from the Loire. With a large army, she took the dauphin across English-held territory and had him crowned Charles VII in Reims. She was captured by the English in 1430 and burned at the stake in Rouen the following year. But within twenty years the English were beaten. Jeanne was an early and enduring symbol of French nationalism.

Songhai

The Songhai people were established at Gao, below the big bend of the Niger, in the ninth century. Later, they came under the sway of Mali to the west. But as Mali grew, so did the difficulty of retaining the loyalty of its outlying provinces. Once it weakened, Songhai's Sunni dynasty absorbed significant parts of the empire. In 1471, Sunni Ali (r. 1464-92) captured Djenne, one of Mali's principal commercial cities. His successor Askia Mohammed (1493-1528) extended the new empire to an even greater size than that of Mali, now totally eclipsed. Although increasingly subject to internal dynastic rivalries, the Songhai empire held its position until 1591 when it was attacked from the north by the Sa'dids of Morocco. They had muskets, a terrifying new weapon to which the Songhai had no reply. Their capital at Gao was taken and the empire split into a series of petty kingdoms.

The tomb of Askia Mohammed at Gao. Askia was ruler of the Songhai empire in the late fifteenth and early sixteenth centuries.

Turkistan

For most of the Middle Ages the high, arid region of central Asia known as Turkistan maintained an independent existence. It was protected more by distance than by any internal cohesion: its tribal way of life was undisturbed either by a centralizing state or by outside conquest. In the long-distant days of the Han dynasty, it had been ruled by China; the Mongols under Genghis Khan overran it but did not alter it fundamentally. The most potent of all outside forces had been Islam which had been introduced by Arab invaders in the ninth century. This region of Asia has remained Muslim ever since, despite being divided between the growing power of Russia and China in later centuries.

A nineteenth-century painting of a mosque in Turkistan by the Russian artist Vereshchagin.

800	1000	1200	1400	1600	1800	2000

■ **1400** Mali empire in decline: Wolof people (modern Senegal) secede, establish their independence.

■ **1401** Rebellion of Owen Glyndwr in Wales develops into war against English rule (-1409).

■ **1402** Ethiopian ambassadors reach Venice, the first of a number of such embassies to Europe.

■ **1403** Prince Paremesvara establishes new kingdom at the tip of the Malay peninsula.

■ **1406** Chinese naval leader Cheng Ho occupies and subdues Sumatra.

■ **1410** Polish-Lithuanian coalition defeats the Teutonic Knights at Tannenberg.

■ **1414** Lollard rebellion in England anticipates the Reformation.

■ **1414** Khizar Khan, governor of the Punjab, captures Delhi, founds Sayyid dynasty.

■ **1415** Battle of Agincourt, worst defeat for the French crown in the 100 Years' War.

■ **1415** Burning of Jan Hus, Bohemian church reformer.

■ **1415** Ethiopian King Yeshaq I overruns Muslim sultanate of Ifat on Red Sea coast.

■ **1417** End of the Council of Constance: Latin church reunited following Great Schism.

■ **1417** Great Chinese naval expedition under Cheng Ho sails as far as East Africa.

■ **1421** Establishment of Chinese capital at Peking (Beijing).

■ **1429** Under inspiration of Jeanne d'Arc, French relieve English siege of Orléans.

■ **1430** Aztecs under Itzcoatl defeat the Tepanaca people who preceded them in Mexico.

■ **1431** Jeanne d'Arc burned at the stake in Rouen, France.

■ **1431** Siamese invasion of Cambodia forces evacuation of Angkor.

■ **1433** Saharan Tuaregs sack Timbuktu.

■ **1433** Portuguese first sail past Cape Bojador (Bulging Cape) on West African coast.

■ **1434** Beginning of Medici power in Florence.

■ **1436** French recapture Paris as 100 Years' War turns against English.

■ **1438** Foundation of Inca empire established in Peru.

■ **1446** After repeated invasions, Ming Chinese finally conquer Burmese kingdom of Ava.

■ **1449** Accession of Montezuma I (-1464) who expanded Aztec power in southern Mexico.

Peking capital of China

Kublai Khan had established his capital at Peking (Beijing) in 1272, calling it Khanbalik. However, the Ming abandoned it in favor of Nanking on assuming power in 1368. But at the turn of the fifteenth century, a dynastic power struggle within the Ming led to the rise of the usurper known as the Yung-lo emperor. It was he who decreed a return to Peking, which has remained the administrative and political center of a unified China ever since—except for a few short periods. The purpose of the move was to make it easier to defend the troublesome northern frontier. To consolidate the status of his new capital, the emperor embarked on an ambitious program of public building: many of the city's most famous structures date from this period, as does the Forbidden City itself.

A gilded bronze lion guards the Emperor's Palace in the Forbidden City, Peking.

The Rise of the Incas

By the mid-1400s, the Incas had been settled for 300 years in the Cuzco valley of Peru. From here, they raided neighboring territories but did not seek to extend their own. In the early fifteenth century, the Inca king Viracocha Inca undertook a modest territorial expansion. Compared with what came later it was unimpressive, but it began a process that within a few generations saw the establishment of one of the most brilliant of all pre-Columbian civilizations in the Americas. At its apogee, it extended from just north of modern Quito in Ecuador to the south of Santiago in Chile. The Incas built a sophisticated road system and had highly developed administrative skills. The autocratic state controlled all economic activity. Yet in 1533, the Spanish conquistador Francisco Pizarro was able to overthrow all this with less than 200 men. Once the king and capital fell, the state fell too.

Gold female figurine wrapped in cloth secured with a gold pin: she represents a concubine of the Inca emperor.

5000	2000	1000	500	AD1	400	600

The Signs of the Blessings *by Al-Jazuli; the names of God and Muhammad highlighted in gold form a clear visual pattern.*

The Sufi in North Africa

The fifteenth century witnessed the spread of the Sufi movement, as Moroccan saint and mystic Al-Jazuli, seeking to revive spirituality within Islam, formed a brotherhood that would be known as the Jazuliya. Typical of the spiritual dimension of Sufi is the book of prayers *Signs of the Blessings* composed by Al-Jazuli himself. The approach adopted is that of repetitive prayer, aimed at focusing the mind on God. Sufi brotherhoods proliferated and the movement spread across the Maghreb and into the Middle East. However laudable its intentions, critics maintained that the Sufi promoted a fatalistic outlook, encouraged saint worship and provided a platform for religious charlatans. Some 300 years after the movement's first appearance, the Sa'ud dynasty of Arabia would launch an anti-Sufi initiative to refocus on the basics of Muslim teaching, promoting a new orthodoxy that would impact upon northern Africa.

The Origins of Balinese Performance

Balinese theatrical traditions trace their origins to the latter days of the Majahapit empire. Founded on the island of Java in 1293 by a Hindu prince, at its peak in the late fourteenth century the Majahapit empire may have extended to include all the islands of present-day Indonesia as well as parts of Malaysia. Certainly it included Java, Bali, and Madura. Lasting into the sixteenth century, the empire began to feel the expanding influence of Islam in Southeast Asia during the fourteenth and fifteenth centuries. The last Hindu-Buddhist court retreated in the face of the Islamic advance from Java to the neighboring island of Bali, which even today retains its Hindu identity in a predominantly Islamic country. Traditional Balinese performance traces its ancestry to the residency of the Majahapit court, although older Indian influence is evident. The *gambuh* is dance drama presenting traditional stories based on ancient Javanese legends. In the *wayang parwa*, shadow puppets are used to tell stories from the *Mahabharata*. Performances are seldom scripted, but usually involve improvisation cued by music from the *gamelan* (gong chime orchestra). Both types are presented at village temple festivals, often at night in order to take advantage of the assumed presence of spirits.

The Balinese Hindu Pura Dalem, or demon temple, is opposite the Pura Puseh, or home of the gods, in each village. The demon temple is intended to placate the deities of death and cremation.

The Incas

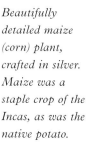

Beautifully detailed maize (corn) plant, crafted in silver. Maize was a staple crop of the Incas, as was the native potato.

Rising from obscurity about 1200, the Incas eventually ruled over the largest territory in the ancient Americas, including most of present-day Peru, Ecuador, and Bolivia, and the northern portions of Argentina and Chile. Much of this area was consolidated during the reign of Pachacuti (1438-1471). Although the term "Inca" is now applied generally, originally it was title of the semi-divine ruler. The Incas called their land Tawantinsuyu, meaning "land of the four quarters" in the Quechua language. Quechua remains the most widely spoken American native language, a legacy from Pachacuti's time, when it became the *lingua franca* uniting the many different peoples of the Inca realm. This realm was also linked by an extensive series of roads and an efficient postal system using human runners. The Incas were extraordinary builders, constructing bridges, tunnels, and aqueducts, and steep mountain terraces for farming, as well as buildings famous for their stone blocks which fit snugly without mortar. They were skillful metallurgists, lining the Temples of the Sun and Moon at Cuzco with gold and silver and crafting fine artifacts. Although they possessed no written language, they kept detailed records by means of colored knotted string (*quipu*) and practiced sophisticated medicine, including brain surgery.

Humanism

By the mid-fifteenth century, Humanism had merged with the Renaissance, as that movement gathered pace. Seeking to develop the talents of mankind to the full, Humanists focused on man's history and past works. This approach owed much to the fourteenth-century Florentines Petrarch and Boccaccio who, while producing literature in the Italian vernacular, collected and studied Latin and Greek manuscripts. Pope Nicholas V (r. 1447-55), striving to build up the Vatican library, paid for the translation of Greek works into Latin. When Constantinople was conquered by the Turks in 1453, he sent clerks to rescue what they could of the city's Classical heritage. One outcome of this interest in the great works of Greece and Rome was a questioning of old ways of thinking. The entire process of knowledge transmission would be revolutionized around the mid-fifteenth century. It is difficult to ascertain who first used a movable metal type printing press; perhaps it was Lourens Coster of Haarlem (Netherlands) *c.* 1440.

Certainly, Johann Gutenberg of Mainz produced an edition of the Bible in 1456. It would take some decades for the importance of this breakthrough to become apparent.

A nineteenth-century French woodcut in the style of c.1520 provides a symbolic depiction of the breakthrough in the medieval conception of the world that occurred at this period.

The Ming Dynasty

The powerful Ming dynasty (1328-1644) was founded by a commoner, Chu Yüan-chang (known as Hung-wu), who was determined to re-establish the values and styles of the earlier Chinese Han and T'ang periods after years of foreign Mongol rule. Hung-wu's son Yung-lo (r. 1402-1424), who usurped the throne from the designated heir, his nephew, used the foundations of the Mongol capital at Peking (Beijing) to build a new city inspired by the achievements of T'ang design. The main city walls, over forty feet high, spanned a circumference of more than fourteen miles. Within stood the walls of the Imperial City, some five miles in circumference, and within those, a two-mile moat surrounded the high red walls of the magnificent Forbidden City, the imperial palace complex. Under Ming rule, scholarship flourished, and one of the accomplishments of Yung-lo's reign was the compilation by over 2000 scholars of an enormous encyclopedia of 11,095 volumes. The arts also prospered during the stable Ming period. Innovations in traditional landscape painting were made by Shen Chou and other artists. Ming patronage encouraged the production of porcelain of remarkable quality and beauty, often of distinctive blue and white design, but also sometimes incorporating the colors of red, green, yellow, and purple.

A classically beautiful blue and white Ming vase, its special underglaze-blue clearly evident. The Ming dynasty emperors took the production of fine porcelain very seriously, establishing and controlling imperial kilns whose directors were royally appointed and whose wares were highly valued in China and beyond.

WONDER AND DEVASTATION

Española is a marvel.
Letter of Christopher Columbus

Christopher Columbus planned his initial voyage to discover a western route to Asia with the best information available to him. He accepted Marco Polo's estimate of the distance between Japan and mainland China (1500 miles, according to Polo), and he also had the still-respected authority of the great second-century Greco-Egyptian mathematician and geographer Ptolemy on the size of the Eurasian land mass and the circumference of the earth. Today it is obvious that Polo greatly overestimated the distance between China and Japan, and equally evident that Ptolemy overestimated the size of Eurasia and underestimated the circumference of the globe. However, with the information he possessed, it is not surprising that Columbus continued to believe until he died that he had landed upon some outlying Asian islands when he discovered the islands of the Caribbean. His truly remarkable accomplishment was being able to travel the vast uncharted distance between Europe and the Caribbean successfully, not merely once but four times.

"O BRAVE NEW WORLD THAT HAS SUCH PEOPLE IN'T!"

When it became clear that Columbus and other explorers had actually stumbled upon a land mass previously unknown to Europeans—a New World—the effect upon Europeans was staggering. Almost everything in the Americas seemed marvelous and fantastical; new plants, new animals, new elements, new … peoples? Europeans were uncertain about how to categorize the inhabitants of the New World. Pope Julius II finally decreed in 1512 that the Indians of the Americas were descended from Adam and Eve, just as Europeans were. Still, nothing in their science or theology prepared Europeans to understand a world literally beyond their imagination. The reverberations of this shock lasted for at least a century. The questions it raised are evident in Montaigne's wry essay "On Cannibals" and in Shakespeare's *The Tempest*, to mention only two examples.

Whether hostile or friendly, the natives apparently found the Europeans equally exotic, although very little direct evidence remains. Most of what is known about Indian reactions to the explorers comes from European accounts. Indians at first found the horses of the Europeans amazing and terrifying; the horse had died out in the Americas in the last ice age. That the Spanish explorer Cortés could convincingly adopt the guise of the deity Quetzalcoatl is persuasive evidence of just how strange and magical he must have appeared in the eyes of the Aztec ruler Montezuma II.

CONQUESTS

The Spanish and Portuguese established the strongest early European presence in the Americas. It seemed natural to them to claim these lands as European territory. It was not unlike what the Islamic Turks were doing in eastern Europe in the mid-fifteenth century. Then, European Christendom trembled in the face of the Islamic advance; less than a century later, the Spanish and Portuguese were possessed of far more vast territories than the Islamic Turks, and the rest of Europe was eager to participate in the conquest of the New World.

The Pope's decree implied that the Indians had human souls in need of Christian salvation. Under the *encomienda* system Spaniards were granted Indian laborers by the Spanish crown for farming and mining. In return they were to provide adequate care for the Indians and instruct them in Christianity. In practice, this often degenerated into cruel slave labor. The native populations of the Caribbean and parts of the mainland Americas were quickly decimated, leading the encomanderos to import slave labor from Africa. Not all Europeans were insensitive to this situation; an early and articulate Spanish defender of the Indians was Bartolomé de Las Casas, who began his American career as a soldier, and then, in 1512, became the first priest ordained in the Americas. De Las Casas's blistering attack on the Spanish treatment of the Indians, *The Devastation of the Indies*, described their abuses in detail and directly affected the passing of laws in Spain designed to protect the Indians. Sadly, these were not always enforced by local officials.

THE WORST DEVASTATION

Perhaps the greatest devastation of the native populations of the Americas came not from brutal conquest and slavery, but from a far more insidious enemy: disease. It is estimated that as many as two-thirds of the native peoples of the Americas died of strange new diseases, such as smallpox, brought by the Europeans. Having no immunity to these diseases, the natives succumbed to them with great rapidity. It has been suggested that if the population of the Inca empire had not been seriously reduced by European infections, Pizarro would never have managed to conquer the Incas. Certainly disease aided the conquest of Mesoamerica. In any case, although both the Aztecs and the Incas had many native enemies who were (at first) eager to join the Spanish and Portuguese conquerors, it is uncertain what might have happened if this tragic biological disaster had never occurred.

S.I.

Although dating from a later period, this book illustration suggests some of the punishments inflicted upon the Indians of Mexico by their Spanish conquerors.

5000	2000	1000	500	AD1	400	600

- **1450** Battle of Formigny: English longbowmen blown away by French cannon.

- **1451** Civil war in the Mayan empire leads to the destruction of Mayapan.

- **1451** Sayyids overthrown in Delhi by Lodi dynasty.

- **1453** Ottoman Turks finally capture Constantinople: end of the Byzantine empire.

- **1453** French victory at Castillon effectively ends the 100 Years' War.

- **1454** Johannes Gutenberg of Mainz produces an edition of the Bible by printing with movable metal type.

- **1455** Beginning of the Wars of the Roses, series of English dynastic civil wars (-1485).

- **1458** Matthias Corvinus (-1490), who made Hungary dominant in central Europe.

- **1460** Collapse of Khmer empire in Cambodia under Siamese assaults.

- **1461** Final expulsion of the English from France, except for Calais (1558).

- **1461** House of York in the ascendant in England (-1485).

- **1462** Accession of Ivan III as Russian ruler; first real tsar.

- **1464** Songhai empire under Sonni Ali expands in region of the Middle Niger.

- **1467** Civil war in Japan.

- **1468** Axayactl, Aztec king, expands the empire's reach to Atlantic and Pacific coasts.

- **1473** War in the Aztec empire ends with city of Tenochtitlan victorious over Tlatilulco.

- **1476** Charles the Bold of Burgundy killed in Swiss wars.

- **1477** Union of Burgundy with the French crown; birth of modern French state.

- **1478** Tsar Ivan III captures Novgorod and begins Muscovite consolidation of Russia.

- **1478** Lorenzo "the Magnificent" de Medici, sole ruler of Florence (-1492).

- **1479** Ferdinand king of Aragon; m. (1469) Isabella of Castile; union of crowns.

- **1480** Tsar Ivan III throws off Tartar yoke; Muscovy dominant in the Russian lands.

- **1485** Battle of Bosworth ends the Wars of the Roses; Henry VII first Tudor king of England.

- **1487** Lodi dynasty of Delhi establishes full control of central Ganges valley.

- **1488** Portuguese Bartolomeu Diaz rounds the Cape of Good Hope.

- **1491** "Golden Horde" in decline; invasion of Poland-Lithuania crushed at Zaslavl.

- **1491** Ruler of Kongo kingdom baptized Christian by the Portuguese.

- **1492** Fall of the Alhambra in Granada: final defeat of Muslim Spain after nearly 800 years.

- **1492** Accession of Rodrigo Lanzol y Borgia as Pope Alexander VI (-1503).

- **1492** Columbus discovers the New World, lands San Salvador, Cuba and Haiti.

- **1494** Temporary eclipse of the Medici in Florence; personal rule of Savonarola (-1498).

- **1496** Jews expelled from Portugal.

- **1497** Vasco da Gama begins his successful voyage from Portugal to India.

- **1499** First appearance of the musket in European warfare.

Passage to India

Cape Bodajor is on the West African coast, just south of the Canaries. Until 1433 Portuguese sailors refused to sail past it for fear of being unable to return against the prevailing north wind. Once that barrier was breached, the advance down the coast began in earnest. In 1482, ships from Lisbon were at the mouth of the Congo. In 1487 Bartolomeu Dias became the first European to round the Cape of Good Hope and stand his ship out to sea in the Indian Ocean. Ten years later, Vasco da Gama rounded the Cape again and sailed up the eastern coast to Malindi, near Mombasa, where he spent the winter. He left there in April 1498 and after a voyage of nearly a month dropped anchor in Calicut, on the Malabar coast of India. The Portuguese were the first Europeans to reach the subcontinent and the last to leave.

The stone cross erected at Malindi by Vasco da Gama en route to India.

800	1000	1200	1400	1600	1800	2000

Consolidation of France

The dukes of Burgundy were the most powerful vassals of the French king. During the Hundred Years' War, they had attempted to establish their independence as a separate kingdom. In 1477, however, Charles the Bold of Burgundy died without a male heir. His territories were divided. The western part became the historic French province of Burgundy. Picardy and Artois also reverted to the crown. The rest, comprising the Franche-Comté and the Netherlands, passed to the Hapsburgs by marriage. King Louis XI (r. 1461-83) added Roussillon, which he bought from John II of Aragon. In 1480 Anjou and Maine passed to the crown, as did Provence in 1481. Louis's successor, Charles VIII (r. 1483-98) married Anne, duchess of Brittany, which was thus joined to France. By the end of the fifteenth century, France had overcome internal division to form a coherent state stretching from the English Channel to the Mediterranean.

The marriage of Charles VIII and Anne de Bretagne at Château Langeais, France. A wax figure reconstruction.

New World

When the Genoese sailor Christopher Columbus sailed west in 1492 he was seeking a passage to China and the Indies. Instead he discovered, not the greater American continent, but the Bahamas, Cuba and Hispaniola. From this first error-strewn voyage, all else followed. The discovery of a vast new continent, bursting with natural riches, reoriented the whole situation in Europe, marking the rise of the Atlantic states over the Mediterranean. For the several cultures of the Native Americans, this moment was doom-laden. Within a couple of generations, the mighty Aztec and Inca empires would collapse before handfuls of Spanish conquistadores. Portugal quickly colonized Brazil. Spain took most of the rest of South America and all of Mexico and Central America. North America saw English settlement on the east coast; French exploration of Canada, the Great Lakes, and the Mississippi basin; and Spanish influence in the southwest.

A contemporary portrait of Christopher Columbus.

Rise of the Yoruba

The Yoruba were a predominantly urban people who settled in southwest Nigeria from the twelfth century onward. They were a mercantile people highly skilled in craftwork of every kind. Positioned as they were between the powerful states of Ife on the one side and Benin on the other, they were influenced by both. Their state, called the kingdom of Oyo, prospered and reached its full power in the seventeenth century. It maintained its influence until the arrival of the British in the nineteenth. The descendants of the Yoruba of Oyo are particularly concentrated in the modern Nigerian city of Ibadan.

A fifteenth-century carved ivory cup. This exquisite piece of work is a good example of Yoruba art.

Muromachi power in Japan

The Ashikaga family held the office of shogun from 1338 to 1573. They were at the height of their power in the second half of the fifteenth century, when they faced fewer internal challenges—either from emperors or from regional warlords—than they had done in the fourteenth or would again in the sixteenth. Possession of the shogunate made them the real hereditary rulers of Japan. In theory they exercised their office in the name of the emperor; in practice the emperor was a cipher. The great feudal nobles of the provinces were much more of a threat. They constantly frustrated the ambitions of the Ashigaka to create a more centralized administration. Nonetheless, they created foundations which would be built on more successfully by the later Tokugawa shogunate after 1603. Their period of power is called Muromachi after the area of Kyoto where they had their family home.

Ginkaku-ji, Temple of the Silver Pavilion. The garden was designed by Soami in the Muromachi period, late 1500s.

Self-portrait of Leonardo da Vinci (d. 1519), Italian painter, sculptor, and designer.

Renaissance

The Renaissance, a great rebirth of culture and learning, owes its origin to the relative political stability and commercial growth of Mediterranean Europe as the Middle Ages closed. This development was preceded by the emergence of Humanism, and was paralleled by an "Age of Exploration" when journeys to the African, Asian and American continents broadened European horizons. From the mid-fifteenth century, the wealthy commercial centers of Florence and Milan, under the Medici and Svorza dukes, patronized the arts and allowed painters and sculptors like Leonardo da Vinci and Michelangelo Buonarroti to flourish. Renaissance painters developed perspective and shading, and realistic representation of the human body based on improved knowledge of anatomy. By c. 1550, this new art was thriving in western and northern Europe, and Palladian architecture, based on the Classical styles of Greece and Rome, was spreading across the continent. Universities were already well established from Oxford and Paris to Prague and Crakow. Vernacular literature was developing in England, France and Spain, while scholars like Nicholas Copernicus from Poland, and later the Dane Tycho Brahe, were establishing demanding new frontiers in astronomy and the physical sciences.

Columbus in the Caribbean

Christopher Columbus was not the first European to arrive in the Americas, being preceded by the Vikings in the tenth century, and perhaps by other Europeans as well. He nonetheless remains inextricably associated with the discovery of the "New World," although he refused to recognize this idea. Columbus called the peoples of the Caribbean islands where he arrived in 1492 "Indians," believing that he had found a western route to Asian riches. Columbus made four voyages to these islands and to the northern coast of South America, and died still believing that he had reached the edges of Asia. He and his crew were initially received in timid but friendly fashion by the peaceable Arawaks (who also peopled the tropical forests of northern South America). The island Arawaks were largely driven away shortly before Spanish colonization by the fierce Caribs, whom the Spanish called Canibales, giving rise to the generic term. Although the Caribs managed to resist the Spanish for almost 200 years in some places, eventually they, too, were driven away, enslaved, or died of contagious European diseases.

Today the Caribbean is populated by a complex mixture of descendants of slaves imported from Africa, various Europeans, East Indians, and others, with little trace of the indigenous inhabitants' existence.

A nineteenth-century depiction of Columbus landing on one of the Caribbean islands he claimed for Spain. Notice the artist's depiction of the frightened natives in the background.

800	1000	1200	1400	1600	1800	2000

The Fall (and Restoration) of Constantinople

The powerful Ottoman Empire emerged from once-scattered nomadic Turkish tribes. Initially united by enthusiasm for Islam, brought to central Asia in the eighth century by the Arabs, Turkish slaves rose to power in the Islamic world through their warrior skills. They considered Anatolia their homeland, and established positions on the edges of the Byzantine empire, where, in spite of their differences, Turkish Islamic culture mingled with Byzantine Christian culture. In 1453, the Ottoman Sultan Mehmed II accomplished a feat often attempted unsuccessfully by others: the capture of the Byzantine capital of Constantinople (Istanbul). The Byzantine empire had long been in decline, and Mehmed II found a city in disrepair. An inexorable conqueror, Mehmed II was also cosmopolitan and pragmatic. He began a program of repopulation and restoration, not only of buildings but of economic and intellectual life. He gathered Muslim, Greek and Italian scholars at his court, and established a policy of tolerance towards monotheistic religions, encouraging Christians and Jews to settle in Constantinople. Although not granted all the privileges of the sultan's Muslim subjects, Christians and Jews were given jurisdiction over their own communities and protected by law. Many Jews fleeing persecution in Europe chose Constantinople as their new home.

A portrait of the Ottoman Sultan Mehmed II, who captured and rebuilt Constantinople. He is sometimes considered to be the true founder of the Ottoman empire, which he continued to expand.

Zen Buddhism

Although the third Ashigaka shogun, Yoshimitsu (1358-1408) managed to reunite the emperor's rival southern court with the northern shogunate court at Kyoto in 1392, the resultant peace lasted for only about thirty years. The later feudal period in Japan was characterized by continual tumultuous warfare between powerful local lords which lasted until the mid-sixteenth century. These warlords embraced as their religion the meditative sect of Zen Buddhism, producing a distinctive culture of powerful simplicity. Zen Buddhism originated in China in the sixth century, but reached its height as a creative force in Japan in the Muromachi (or Ashigaka) feudal period. The sect was introduced to Japan by monks who had studied in China in the twelfth century. One of these, Eisai, popularized tea in Japan. The quiet rigor of Zen, which requires the initiate to seek his own attainment of enlightenment through meditation, combined with the warrior ethos to produce a culture of refined selectivity and strength. The ordered serenity of the tea ceremony and the carefully arranged intimacy of Zen gardens are perhaps its most typical expressions. The disciplined and expressive *Nō* drama which developed in this period was also inspired by the Zen warrior ethos.

Great Zimbabwe

There has been much debate about the origins of Great Zimbabwe, the development of which was arguably inspired by the East African trading center of Kilwa. Some would see an Arab influence in the layout of Great Zimbabwe (near modern Masvingo), others look to earlier Shona villages as a source of inspiration, although the great conical tower has no known precedent in indigenous tradition. Certainly the city which developed here from the thirteenth century featured houses of stone, especially granite, and under the Rozwi dynasty from the late fifteenth century it was surrounded with massive stone walls. The Shona-speakers brought mining skills and exploited local gold and copper. They produced fine ornaments in these metals, and practiced other crafts including pottery. Their trade links extended to the East African coast, exporting ivory and importing glass beads and iron tools. The religion of Great Zimbabwe emphasized ancestor worship and there was a professional priestly class. Many burials of nobility in the Zambezi Valley feature grave goods, including pottery and artifacts obtained through trade.

Tower of Great Zimbabwe, with walls dating from the Rozwi dynasty (c. 1500 AD).

5000	2000	1000	500	AD1	400	600

Cortés conquers the Aztecs

Hernan Cortés came of a noble family in the remote inland province of Estremadura, Spain. In 1518, he took a mere 550 men, seventeen horse and ten cannon and with this improbably small force invaded the Aztec empire of Mexico, one of the most powerful and sophisticated of all Native American civilizations. He first conquered the Yucatán peninsula and skillfully embraced the support of disaffected elements in the Aztec provinces. In the end, his victory was the product of two things: vastly superior military technology, especially cavalry and artillery, which more than compensated for lack of numbers; and gross treachery in his dealings with the Aztec emperor Montezuma, who had received him well, but whom he abducted and forced to submit to Spain. An Aztec revolt forced Cortés first to withdraw but he returned to besiege and capture Tenochtitlan, the Aztec capital, which fell to him in 1521.

Cortés meets Zempuala, an Aztec prince.

Decline of the Egyptian Mamelukes

The Mamelukes had originally been slaves who had risen by their own efforts and talent to high military office in Egypt. Islam had always recognized the institution of slavery but followed the Prophet's dictum that slaves should be well treated, so that there was no chattel slavery in the Islamic world similar to that in the Americas. Since the 1250s two dynasties of Mamelukes had actually ruled Egypt. But in 1517 they felt the full force of the ever-expanding Ottoman empire. Having captured southeast Europe, it then spread into Palestine and Arabia, bringing most of the Islamic holy places within the empire, and annexing Egypt. The country was now subject to the Turkish pasha, who was directly responsible to the sultan in Istanbul. However, the Mamelukes survived as *beys*, or provincial governors, and remained an important element in Egyptian life until finally destroyed by Napoleon in 1798.

Selim the Grim, who brought Palestine, Arabia, and North Africa within the Ottoman empire and limited the Egyptian Mamelukes' power.

Foundation of the Mughal Empire

The sultanate of Delhi never extended its power to the entire subcontinent, nor was it so much a unified state as the center of a loose confederation. Successive invasions— of which Timur's was the most celebrated—weakened it. In the 1520s it was in the hands of the ineffectual Lodi dynasty. In 1526, Babur, a descendant of Timur, invaded the Ganges valley, defeated the Lodi and occupied their capital Agra. He proclaimed himself the emperor of Muslim India. He was able to confirm his claim by building a centralized, efficient state in a way that the sultanate had not. He extended his empire ever southward, but it was left to his grandson and successor, Akbar the Great, to bring the empire to its apogee. He conquered nearly all the subcontinent in the second half of the century. The Mughal empire was later a model for the British Raj.

Babur, Shahir ed-din Mohammed, India Grand Mughal, in his garden. From the Babur-Nama manuscript, 1589.

Burma Reunited

Tabin Shwehti was ruler of Toungoo, a petty kingdom in southern Burma. In 1539 he captured Pegu, the leading city in the south, and declared himself king of Lower Burma three years later. In 1546 he launched himself against Pagan in the north, conquered it and was crowned king of all Burma. However, his kingdom did not embrace all of modern Burma (Myanmar) because Tabin Shwehti's campaigns against Arakan— the west coast kingdom on the Bay of Bengal—were unsuccessful and Arakan remained an eastern buffer between India and East Asia until the days of the British Raj. Nor did the new kingdom fare any better in the south, failing to make significant gains in Siamese territory. Finally, military overreach destroyed the kingdom in 1600, the latest failed attempt to create a permanent united Burmese state.

1500 Pedro Cabral claims Brazil for Portugal.

1501 Ismail I (-1524) first Safavid Shah of Iran; introduces Shi'ism as state religion.

1501 First African slaves shipped to Hispaniola.

1502 Montezuma II emperor of the Aztecs.

1502 Final victory of Russia over remnants of the "Golden Horde," the Mongol army.

1505-7 Portuguese found Mozambique on the coast of East Africa; trade with Africans begins.

1509 Battle of Diu establishes Portuguese control of Indian seas.

1510 Albuquerque annexes Goa on the west coast of India for Portugal.

1511 Spaniards capture Puerto Rico.

1513 Battle of Flodden, the greatest military disaster in Scottish history.

1513 Balboa reaches the isthmus of Panama and the Pacific.

1514 Russian-Polish war: Russia captures Smolensk.

1514 Portuguese reach Canton; first Europeans in China.

1514 War between Turkey and Persia: the Persians are defeated at the Battle of Chaldiran.

1516 War between Ottoman empire and Egypt (-1517): Cairo captured.

1517 Martin Luther formulates his 95 theses, the first act of the Reformation.

1517 Fall of the Egyptian Mameluke rulers; Egypt now part of Ottoman empire.

1519 Ferdinand Magellan begins the first circumnavigation of the globe.

1520 Accession of Sultan Suleiman I (the Magnificent) of Turkey (-1566).

1521 Cortés completes the conquest of Mexico for the crown of Spain.

1525 Battle of Pavia: Holy Roman Empire defeats France.

1526 Turks crush Hungarians at Mohacs, capture Buda.

1526 Babur, a descendant of Genghis Khan and king of Kabul in Afghanistan, defeats last Delhi sultan and founds Mughal empire in India.

1527 German and Spanish troops sack Rome and take Pope Clement VII prisoner.

1529 First Turkish siege of Vienna ends with onset of winter.

1529 Muslims defeat Ethiopian Christians at the Battle of Shimbra Kure. Rule until 1543.

1533 Ivan IV, "the Terrible", Tsar of Russia (-1584).

1533 Pizarro overruns the Inca empire, captures capital Cuzco.

1534 King Henry VIII assumes leadership of English Church, denying papal authority.

1535 Jacques Cartier in Quebec.

1536 Foundation of Ascunción (Paraguay) and Buenos Aires.

1536 France forms an alliance with Turkey.

1539 Spanish forces under Hernando de Soto conquer Florida and the Gulf Coast.

1541 De Soto's expedition reaches the Mississippi.

1541 Henry VIII of England claims title of King of Ireland, ending medieval lordship.

1541 Turks conquer Hungary.

1545 Opening of Council of Trent, first major event of the Counter-Reformation.

1546 Tabin Shwehti re-creates united kingdom of Burma (-1600).

1549 Spanish Jesuit St Francis Xavier the first European presence in Japan; he introduces Christianity.

Italy and the Franco-Hapsburg Rivalry

Political disunity made Italy vulnerable. In 1494 France invaded, reviving an old claim to the kingdom of Naples. Since 1292 Naples had been ruled by Aragon, now part of Spain. The French occupied Naples but the Spaniards mobilized a coalition against them. France invaded Italy again in 1499 and 1524. In the meantime, the Hapsburgs had acquired the Spanish throne through marriage. In 1519, the king of Spain, Carlos I, united the two branches of his house when he was elected Holy Roman Emperor as Charles V. In Italy, Charles controlled much of Lombardy and Tuscany and everything south of Rome, thwarting French ambitions. The independence of most Italian city states was extinguished. France, fearing encirclement by the various Hapsburg kingdoms, eventually made an alliance with the Turks to threaten both Hapsburg flanks. Franco-Hapsburg rivalry was to be the central strategic reality in Europe for the next three centuries.

A nineteenth-century depiction of Charles VIII of France entering Naples in 1495.

5000	2000	1000	500	AD1	400	600

Reformation of the Church

 Even as the Renaissance gathered pace, it had emerged that western Christendom was in urgent need of reform. It was clear that the Church of Rome had long been poorly managed and was riddled with abuses. Some theologians like Erasmus (d. 1536) of the Netherlands and Thomas More (d. 1535) of England, breaking from scholastic tradition, developed an approach known as Christian Humanism, which focused on human values rather than on dogma. They clashed with Martin Luther, an Augustinian theologian at Wittenberg University in Germany, whose strong arguments for reform of the Church's affairs led to excommunication in 1520 and a break with Rome. Numerous earlier reformers had been overwhelmed by the power of the papacy, but in Germany of the 1520s heavy ecclesiastical taxation prompted popular support for change, while many princes anxious to assert their power offered protection to the emerging reform movement. Those who protested in support of Luther called themselves Protestants, and soon new national Churches emerged across Europe. Doctrinal reform paralleled organizational change and the spread of Protestant teaching was greatly facilitated by the printing press.

Portrait of Martin Luther, in an early printed account of his life and teachings.

Clash between Old and New Worlds

The concept of a "New World" was ratified in 1507 in a map by Martin Waldseemüller, which showed South America separate from Asia for the first time. Waldseemüller also used the name "America" in honor of the Italian geographer Amerigo Vespucci, who had explored the coast of Brazil. Vespucci recognized, as Colombus refused to, that the latter had indeed stumbled upon a land mass previously unexplored by Europeans. Vespucci published his conclusions, actually titling one of his writings *Mundus Novus*. As Europeans of many nationalities rushed to discover, chart, and seek wealth in the New World, European and American cultures clashed in often tragic mutual incomprehension. The Spaniard Hernán Cortés was able to make use of this in his conquest of the Aztecs (1519-21). Cortés adopted the persona of the leader-deity Quetzalcoatl, who had promised to return to his people, and by the time the Aztec leader Montezuma II perceived his mistake, it was too late. Another Spaniard, Francisco Pizarro, lured the Inca ruler Atahualpa into a trap, and then demanded a ransom. Although Pizarro was paid an estimated thirty million dollars' worth of gold and silver, Atahualpa was garrotted, and the once well-organized Inca state was plunged into disorder.

Cortés being welcomed with a garland. Horses, extinct in the Americas by the end of the Ice Age, were re-introduced by Europeans.

800	1000	1200	1400	1600	1800	2000

Ein Artinus Luther bin ich gnant
Von Gott dem Deudschen land gesant
Welchs durch des Babsts vnd teuffels
War gantz vnd gar vorfüret seer lehr
Mit lügen vnd Abgötterey
Falsch Gottes dinsts vnd heucheley
Das rechte reine Gottes wort
Von Jhesu Christ/ward nicht gehort
Das schafft des Babst dreikronich hut
Betrog vns vmb leib seel vnd gut
Solchs grossen jamers hat Gott sich
Aus gnad erbarmet Veterlich
Dem armen volck wolln zeigen an
Wie er dan zusag hat gethan
Vorm Jüngsten tag den widderchrist
Des Teuffels kind/mit seiner list
Hat mich zum Predigampt erweckt
Jnn grosse fahr vnd müh gesteckt
                         A iij   Sein

Africa: European Exploration

By the early sixteenth century, following on the early initiatives of Dom Henrique the Navigator and such explorers as Vasco da Gama, a Portuguese presence had been established around the coast of Africa from Morocco to Kenya. The Portuguese advance from the Cape of Good Hope northwards along the coast of East Africa had as early as 1498 encountered Arab settlement in what is now Kenya and Tanzania. Built on a flourishing trade in ivory and slaves, Gedi and Kilwa had been thriving towns since the thirteenth century. By the late fifteenth century, other centers such as Malindi and Kunduchi had developed, and trade links extended inland as far as the Zambezi. In cultural terms, these traders were responsible for the spread of Arabic architecture and of the Muslim faith in East Africa. The Portuguese, who in 1505 sacked Kilwa and established a base there, sought to introduce Christianity. In 1542, the Jesuit missionary Francis Xavier consecrated a chapel at Malindi. Meanwhile, in West Africa, Nzinga Mbemba (d. 1543), monarch of the wealthy centralized Kongo state, embraced Christianity, taking the Portuguese name Afonso. His son Henrique became a Roman Catholic bishop.

Suleiman the Lawgiver

The Ottoman empire reached its height under Suleiman I (1520-1566), known in the Islamic world as the "Lawgiver" (*Kanuni*) for his extensive legal, educational, and military reforms. A contemporary of Henry VIII of England, François I of France, and the Holy Roman Emperor Charles V, Suleiman I was far richer than any of them; in Europe he was called the "Magnificent". Since the Turks themselves had risen to power in the Islamic world as military slaves, the practice of *devshirme* ("collecting") Christian boys, converting them to Islam, and training them as soldiers of the Ottoman empire must have seemed not unreasonable to them. Apparently it caused surprisingly little outcry in the mostly Christian Balkans, perhaps because it could result in wealth and prestige. One such boy became the famous architect Sinan, responsible for Suleiman's splendid royal mosque. Suleiman's reign is also noted for new colors and motifs in both ceramics and sumptuous textiles. Conflict between the Shi'ite Safavid dynasty of Persia and the Sunnite Ottomans (from which the Ottomans emerged victorious) encouraged an already strong Ottoman presence in the west. Suleiman I turned his attention to Europe, where the Ottomans established their rule in Hungary, formed an alliance with François I against the Hapsburgs, and dominated the Mediterranean.

A portrait by a Venetian artist from the school of Titian depicts Sultan Suleiman I, who presided over the Ottoman empire at the height of its prosperity.

A detail from a Japanese folding screen shows Portuguese merchants and Jesuit missionaries. The Japanese were fascinated with the exotic physiognomy and strange costumes of these namban jin, or "southern barbarians."

Portuguese Traders and Jesuit Missionaries

Intrepid Portuguese traders led European maritime exploration into East Asia. Rounding the Cape of Good Hope and reaching India in 1498, they reached China some years later and by 1559 had established a permanent trading post at Macao. From China the Portuguese sailed to Japan, arriving about 1543. A very few years later, they were followed by the Jesuit missionary St Francis Xavier, who arrived in Japan under the auspices of King John III of Portugal in 1549, and stayed until 1551. The Japanese warlords Nobunaga and his successor Hideyoshi, who finally unified Japan again, were both courteously welcoming to the early Christian missionaries, partly in the hope of securing good trade relations with Portugal. The Portuguese traders in Macao, on the other hand, did little but confirm the Chinese impression of them as uncivilized barbarians. Jesuit missionaries had greater success; a few studied Chinese thought and mores and were granted positions at the court. Among them was the striking Italian Jesuit Matteo Ricci who, with his colleagues, converted some 200 Chinese, including high officials. Some years later, the German Jesuit Johannes Adam Schall earned favor with his skills as an astronomer, helping the Chinese imperial astronomers to recalculate their calendar.

EUROPE'S QUEST FOR THE "SPICE ISLANDS"

Beyond Cape Bojador the sun's heat intensifies, the sea boils and becomes covered with a scum of green weeds and hideous serpents.

Medieval Arabian traveler's tale

Doubtless the swirling seas around the rocky promontory of Cape Bojador (western Sahara) were suggestive of boiling water to early mariners: to the medieval mind the uncharted was invariably the realm of monsters or spirits. Yet in the fifteenth century, European explorers would brave what was for them the unknown, circumnavigating the continent of Africa and ultimately reaching India; in the process they facilitated the emergence of the Atlantic as a sea highway for world trade. Commercial considerations were indeed an important driving force in these developments. The spice trade with the Far East was crucial for Europe; spices were used not merely as food flavorings but as preservatives and as the basis for medicines. From the late 1300s, the contraction of the Mongol empire and Turkish expansion into the Mediterranean, as Ottoman power systematically strangled the rump Byzantine empire, posed difficulties for European merchants.

ADVANCES IN GEOGRAPHY

Portuguese control of Ceuta from 1415 presented an opportunity to open new routes. Fortuitously, this coincided with significant advances in European geographical knowledge. A few years earlier, Florentine merchant Palla Strozzi obtained from Constantinople a copy of *Geography* compiled by second-century Greco-Egyptian Ptolemy of Alexandria. This included a world map with details of the northwest and northeast African coasts with an outline of the Indian Ocean, long familiar to Arab merchants. Ptolemy had considered the earth to be spherical, and had worked out a means of calculating latitude and some

notion of longitude. The adoption of such geographical information for navigational purposes would greatly assist future exploration by sea.

THE CONTRIBUTION OF DOM HENRIQUE—"HENRY THE NAVIGATOR"

Dom Henrique (Prince Henry), styled "the Navigator," son of King John I of Portugal and governor of Ceuta in North Africa, established a navigational school at Sagres in south Portugal. The prince's campaigns in North Africa prompted his interest in further exploration. Aside from compiling maps and charts, Henrique's researchers worked on the development of the caravel, a ship which combined square- and triangular-shaped lateen sails, enabling it to cope more effectively with adverse winds. The Sagres school instructed master mariners in navigation techniques including use of the quadrant, and improved the compass (hitherto floated in a basin) by fixing it on a pivot. As appears from the account of his confidant Gomez de Azurara, a new trade route to the east was but one consideration underlying Dom Henrique's zeal. He desired to extend the power of the Portuguese crown, and to spread the Christian faith. Conscious of the steady advance of Islam towards Europe, he sought to ascertain the extent of Muslim power in North Africa. He was also hopeful of establishing contact with the kingdom of Prester John, a legendary Christian realm believed to have existed somewhere in the east. Portuguese mariners rounded Cape Bojador in 1434 and, by the time of Henrique's death in 1460, had reached the coast of Sierra Leone.

THE VOYAGES OF DIAS AND DA GAMA

By the later decades of the 1400s, European exploration of the African coasts had a fresh impetus. Constantinople had fallen to the Turks in 1453. By this time the Portuguese had become involved in the lucrative slave trade and, by 1480, had penetrated as far south as Congo. At the instance of King John II, master mariner Bartolomeu Dias undertook to sail around the south of Africa. He achieved this in January 1488, planting a

On Friday, 18 May 1498, Portuguese explorer Vasco da Gama anchored off Calicut. He arrived at the royal court to meet a cool reception. In this nineteenth-century engraving, da Gama presents a letter from King Manuel of Portugal to the king of Calicut.

stone pillar on the headland that would be known as the Cape of Good Hope, as optimism grew that a sea route to India would soon be found. Ten years later, Vasco da Gama sailed from Lisbon with three ships, *St. Gabriel*, *St. Raphael*, and *Berrio*, rounding the Cape and at Christmas sighting a land which he named Natal in honor of the feast of Christ's birth. There is evidence that the Arab traders resented the arrival of the

Portuguese. Clearly, they understood the commercial motives behind da Gama's explorations. The Portuguese were greeted with suspicion in Mozambique and open hostility in Mombasa. At Malindi in Kenya, da Gama secured the services of a pilot by holding hostage an official of the local viceroy. This conduct on their part may explain the coolness of their reception at the royal court of Calicut (Calcutta). Even so, a

sea route from Europe to India now existed and soon the Portuguese established bases at Goa, Diu, and on the island of Ceylon (Sri Lanka). In 1504, Francisco d'Almeida was viceroy of the Portuguese Indies. Ferdinand Magellan, serving with the viceroy's fleet, helped to capture Malacca (in Malaysia) in 1511. The route to the islands of Indonesia—the Spice Islands—was now open to European trade.   *A.M*

5000	2000	1000	500	AD1	400	600

The Portuguese in Angola

 The Portuguese presence along the West African coast was principally to do with trading and missionaries. They converted a number of African kingdoms, most notably that of Nzinga Mbemba, who was king of Kongo from 1507 until 1543. He tolerated the slave trade, without showing much enthusiasm for it: it had always been part of West African life. What changed everything was the founding of the great Portuguese colony in Brazil, on the far side of the South Atlantic. Suddenly the demand for slaves to work the Brazilian plantations grew enormously. In 1575 Paulo Dias de Novais established a base at Luanda, just south of the kingdom of Kongo, and founded the colony of Angola as a center for the South American slave trade. He and his successors made pitiless war on African people, Christian and pagan alike, in order to supply the trade.

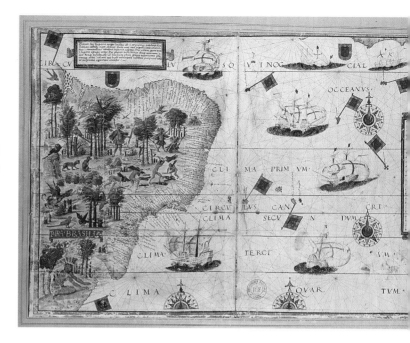

A sixteenth-century Portuguese map showing the South Atlantic and Brazil. This route brought thousands of slaves to the plantations.

Persia: Abbas the Great

 Abbas I came to the throne of Persia in 1587, the fifth shah of the Safavid dynasty. Earlier in the century, the empire had come under the effective control of the Ottomans. Abbas, in the course of a reign which lasted until 1629, regained all the concessions made not only to the Turks but also to the Uzbeks. He moved his capital from Qazvin to Isfahan, which he rebuilt in a style appropriate to the magnificence of his empire. By the time of his death, this stretched from the valley of the Tigris to that of the Indus and from the Gulf to Armenia and Azerbaijan in the north. Thus Abbas the Great restored the integrity of one of the world's oldest political units.

A seventeenth-century wall painting of a man and a girl taking refreshment in a garden. The Hall of One Hundred Pillars, Isfahan.

Europeans in the Americas

Claiming lands in the Americas became a competition between European nations who appreciated the Americas as a potential source of riches and a repository of human labor and lands. The Spanish colonized the Caribbean and Mesoamerica, moving north into North America; they also attempted to control the west coast of South America, and to expand into the interior. Here the Amazon basin tropics and the hostile populations of Tupi-Guarnari peoples proved difficult for the Spanish and Portuguese, although the Portuguese did settle on the coast of present-day Brazil, repulsing Dutch and French attempts to colonize. When the natives were decimated by European diseases, slaves were imported from Africa (see above left). In North America, the English and Dutch competed for the east coast, with some interference from Sweden; and the French progressed south from their claims in the north (as far west as the Great Lakes) to the area they called Louisiana.

Natives of Mesoamerica attack the invading Spanish.

| 800 | 1000 | 1200 | 1400 | 1600 | 1800 | 2000 |

1554 Turkey begins conquest of North Africa (completed 1556).

1555 Treaty of Amasia ends Turkish-Persian wars: major Turkish gains.

1556 Akbar the Great rules India (-1605).

1556 Philip II king of Spain (-1598).

1557 Portuguese settle at Macao, China.

1557 Russia completes conquest of Kazan and Astrakhan.

1558 French take Calais, last English possession on the European continent.

1558 Elizabeth I queen of England (-1603).

1567 Foundation of Rio de Janeiro by the Portuguese.

1567 Abdication of Mary Queen of Scots in favor of her son James VI.

1568 William the Silent begins Dutch revolt against Spanish rule.

1569 Apogee of kingdom of Burma under king Bayinnaung (r. 1551-81).

c. 1570-*c.* 1610 Kanem-Bornu kingdom in Central Africa flourishes.

1571 Battle of Lepanto: Spanish-Venetian fleet destroys Turkish navy.

1572 St. Bartholomew's Day massacre in Paris, thousands of Huguenots killed.

1573 End of the Muromachi shogunate in Japan.

1575 Akbar the Great takes Bihar and Bengal for the Mughal empire.

1576 First voyage of Martin Frobisher in search of the Northwest Passage.

1577 Akbar the Great unifies northern India.

1581 Russia begins colonization of Siberia.

1583 Spain conquers the Philippines.

1587 Roanoake, first English colony in North America.

1588 Accession of Abbas I, "the Great", as Shah of Iran (-1629).

1588 Defeat of the Spanish Armada in the English Channel and its eventual scattering by storms.

1589 Assassination of King Henry III of France, the last of the Valois kings.

1590 Political unification of Japan under warlord Hideyoshi.

1592 Akbar the Great conquers Sind.

1592 First of a succession of devastating Japanese invasions of Korea.

1593 War between Austria and Turkey (until 1606).

c. 1598 Foundation of Dutch trading posts on the Guinea coast of West Africa.

1598 Edict of Nantes grants religious tolerance to French Huguenots.

The Rise of Russia

Ivan IV, better known as Ivan the Terrible, was the first ruler of Russia to take the name "Tsar," a derivation from the Roman imperial title "Caesar." Indeed, Moscow saw itself quite consciously as the "Third Rome" after Rome itself and Constantinople: much of Russian history was driven by this vision of itself as the leader of the Orthodox Christian and Slav world. Ivan's grandfather, Ivan III, had established the primacy of Moscow within Russia. Ivan IV (r. 1547-84) built on this, capturing Kazan, Astrakhan and spreading Russian power to the Baltic and Siberia for the first time. His Service Regulations of 1556 began the process whereby the *boyars* —the high nobility— had their authority curtailed. Henceforth they were tied to the state and forced to render service, either directly or through material contributions in serfs and horses. Such limiting of the regional autonomy of magnates by an expanding central power was a feature of state-building throughout Europe.

A contemporary woodcut of Ivan the Terrible.

End of Disunion

As Muromachi power declined in Japan, that of the *daimyo*, or provincial warlords, increased. The danger of Japan dividing into a patchwork of feudal petty kingdoms increased too. Then in 1568, the so-called "three heroes"—Oda Nobunaga, Toyotomi Hideyoshi and Tokugawa Ieyasu—began the process which ended this chaos. Nobunaga fought his way to supremacy and occupied Kyoto, ousting the last Muromachi shogun five years later. He imposed his rule on most of the country, a process that was continued by Toyotomi following Nobunaga's assassination in 1582. Eventually, it was the last of the trio, Tokugawa, who founded a lasting shogunate in 1603. He and his successors established an ordered system of feudal hierarchy for the governance of Japan. Daimyos and bureaucrats, as well as the court itself, were made responsible to the shogunate. *Bushido*, the ethical code observed by the samurai, was formalized and adopted by the aristocracy.

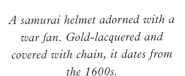

A samurai helmet adorned with a war fan. Gold-lacquered and covered with chain, it dates from the 1600s.

5000	2000	1000	500	AD1	400	600

A headdress made of feathers from the birds of the tropical Amazon region. Perhaps the (possibly imaginary) female warriors sighted by the Spanish explorer Francisco de Orellana wore such adornments?

Claiming Brazil

Brazil was named by Portuguese explorers after the reddish wood that grew in the abundant coastal forests of South America, which became an important early export. The Spaniard Vicente Pinzón touched the northern coast in 1500; in the same year Pedro Cabral claimed the land for Portugal. Eventually the Portuguese claim superseded other European attempts, notably by the Dutch and the French, and the first permanent Portuguese settlement, at São Vicente, was founded in 1532. Sugar plantations developed rapidly in the 1530s. Because the native peoples were widely scattered and rather sparse, the Portuguese began importing slaves from Africa to work the plantations as early as 1538. Native Brazilians included Tupi-Guarani, Carib, Arawak, and Ge peoples, some of them aggressive and cannibalistic. The vast area of Brazil comprises many terrains, including much of the tropical Amazon River Basin. The powerful Amazon was named by the Spanish explorer Francisco de Orellana, who was the first European to descend from the headstream in the Peruvian Andes to the Atlantic, in 1541. Orellana was reportedly attacked by female warriors, and named the river after the legendary warriors of ancient Greece.

Momoyama Japan

Firearms and cannons introduced by Europeans changed the character of warfare in Japan, and also inspired new architectural styles. The military leader Oda Nobunaga (1534-1582) set the standard with his moated fortress castle at Azuchi (built 1576-79), and his successors, the military hegemons Hideyoshi (1536-98) and Tokugawa Ieyasu (1542-1616), followed suit with structures grander than anything previously built in Japan. Although none of Hideyoshi's castles survive, the one he built at Momoyama has given its name to this period (1573-1616) characterized by vigorous splendor. Even the meditative serenity of the traditional tea ceremony sometimes took on grandiose aspects: Hideyoshi sponsored a public tea ceremony in 1587 in Kyoto that was attended by thousands over a ten-day period, and included dancing and dramatic performances as well as art exhibits. The art of screen painting reached its boldest expression in this period. Kano Eitoku (1543-90), the grandson of the founder of the Kano artistic family, created the style that is associated with the great military castles, and which lasted until late in the seventeenth century. Eitoku used gold leaf in the backgrounds of his paintings, and was noted for powerful foreground composition, exemplified on one screen by the depiction of a lone strong cypress tree.

Hideyoshi's audience chamber, formerly in his Fushimi castle. The walls and screens are covered with paintings by artists of the Kano school, characterized by bold composition and the use of gold.

Counter-Reformation

Before the Protestant Churches had quite taken shape, the papacy initiated a program of reorganization and doctrinal redefinition—the Catholic or Counter-Reformation. While doctrinal divergence between Protestantism and Roman Catholicism cannot be denied, the most observable differences relate to custom. Roman Catholic practice emphasized the ceremonial aspect of worship; the cult of saints was encouraged, with processions to celebrate their feast days. The Jesuit order popularized Baroque church architecture with Classical façades, columned interiors and elaborate high altars. Richly vestmented clergy conducted services in such church buildings, which were often adorned with statues of saints.

| 800 | 1000 | 1200 | 1400 | 1600 | 1800 | 2000 |

St. Peter's, Rome; the dome (originally designed by Michelangelo) was completed in 1593. The canopy is seventeenth century.

In contrast, Protestant clergy adopted plain vestments while their church interiors displayed little or no decoration; statues and religious paintings were eschewed—it being felt that, rather than inspire the faithful, they served only to distract. Parallel to this reform of Western Christendom, the European Renaissance in the arts continued to flourish. Vernacular writers of the caliber of Rabelais (d. 1553) and Cervantes (d. 1616) emerged in France and Spain. In England, Shakespeare (d. 1616) brought vernacular literature to new heights with superb poetry and drama, his plays being staged at London's Globe Theatre.

Benin

In the 1550s English traders reached Benin seeking gold and slaves. Centered on the Niger, Benin was a large state encompassing both Yoruba and Edo languages. Culturally, it was heir to the Ife kingdom and some common traits can be discerned. Having emerged some 300 years previously, Benin had been transformed by the fifteenth-century Oba (King) Ewuare, whom tradition credits with introducing autocratic kingship and succession by primogeniture (i.e., father to son). Ewuare rebuilt the palace at Benin and surrounded the city with massive walls. The kingdom gradually expanded, subjecting neighboring states such as Igala, and reached its apogee in the mid-sixteenth century. Its towns included Ketu and Dassa Zoume, where stone houses with potsherd floors have come to light. Benin art combines naturalism and stylization, in such media as brass, terra cotta and ivory. Human imagery predominates. Ancestral spirits were important in the religion of Benin, although contact with European merchants and with the Muslim Upper Niger meant that Christianity and Islam would make inroads.

Brass head of Idia, mother of Oba Esigie. Securing victory over Igala through mystical means, she was, as a reward, granted her own palace and ancestral altars.

Akbar the Great crossing the Ganges, in a miniature from a Mughal manuscript. Many artistic influences were blended in innovative paintings during the Mughal period.

Akbar the Great

The greatest Mughal emperor, Akbar, ascended the throne in 1556 when he was only thirteen. "Mughal" is derived from the Persian word for "Mongol" (and is the origin of English "mogul"), but Akbar's grandfather Babur, the dynastic founder, claimed descent from the Turkish Timur the Lame as well as the Mongol Ghengis Khan, and his adopted culture was Persian. During his remarkable and lengthy reign (to 1605) Akbar forged a great empire, determined to rule not as a foreigner but to unite diverse peoples into one Indian state. He abolished his predecessors' tax on non-Muslims, granted freedom of worship, and appointed Hindus to office. Akbar was as energetic in pursuit of knowledge and art as he was on the battlefield. He was deeply interested in religion, and organized debates among religious scholars of many faiths, questioning them intently. In 1581 he devised his own "Divine Faith" which included Muslim, Hindu, Parsee, and Christian elements. He possessed a huge library of finely illuminated manuscripts, although he remained illiterate. He invented artillery improvements and was a gifted musician. Also trained in painting, Akbar sponsored over one hundred painters, including one woman, and constructed a beautiful city, Fatehpur Sikri, which unfortunately had to be abandoned when its water supply failed.

5000	2000	1000	500	AD1	400	600

Kingdom of Benin

During the seventeenth century Benin, successor to an ancient state of the same name, flourished in what is now southern Nigeria. Its capital, Benin City, still stands. It established early contacts and trading relations with Portugal, with which it dealt in textiles, pepper, palm oil and ivory. It also dealt in slaves, although by a curious royal ordinance only female slaves were allowed to be exported. A Dutch visitor in the early seventeenth century compared Benin City favorably with cities in Europe. He described a broad main street, three miles long and very straight, as well as a huge royal palace complete with courtiers, attendants, horses and slaves. By the end of the century, Benin had been supplanted by the kingdom of Oyo which was a more efficient conduit for the passage of European goods to Africans as well as for the passage of African slaves to the Americas.

A Benin brass relief of a Portuguese man with a helmet and trident, c. 1600.

Thirty Years' War

This complicated series of wars was fought to determine different but related issues. Would the Hapsburg emperors or the local princes hold sway in Germany? Would Catholicism or Protestantism dominate in central Europe? Would France or the Holy Roman Empire be the greatest continental power? The war began with the Bohemian revolt against the empire in 1618 but later spread as other powers—principally Sweden and France—intervened against the empire. Sweden feared it because it was Catholic. France feared being surrounded by Hapsburgs in Germany and Spain. The Treaty of Westphalia of 1648 ended the war, leaving France the leading state in Europe, a position she was to hold until 1870. The physical destruction in Germany was enormous. Successful centralized states like France and Sweden counterpointed the political disunion of the German lands. The settlement left a power vacuum in Germany, only partially filled by the rise of Prussia.

Cardinal Richelieu, chief minister to King Louis XIII and architect of modern France.

- **1600** Foundation of East India Company in London.

- **1602** Holy war between Persia under Shah Abbas I and Turkey (until 1618).

- **1603** James VI of Scotland assumes English throne as James I: first Stuart king.

- **1603** Establishment of Tokugawa shogunate (-1867) in Japan.

- **1604** Russia's Time of Troubles (-1613).

- **1605** Gunpowder Plot in London; execution of Guy Fawkes and others.

- **1607** Jamestown colony in Virginia first successful English settlement in North America.

- **1608** Champlain founds settlement at Quebec.

- **1609** Kepler's first two laws of planetary motion.

- **1610** Galileo, first telescopic observations.

- **1610** Assassination of King Henry IV of France.

- **1613** Tsar Michael of Russia, first Romanov ruler.

- **1613** Turks invade Hungary.

- **1618** Defenestration of Prague by Bohemian Protestants, prelude to Thirty Years' war.

- **1620** Battle of the White Mountain: imperial troops rout Bohemian Protestants.

- **1620** Voyage of the *Mayflower*.

- **1624** Queen Nzinga (r.-1663) assumes Angolan throne and makes war against Portuguese slavers.

- **1624** Richelieu chief minister of France (-1642).

- **1626** Peter Minuit buys Manhattan Island from Native Americans for $24; founds New Amsterdam.

- **1630** First general court of Massachusetts Bay colony meets at Boston.

- **1631** Battle of Leipzig, in which King Gustavus Adolphus II of Sweden defeated imperial army.

- **1636** Harvard, first North American university.

- **1638** Scottish National Covenant.

- **1638** Shimabara uprising in Japan crushed; Japanese Christianity wiped out.

- **1638** Turks conquer Bagdad.

- **1639** Treaty of Kasr-I-Shirim establishes border between Persians and Turks.

- **1640** Catalan revolt against Castilian rule, not suppressed until 1652.

- **1640** Successful revolt in Portugal, regains independence from Spain lost in 1580.

- **1642** Beginning of English Civil War.

- **1642** De Maisonneuve founds Montreal.

- **1643** Battle of Rocroi: France defeats Spain, ending its continental supremacy.

- **1644** Last Ming emperor of China commits suicide; start of Manchu dynasty (-1912).

- **1648** Treaty of Westphalia ends Thirty Years' War.

- **1649** Execution of King Charles II; establishment of Commonwealth in Britain under the Puritan Cromwell.

Mughal Empire: Apogee and Decline

Akbar the Great (1542-1605) brought the Mughal empire to its zenith. At his death, it controlled all of north and central India, as well as Afghanistan and Kashmir. Akbar was succeeded by Jahangir (r. 1605-27) and Shah Jahan (r. 1627-58), the builder of the Red Fort. Both maintained religious toleration and an equitable system of taxation. Shah Jahan's son and heir, Aurangzeb (r. 1658-1707) began the process of decline, although it was during his reign—in 1691—that the empire was at its greatest extent. First, Aurangzeb was a Muslim rigorist. He discriminated against Hindus, reintroducing a special tax on them called the *jizya* which Akbar had abolished. He attacked and destroyed Hindu temples. The Marathas of central India and the Punjabi Sikhs seceded. The weakened empire was also prey to the European powers—England, France, Portugal and Holland—who were established along the coast of the subcontinent by 1700.

The Throne Room of the Great Mogul Shah Jahan in the Red Fort in Delhi.

End of the Ming Dynasty in China

While the early Ming emperors had been full of energy, their power came under increasing threat with the passage of time. First, China abandoned the curiosity and sense of adventure that had typified Cheng Ho's voyages and turned in on itself. Rebellions and border incursions from Mongols and others made internal security an ever more pressing matter. The quality of the emperors declined sharply and they became increasingly

subservient to manipulating courtiers. Then came the penetration of China by Europeans, especially by Portuguese and Dutch traders and by Jesuit missionaries. Finally, in the 1640s a serious famine occurred which caused a rebellion against the government. The Ming sought the assistance of the Manchu, a non-Chinese people recently come to power in Manchuria. The Manchu helped put down the rebellion, then seized power in Peking (Beijing) themselves. The last Ming emperor committed suicide in 1644.

Portrait of an ancestor. Chinese painting from the late Ming or early Manchu dynasties.

The Pilgrims in America

In 1607 Sir Thomas Smith established the first successful English settlement in North America at Jamestown in Virginia. They were not the first Europeans on the continent. The Spaniard Juan Ponce de León had landed in Florida in 1512. The Frenchman Cartier had explored the St. Lawrence in the 1530s and French explorers would open up the Great Lakes and the Mississippi basin during the seventeenth century. It was the English, however, whose future influence would be greatest. In 1620, 101 men and women—all Protestant dissenters, or Puritans, who had already fled from the anti-Calvinist atmosphere of James I's Anglican kingdom—sailed from Leyden in Holland aboard a tiny ship, the Mayflower. They landed at Massachusetts Bay, in virgin territory beyond any existing legal jurisdiction. Under the Mayflower Compact, they bound themselves to observe laws made by their own elected representatives. This was the foundation moment of Puritan New England.

A nineteenth-century picture of the first Thanksgiving Day, November 1621, when the Puritans thanked God for their first year in America.

A seventeenth-century painting depicting Galileo before the Inquisition in Rome between 12 April and 22 June, 1633. There the scientist was forced to renounce the theories of Copernicus.

Pocahontas, also known as Lady Rebecca Rolfe

 Jamestown, the first permanent English settlement in America, was established in Virginia in 1607 by 120 colonists. The settlers could not agree about whether to stay or whether to seek gold and silver. Neglecting to plant crops, they found themselves starving. The colony was held together by Captain John Smith, who managed to win the respect of a powerful local native, Wahunsonacock. Wahunsonacock headed a confederation of thirty-two tribes and 200 villages, which regarded the quarrelsome colonists with some suspicion. John Smith claimed that Wahunsonacock's daughter Pocahontas prevented her father from killing him, and persuaded Wahunsonacock to aid the starving colonists, although this may be a pleasant fiction. However, it is documented that Pocahontas was converted to Christianity in 1613, and that she married a colonist named John Rolfe with her father's approval in 1614, initiating a peaceful period in relations between the Indians and colonists. Pocahontas's husband was a successful tobacco farmer; this cash crop, much in demand in England, became the mainstay of the colony. Pocahontas, now Lady Rebecca Rolfe, died in 1617 during a visit to England. Relations between the English colonists and native Americans soon deteriorated.

Early Modern Europe

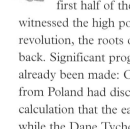 The Renaissance having awakened a new spirit of enquiry in Europe, the first half of the seventeenth century witnessed the high point of a scientific revolution, the roots of which lay further back. Significant progress in astronomy had already been made: Copernicus (d. 1543) from Poland had discovered through calculation that the earth orbited the sun, while the Dane Tycho Brahe (d. 1601) built the Uraniborg observatory. As the century progressed, further advances were made in the sciences, mainly in western Europe. The Italian Galileo (d. 1642) improved the telescope, confirmed Copernicus's theories and experimented with gravity. The Frenchman Descartes (d. 1650) advanced scientific calculation and geometry and Boyle (d. 1691) from Ireland discovered properties of gases. Pioneering work in anatomy by Vesalius (d. 1564) of Brussels inspired others; in 1619 Irish doctor Thaddeus Dunn, working in Switzerland, produced a book on diseases in women. In 1628 English physician William Harvey published *On the Motion of the Heart and Blood*. Further east in Russia, during the reigns of tsars Michael and Alexis, gradual replacement of agriculture-based with modern scientific-based industries including glass, paper and silks reflected that empire's growing confidence.

Pocahontas in English dress on a visit to England in 1616.

800	1000	1200	1400	1600	1800	2000

Isfahan under Shah Abbas I

The interior of the Royal Mosque (Masjid-i-Shah) at Isfahan, built by Shah Abbas I, one of the greatest Persian rulers.

Shah Abbas I (r. 1587-1629) revitalized the Safavid dynasty of Persia. Founded as a Sufi mystical order in the thirteenth century, the Safavids later converted to Shi'ite Islam, which became the state religion under the dynasty founder, Ismail I (1502-1524). Rivals of the Ottoman empire, the Safavids were defeated by them in 1514, and then pursued an isolationist policy until the advent of Shah Abbas I. He enlarged the empire and encouraged production for the world export market. The new capital city of Isfahan became known for its silk weaving, carpets, ceramics and arms. Originally Sassanid, Isfahan had been captured by Seljuk Turks in the eleventh century, and devastated by Timur in the fourteenth. Abbas I rebuilt Isfahan as one of the world's most beautiful cities, employing the finest traditions of Islamic architecture. Although Islamic secular art is often figurative, the strong prohibition against idolatry in the Koran has been interpreted as an injunction against figurative representation in religious art. Therefore the beauty of Islamic religious architecture is in line and form, and the limitations placed upon representation have become the strengths of its decoration. Abstract pattern and calligraphy find their most exquisite expression in the Islamic mosque.

Portuguese Cultural Influence

By the early seventeenth century Portuguese influence was becoming increasingly explicit, especially along the western coast of Africa. Kongolese ruling classes, from the time of King Afonso, had been open to Catholicism and to the adoption of Portuguese names. From the first settlement of Angola in 1575, this trend would increase. However, in alliance with nomads, the Portuguese encroached upon Kongo occupying a sizable part of the kingdom by 1621. Ironically, Kongolese independence was preserved partly through diplomatic alliance with the Vatican. Missionary efforts were renewed in Angola and in Kongo from 1645, and the magnificent Church of Our Lady of Nazareth was built at Luanda. Kongolese king Antonio I would be buried here in 1665. Meanwhile, Portuguese and other European merchants became more established in such western states as Benin. They traded manufactured goods, including guns, for gold, slaves, spices and salt. Curiously, later Benin art features many representations of Portuguese merchant and military classes, whose dress, armaments and caravel ships had become familiar sights.

Benin-style ivory salt-cellar, with figures of Portuguese noblemen surmounted by a caravel.

European Pacific Exploration

More than a century after Magellan's ships were the first European vessels to cross the Pacific as part of their global circumnavigation between 1519 and 1522, this ocean was still largely unexplored by Europeans. In 1606, the Dutch explored part of the coasts of New Guinea (sighted as early as 1511 by the Portuguese) and of Australia, without realizing the extent of either. Further European exploration was encouraged by rumors of a rich "unknown southern land" (*Terra Australis Incognita*). Dutch explorers set foot on Tonga in 1615, where both parties engaged in alternately friendly and unfriendly exchanges. In 1642, the Dutch Governor-General at Batavia, Antony van Diemen, sent Abel Tasman to explore the South Pacific. Sailing south, Tasman found an island which he called Van Diemen's Land (Tasmania). They found no inhabitants, and set sail again, finally reaching New Zealand. The Maoris were aggressive and the Dutch left hastily. On their return voyage, they stopped at Tonga and Fiji. The encounter on Tonga seems to have been the first significant contact between Europeans and Pacific Islanders without bloodshed.

An engraving of Fiji Islanders in an elaborately carved canoe, inspired by a drawing made by Abel Tasman in 1642.

109

ASIAN DYNASTIES

An ancient pond

A frog jumps in

The sound of water.

Basho, Japanese poet

Three magnificent dynasties flourished in Asia during the seventeenth century, about the time Louis XIV was defining European absolutism during his long reign (1643-1715) as king of France. Although the Mughal dynasty of India disintegrated rapidly after 1707, the Tokugawa shogunate of Japan and the Manchu dynasty of China proved remarkably durable, the first lasting until 1868, and the latter until 1911. Each dynasty had its own unique character and, although ultimately replaced by very different regimes, all left distinctive traces in their respective cultures. Although Japan remained isolated from Europe for most of the Tokugawa period, both China and India experienced influence from Europe, and were influential in turn on Europeans.

THE MUGHALS OF INDIA

The heritage of the dynastic founder Babur (of Turkish and Mongol descent, with a Persian education and a Persian wife), merged with traditional Indian cultures in a cosmopolitan blend that characterized most of the great Mughal rulers. To this was added a dash of European influence: although Babur's grandson Akbar the Great disappointed the Jesuit missionaries at his court, his lively curiosity resulted in the importation of European prints which influenced Mughal painting. Painting flourished especially during the reign of Akbar's son Jahangir (r. 1605-1627). Intelligent, dissipated and probably a patricide, Jahangir was a cultivated connoisseur of the arts, which he preferred to statecraft. His son Shah Jahan (r. 1627-1658), who also spilled some family blood, compensated for his father's lack of interest in architecture by extravagant expenditure on splendid buildings such

as the Taj Mahal at Agra and a palace in the Red Fort at Delhi. In spite of conducting numerous wars in the Deccan, Shah Jahan, like his father, did little to enlarge the Mughal empire beyond the extensive territory already established by Akbar, including northern India, much of Persia, and parts of the Deccan. This task was left to the fierce and energetic Aurangzeb (r. 1658-1707), who killed several of his brothers and imprisoned his father Shah Jahan. Aurangzeb's conquests, accompanied by persecution of any faith other than orthodox Islam, ultimately weakened the dynasty. Internal conflicts in India aided the rise of the next great empire, which was British.

THE TOKUGAWA SHOGUNATE IN JAPAN

In Europe feudalism was superseded by the rise of centralized nation-states, but Japanese feudalism actually became the foundation of centralized power. The samurai aristocracy that emerged as a potent political force in the twelfth century gradually became associated with local war lords called *daimyo*. Daimyo domains, whose boundaries were defined through centuries of warfare, formed a surprisingly solid basis for unification. Three successive military leaders, Oda Nobunaga, Hideyoshi, and Tokugawa Ieyasu were able to accomplish this with the aid of European firearms and cannons, introduced by Portuguese traders. Nobunga and Hideyoshi left infant heirs, provoking quarrels over the succession; this problem was solved by Tokugawa Ieyasu. In 1605, two years after establishing himself as shogun, he retired in favor of his adult son Hidetada, although Ieyasu maintained effective power until his death in 1616. Hidetada

resigned in favor of his own son Iemitsu, who ruled as shogun from 1623 until 1651. Under these three Tokugawa shoguns, the pattern of government that was to persist for centuries took shape.

Jesuit and Franciscan missionaries arrived with European traders, hoping to Christianize Japan. Although welcomed courteously by Nobunga and Hideyoshi, who hoped for trade, the Japanese soon suspected the missionaries of being spies, and also found the egalitarian principles and monotheism of Christianity in conflict with both ancient Shintō beliefs and Confucian principles of government. Shintōism, in which the divine and human worlds merge imperceptibly, supported Japanese belief in the divinity of their emperors, who, even though they rarely exercised political power, were symbolically important as the spiritual leaders of the state. Confucianism, absorbed from the Chinese, emphasized a balanced, stratified society. These conflicts culminated in a slaughter in 1638 that virtually ended Christianity in Japan. Henceforward the Tokugawa shogunate adopted a strict isolationist policy.

CHINA UNDER THE MANCHUS

Manchurian nomads were descendants of the Jurchens who established the Chin (Jin) dynasty of north China in 1122, later conquered by Genghis Khan. Nurhachi unified the Manchurian peoples, adopting the title of emperor of the Later Chin in 1616. He began an aggressive challenge to Chinese Ming power which was continued by his son Abahai. Abahai made Korea and Inner Mongolia into vassal states of the Manchus, and renamed his father's dynasty

Ch'ing (Qing), or "Pure," in 1636. In 1644, Abahai's younger brother Dorgon finally captured the Ming capital, Peking, with the help of Chinese rebels, marking the official transfer of power to the Manchus. The final conquest of Chinese-held territory, however, was not accomplished until 1683, when the island of Taiwan was taken during the reign of Nurhachi's great-grandson, the K'ang-hsi emperor (r. 1661-1722). The Manchu regime was at its height during the reign of this remarkable emperor (contemporary with Louis XIV, and probably the better statesman) and that of his grandson, Ch'ien Lung (r. 1736-1799).

The Manchus were more willing than the Mongols had been to incorporate Chinese scholar bureaucrats into their government, resulting in a sense of continuity in spite of the conquest. Under the intellectually curious K'ang-hsi emperor, the Jesuits who had weathered the transition from Ming to Manchu power were still welcomed at court. A dispute with the pope over whether traditional ancestor rites were compatible with Christianity, however, led to increased dislike and suspicion of Christians, and the religion was finally suppressed in the eighteenth century. Nonetheless, some contact (carefully controlled) continued between Europe and China. Although a Chinese-baroque palace was designed for Ch'ien Lung in the eighteenth century, perhaps the most powerful influences traveled from China to Europe. European political philosophy and artistic design were deeply affected, and the popularity of tea imported from China soon made it the world's favorite beverage.

S.I.

An Indian miniature, probably from the Mughal capital of Delhi, painted during the reign of Shah Jahan.

5000	2000	1000	500	AD1	400	600

- **1651** Yetuna, new Japanese shogun (r.-1680), overcomes two rebellions in Edo.

- **1652** Dutchman Jan van Riebeeck founds Cape Town.

- **1652-4** First Anglo-Dutch war.

- **1654** War between Russia and Poland.

- **1657** Great Fire of Edo in Tokyo.

- **1654** Aurangzeb (1618-1707) imprisons his father, Shah Jahan, and becomes Mogul emperor.

- **1660** Restoration of the British monarchy.

- *c.* **1660** Ethiopia expels Portuguese missionaries.

- *c.* **1660s** Sultanate of Morocco restored by Mawlay al-Rashid.

- **1660** Treaty of Oliva ends Swedish-Polish war; Swedish gains.

- **1661** British acquire Bombay, India.

- **1661** d. Cardinal Mazarin; Louis XIV assumes sole power.

- **1664** Dutch cede New Amsterdam to English, who rename it New York.

- **1664** First Russian trade mission to Isfahan opens up Persian trade route.

- **1665** Second Anglo-Dutch war, nadir of English naval fortunes.

- **1666** Great Fire of London.

- **1669** Mughal empire prohibits Hinduism and destroys Hindu temples.

- **1670** First independent Ashanti kingdom established with capital at Kumasi.

- **1677** First Turko-Russian war (-1681).

- *c.* **1681-2** French explorer La Salle travels the full length of the Mississippi River and founds Louisiana, named after the French king.

- **1682** Turkey at war with Austro-Polish coalition (-1699).

- **1682** William Penn, Englishman, arrives in Pennsylvania and founds Philadelphia.

- **1683** Turkish siege of Vienna finally relieved by Poles.

- **1685** All Chinese ports opened to foreign trade.

- **1688** Glorious Revolution: William III replaces James II on English throne.

- **1689** War of the League of Augsburg (-1697), France opposed by imperial coalition.

- **1689** Peter I "the Great" tsar of Russia (-1725).

- **1689** Natal, South Africa, becomes a Dutch colony.

- **1690** Foundation of Calcutta.

- **1692** Salem witchcraft trials lead to dozens of arrests in Puritan New England.

- **1698** Portuguese expelled from Mombasa on Africa's east coast.

- **1697** China conquers western Mongolia

- **1699** Treaty of Karlowicz confirms Hapsburg gains from Turkey.

King Jan III Sobieski after the relief of Vienna.

Last Turkish Siege of Vienna

 The Holy Roman Empire of the German Nation, since 1427 a hereditary possession of the Hapsburgs, existed for two principal reasons: as a counterweight to the power of France, at its pre-Napoleonic apogee in the 1670s and 80s under Louis XIV; and as a central European collective defense system against the Turks. As recently as 1526, the armies of Suleiman the Magnificent had stood at the gates of Vienna. Now, in 1683 their successors returned. Although the city was well defended with ramparts, walls and ditches —all recently renewed—the Turks still outnumbered the defenders by ten to one. They had actually breached the walls when the relieving army, commanded by Jan III Sobieski, king of Poland, appeared on the Kahlenberg Hills, worked its way down, charged straight at the Turks and routed them. It was a turning point, the beginning of the Turks' long decline.

New Amsterdam becomes New York

 The Dutch had founded New Amsterdam on the island of Manhattan in the early seventeenth century. One of the first settlers, Peter Minuit, bought the island from the Native Americans for trinkets worth 60 guilders (about $24). Later a tough, one-legged Dutchman, Peter Stuyvesant, was sent out as governor. In the meantime, English colonists from Massachusetts had moved south and some had even set up on Long Island just across the East River from Manhattan. By the 1660s, the little Dutch colony was surrounded and outnumbered by Englishmen. Then King Charles II made a grant of territory between the Delaware and Connecticut rivers to his brother, the Duke of York. English ships sailed to capture their prize and the inhabitants of New Amsterdam, now thoroughly frightened, forced Stuyvesant to surrender. The little town changed its name to New York on 8 September 1664.

Peter Stuyvesant, the first governor of New Amsterdam, later to be named New York.

800	1000	1200	1400	1600	1800	2000

First Europeans in South Africa

On 6 April 1652, the Dutchman Jan van Riebeeck sailed into Table Bay, at the southwestern tip of Africa, with three ships. The Dutch were concerned with the high mortality rates on long ocean voyages, mainly caused by scurvy. They needed a source of fresh vegetables, the best protection against scurvy, and a hospital where those who did succumb could be treated. In 1657 they founded a colony, as distinct from a mere way-station. In 1679, Simon van der Stel arrived as governor and the first grant of land was made in Stellenbosch. In 1689 Huguenot refugees, fleeing France following the revocation of the Edict of Nantes, began to arrive. They were obliged by the authorities to speak Dutch, not French. This mixture of peoples slowly welded together until in 1707 one of them, Hendrik Bibault, described himself as an "Afrikaner," the first known use of the word.

Table Mountain from Cape Town, Table Bay, South Africa, where the first Europeans came ashore.

India: Foundation of Calcutta

In 1690, Job Charnock of the British East India Company founded a trading post not far from the mouth of the Hooghly river. Six years later, Fort William was established nearby in order to protect it. In 1698, three neighboring villages were bought by the company from the Mughal emperor. One of them, Kalikata, was to give its name—in slightly corrupted form—to the great city that gradually arose on the site. In June 1756, Calcutta was captured by Siraj ud-Daula, nawab of Bengal. He imprisoned 146 British captives in a small, subterranean, ill-ventilated room. By morning, all but twenty-three had died in the infamous "Black Hole of Calcutta" This outrage was avenged by Robert Clive, who defeated the nawab and became governor of Bengal on behalf of the East India Company. Calcutta, one of the company's great subcontinental ports, was capital of British India from 1772 until 1912.

Nijo Castle, Kyoto, the principal palace of the Tokugawa shoguns.

Japan: Tokugawa Shogunate

The last of the shogun dynasties ruled Japan from 1603 until 1867. Its founder, Tokugawa Ieyasu (1542-1616), defeated a coalition of rival clans at the Battle of Sekighara in 1600. The dynasty encouraged centralization. As in many contemporary European states, the power of the landed magnates was curtailed. Under the so-called alternate attendance system, each warlord had to live in the capital Edo for half of each year, under the eye of the court. On his return, his family stayed behind, effectively hostage for good behavior. Property rights were vested in the shoguns. The state monopolized foreign trade, which it gradually discouraged. Christian missionaries, previously tolerated, were banned from the 1620s: they were seen as Trojan horses for European powers. In sum, the Tokugawa encouraged rigidity and isolation, but they ensured social stability in return, until the pressures of modernity began to tell in the nineteenth century.

Mughal troops loading an artillery piece mounted on a gun carriage. An Indian painting of the seventeenth century.

5000	2000	1000	500	AD1	400	600

The Last of the Great Mughals

Although he displayed an energy reminiscent of his great-grandfather Akbar, the Mughal emperor Aurangzeb (r. 1658-1707) probably did more to undermine the dynasty than his more languid predecessors. The arts, at least, continued to flourish under Akbar's son and grandson. Jahangir, his son, was not much interested in ruling, and allowed political matters to fall into the hands of his favorite wife, the Persian Nur Jahan. Under his reign (1605-1627), and that of their son, Shah Jahan (1627-1658), however, Mughal painting reached its triumph, blending a Persian and Indian heritage with influences from Europe. Architecture was the passion of Shah Jahan. He is best remembered for the breathtaking Taj Mahal in Agra, a memorial to his favorite wife, Mumtaz. In contrast, Aurangzeb, intractably Muslim, detested all arts except calligraphy. He revived persecution of the Hindus and other sects. Although he extended the Mughal empire, his gains were short-lived and ultimately weakened the dynasty. Aurangzeb also earned the enmity of the Sikhs, an independent religious sect. Originally oriented towards peaceful brotherhood, the Sikhs developed into a fierce military order as a consequence of Mughal persecution.

The Taj Mahal, Agra, often styled "a dream in marble." Perfectly proportioned, this world-famous mausoleum represents the most sophisticated stage of Mughal architecture.

A church door at Dabra Birhan, Gondar.

Christian Ethiopia

The later seventeenth century witnessed the last artistic and intellectual flowering of Christian Ethiopia. This empire, centered on Gondar, had a long tradition of Coptic Christianity, although several tributary Islamic states lay within its bounds. Outward-looking and customarily trained in Egypt, Ethiopian clergy had monasteries in Jerusalem and Cyprus through which they had contact with Europe. Production of illuminated manuscripts was an established practice in Ethiopia. Breakdown occurred when Emperor Susenyos imposed Roman Catholicism, precipitating civil wars which weakened the empire, leaving it isolated and culturally stagnant. However, the last powerful ruler Iyasu I (r. 1682-1706), who strove to re-establish Coptic Christianity and to restore contact with the southwest, actively patronized the arts and sciences. The emperor commissioned many castles, libraries and churches, including that of Dabra Birhan at Gondar. It appears that court patronage prompted stereotypes in art as it did in literature. Lacking the originality of earlier rock-cut churches, this "Abbey of Light" is extensively decorated with frescos, some of which reflect foreign, notably Indo-Portuguese, influences. The effect is nonetheless impressive.

European Absolutism

The growing prosperity of Russia from the mid-seventeenth century accelerated in the reign of Peter the Great after 1689. This enterprising tsar compelled his nobles to abandon Muscovite traditions, like the wearing of beards and long coats, in favor of western European styles. Founding an academy of sciences, he avidly promoted navigation and trade. It is clear that his ideas were greatly influenced by the France of Louis XIV. This "Sun King," who represented the epitome of absolute monarchy, presided over a golden age of French culture in the latter part of the seventeenth century. New developments in architecture included the classicist style, inspired by the heritage of Greece and Rome and best represented by the Louvre Palace and the church of Les Invalides, Paris. Theatre flourished with the comedies of Molière and the tragedies of Racine, while Lully introduced opera to French society and composed music for ballet. Such outlets, however, existed only for an elite. Like most other parts of Europe at this time, France had a large, impoverished peasantry while its urban population endured overcrowded conditions with wooden houses in narrow, dirty streets.

Louis XIV, painted in 1701 by Rigaud.

North American Native Arts

Some native North American art forms persisted with little change for centuries, and others were altered by contacts with Europeans and their descendants. Inuit arts appear to be very ancient: small incised sculptures of shamanistic figures and useful objects (such as buttons and toggles) in bone, wood, and ivory. Their style has been described as highly abstract, surreal, and humorous. The evergreen forests of the Northwest provided materials for superlative wood sculptures by the peoples who lived there. Perhaps the most famous are magnificent totem poles, carved to commemorate special events or honor ancestors; but equal artistry is shown in smaller objects such as masks, bowls, and toys. Iron and steel tools adopted from "the white man" sparked an explosion in these arts. California, Great Basin, and Plateau peoples produced remarkably complex basketry, while the arts of the Plains Indians developed in conjunction with dramatic changes in Indian life. Europeans reintroduced the horse, which made the life of the buffalo hunter possible. Colonial expansion in the seventeenth century made this life necessary; and so new clothing and equipment was created and distinctively embellished, with both native materials such as feathers, and European imports such as glass beads.

Mechanical masks such as this one from the Kwakiutl of the Northwest were manipulated by performers in ceremonial dances.

Performance Traditions in Japan

Kabuki, one of many traditional Japanese theater forms, was invented early in the seventeenth century in Kyoto by a female dancer named Okuni. At the time *kabuki* was unorthodox, the first Japanese dramatic form to present scenes of contemporary urban life to its audiences. Female performers were banned by the shogunate in 1629, and henceforward both male and female roles were played by men. *Nō* drama, developed earlier as the theatre of the samurai, is also performed by men. The stories that unfold in *nō* are familiar heroic histories and legends. The minimalist performance style of *nō* ("skill") was strongly influenced by Zen Buddhism, the chosen religion of the samurai, and demonstrated physical discipline as well as vocal techniques derived from Buddhist chants. *Nō* dramas are usually accompanied by a comic companion form, *kyogen*. *Nō*, *kyogen* and *kabuki* all remain popular today. As with many Asian theater forms, the playtext or plot is relatively unimportant, since it is usually already quite familiar; and in contrast to many familiar European plays, the texts are usually not considered part of a literary canon. Rather, the performance itself and especially the skill of the performers is valued. Today, the greatest *kabuki* actors in Japan are granted the status of "Living National Treasures."

An influential early kabuki *actor supposedly modelled his poses and expressions on the guardian figures of Buddhist temples. This nineteenth-century woodcut shows the continuity of style in* kabuki, *still popular now.*

5000	2000	1000	500	AD1	400	600

Ashanti Kingdom in West Africa

In the first years of European contact along the West African coast, those states on the coast benefited most. But in the early 1800s, a number of new states began to develop, all of them based inland. Of these, one of the most potent was the kingdom of the Ashanti, a confederation of different tribes which in turn secured the allegiance of subject tribal groups in the interior in return for protection and orderly administration. This gave the Ashanti secure access to the commerce of the interior: European influence was confined to the coast. In the nineteenth century, the British built forts along the coast and in time the Ashanti came into conflict with them in the British-Ashanti wars. Eventually the kingdom was incorporated into the British Gold Coast colony in 1901, later to become the Republic of Ghana.

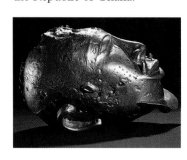

An Ashantic gold head, once probably attached to the royal stool, a symbol of Ashanti kings.

- 1700 Great Northern War (-1721) between Russia and Sweden.

- 1701 Detroit founded by Antoine de Cadillac.

- 1701 War of the Spanish Succession (-1714).

- 1701 Elector of Brandenburg becomes Frederick I, first king of Prussia.

- 1702 Queen Anne succeeds King William III.

- 1703 Russian capital moves to new city of St. Petersburg.

- 1704 English capture Gibraltar.

- 1705 Hussein ben Ali ejects Turks from Tunis, founds Husseinite dynasty of beys.

- 1707 Union of England and Scotland.

- 1709 Russian victory at Poltava, the decisive battle of the Great Northern War.

- 1709 Afghan rebels under Mir Vais overthrow Persian rule.

- 1713 Treaty of Utrecht ends War of Spanish Succession.

- 1714 George I of Britain first Hanoverian monarch.

- 1715 King Louis XV of France (-1774).

- 1716 Cambodian War of Succession ends: victory for Siamese candidate over Laotian-Vietnamese.

- 1718 Spaniards from Mexico occupy Texas, found San Antonio.

- 1719 Battle of Heart: Afghanis consolidate independence by defeating Persians.

- 1719 Civil war in Mughal empire ends: Mohammed Shah new emperor.

- 1720 China asserts dominance in Tibet.

- 1724 King Agaja of Abomey captures port of Allada, West Africa, temporarily disrupting the slave trade. Founds kingdom of Dahomey.

- 1733 War of the Polish Succession (-1738).

- 1733 Founding of Georgia, last of the 13 English colonies in America.

- 1739 Battle of Karnaj: Persians defeat Mughal army and take Delhi, slaughter thousands.

- 1740 War of the Austrian Succession (-1748).

- 1740 Frederick II, the Great, king of Prussia (-1786).

- 1740 Bengal wins independence from Mughal empire.

- 1745 Great Jacobite rebellion in Scotland crushed at Culloden (1746).

- 1746 Mazrui dynasty wins Mombasa's independence from Oman.

- 1748 Peace of Aix-la-Chapelle ends War of Austrian Succession.

- 1749 After many years of war, kingdom of Oyo in West Africa finally defeats the kingdom of Dahomey.

Russia in Europe

Peter I, known as "the Great," of Russia (r. 1689 -1725) succeeded to the throne of a unified state but one which still stood at the far margins of European life and power, regarded as Asiatic and barbarous by the rest of the continent. He was a brutally urgent modernizer, borrowing freely from the more developed countries of the west. He founded a new capital, St. Petersburg, on the banks of the Neva in the far north west. And for twenty-one years he fought the Great Northern War with Sweden, hitherto the dominant power in the Baltic region. The decisive battle of the war was waged at Poltava, deep in the Ukraine, in 1709. The Swedes were routed. When peace finally came in 1721, Russia gained parts of Finland, Estonia and Latvia, she had a navy on the Baltic and she was part of the European state system for the first time.

An interior view of Peter the Great's house in Archangel.

China in Tibet

Tibet had existed as an independent kingdom since time immemorial. It is the highest country on earth—its southern regions are wholly in the Himalayas—and it is a place that has always presented a remote and forbidding face to foreigners. This isolation was the best guarantee of its independence. Since the introduction of Buddhism in the seventh century, there developed an orderly state with an administrative class based on the Buddhist lamas. But faction weakened this kingdom in time and in 1206 it fell to Genghis Khan. By the end of the thirteenth century, however, independence had been

restored. Only the growing menace of Manchu China now threatened, and in the early eighteenth century China claimed suzerainty over Tibet. Over the next two centuries, this claim was to prove little more than nominal but it provided the dubious legal basis for the Chinese invasion of 1950.

A Tibetan reliquary figurine in gold decorated with stones.

Persians Sack Delhi

The Mughal empire had passed its best by the early eighteenth century and its impressive unitary purpose had been diminished. But in 1739 the Persian ruler Nadir Shah invaded the empire and defeated the Indian forces at the battle of Karnaj before capturing and looting Delhi with great slaughter. Among the many priceless artifacts stolen was the famous Peacock Throne, built for Shah Jahan nearly a century earlier. Nadir Shah, who had overthrown the Safavids in Persia itself, had previously captured Afghanistan and recovered Mesopotamia from the Ottomans. An adventurer, he was briefly the most powerful figure in Western Asia. His rule was personal, however, and his empire collapsed following his assassination in 1747. But he had fatally weakened the Mughal empire. The Marathas, a Hindu confederation, gradually filled the vacuum until the arrival of the British.

A battle between Persians and Indians from a book illustration of the Mughal school dating from the mid-seventeenth century.

A seventeenth-century Spanish painting showing Spanish colonial gentlemen and Native Americans dancing together.

Spaniards in Texas

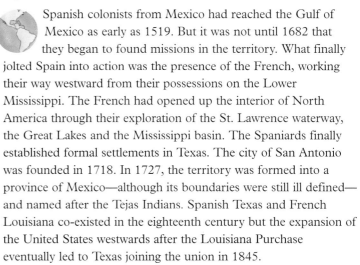

Spanish colonists from Mexico had reached the Gulf of Mexico as early as 1519. But it was not until 1682 that they began to found missions in the territory. What finally jolted Spain into action was the presence of the French, working their way westward from their possessions on the Lower Mississippi. The French had opened up the interior of North America through their exploration of the St. Lawrence waterway, the Great Lakes and the Mississippi basin. The Spaniards finally established formal settlements in Texas. The city of San Antonio was founded in 1718. In 1727, the territory was formed into a province of Mexico—although its boundaries were still ill defined—and named after the Tejas Indians. Spanish Texas and French Louisiana co-existed in the eighteenth century but the expansion of the United States westwards after the Louisiana Purchase eventually led to Texas joining the union in 1845.

117

5000	2000	1000	500	AD1	400	600

Puritans and Witches

The ethical egalitarianism promulgated by New England Puritans was deeply influential throughout the colonial period; it might be said that the political ideal of congregational democratic government was inspired in part by early Puritan theocratic settlements such as Plymouth (1620) and the Massachussets Bay Company settlement (1630). Puritan idealism suffered a tragic contortion in the witch trials held in the village of Salem in 1692, however. After playing at fortune-telling with a household slave, two young girls began behaving oddly; and after being examined by a doctor, and several ministers and magistrates, it was concluded that they were bewitched. Special hearings were begun; within a few weeks, 100 people were in jail. Within a few months, twenty-seven people had been tried and convicted. Nineteen of them were hanged. Some fifty people confessed, and still 100 more were awaiting trial. Although belief in witchcraft was common at the time, the virulent hysteria in Salem eventually drew the condemnation even of believers such as the pious minister Cotton Mather, and the governor ordered a halt to all proceedings and the release of the prisoners.

Tituba, a West Indian slave, triggers an obsessive witchhunt by her storytelling.

A Rajput illuminated manuscript page depicts the wedding of Rama, an episode in the ancient Hindu epic of the Ramayana.

Rajput Arts in India

With the decline of the Mughal dynasty, rival Indian kingdoms once again asserted their independent power. The Hindu Rajputs of the northern hills had long struggled against Islamic dominance. During the reigns of Jahangir (1605-1627) and Shah Jahan (1627-1658), however, some Rajputs found positions at the Mughal court, and absorbed its artistic influences. As Mughal arts declined, these influences found new expression in traditional Rajput art, which already had a distinctive character of its own, and the result was a fresh creative outburst in Rajput painting. Rajput traditions in painting and poetry were shaped as early as the tenth century by Hindu concepts of chivalry and honor. Rajput princes were taught to emulate the epic hero Rama, and the love story of Krishna and Radha, celebrated in the Rajput *Gita Govinda*, was especially prized as the exemplar of a love that was at once divine and secular. The Rajput strain of romantic mystical Hinduism had developed early, influenced by the Buddhism of the neighboring Pala kingdom, which emphasized the mystery of divine union. Rajput depictions of these Hindu themes became increasingly realistic under the influence of Mughal painting, while retaining their own individual character.

Asante

Asante emerged on the Gold Coast in the early eighteenth century, absorbing the former Denkyira hegemony west of the River Pra. A military empire, Asante reached its greatest extent *c.* 1750, stretching from the Volta to the Komoë River. Like earlier Songhai, Asante had a complex structure of government with ministries of finance, trade, home and foreign affairs. The emperors were patrons of the arts and promoted special centers for individual crafts. High standards were achieved in casting gold and brass, with human imagery frequently featured. There were centers for pottery and for cloth, while particular attention was devoted to silk. Traders exported gold, kola nuts and slaves, while guns were included among European imports. Members of the Asante merchant class, many of whom were highly literate, accumulated wealth as middlemen in commercial dealings with the Portuguese and British. As the century progressed, two imported religious faiths impacted upon Asante: Christianity was introduced by the Europeans as commercial bases developed, and Islam made its way down from the Niger region.

Cast gold jewelry: insignia worn by senior officials at the Asante court.

A seventeenth- or eighteenth-century gilt bronze sculpture of Padmasambhava, the original Indian founder of Tibetan Buddhism.

Tibetan Lamaist Buddhism

The Manchu Ch'ing (or Qing) dynasty, which replaced the Chinese Ming dynasty in 1644, continued the expansion of China's borders and annexation of border regions. Incorporating Inner and Outer Mongolia into their state, they recognized the strategic importance of Tibet, which lay in its religious influence over the Mongols. The Lamaist Buddhism that had developed in Tibet had spread rapidly among the Mongols during the Mongol (Yüan) period in the thirteenth and fourteenth centuries. Tibetan Buddhism was a mixture of a strain of Buddhism with Hindu elements from eighth-century India with an indigenous shamanistic tradition called Bon. In the 1400s, a reformist *lama* (or priest) reshaped Tibetan Buddhism, and a Mongolian prince endowed the third successor of this reformer with the title of *Dalai* (all-embracing) in addition to his title of *Lama* (superior one). The Dalai Lama eventually became, in part through the influence of his powerful neighbors, the temporal as well as religious leader of Tibet. The Mongols intervened in 1641 to establish the fifth Dalai Lama in his spiritual palace at Lhasa, and in the eighteenth century a Ch'ing army marched in to quell Tibetan civil war and install the Dalai Lama as official temporal ruler.

The Enlightenment

Prompted by the Scientific Revolution, the application of reason to traditional views of politics, society and religion generated the intellectual movement known as the Enlightenment. The notion of absolute monarchy was attacked; already in Britain, John Locke (d. 1704) had argued that parliament provided a counterbalance to royal power. In France, Montesquieu (d. 1755) advocated limited monarchy while French-Swiss Rousseau (d. 1778), in his *Social Contract*, argued that political power derived not from Divine Right but from the people. He maintained that unjust government caused much disorder in society. Voltaire, whose *Philosophical Letters* appeared in 1734, went further, proposing freedom of thought, religious toleration and justice for all. Although a deist he rejected Christian teaching, attacking what he saw as tyrannical churches in whose names religious wars were fought. Like Diderot, whose *Encyclopedia* appeared from 1751, Voltaire could not reconcile privileged and oppressive Churches with reason. Such thinking encouraged anti-clericalism, which characterized Revolutionary France, but also present were the seeds of modern democracy, which would ultimately transform government worldwide.

Jean-Jacques Rousseau, French philosopher.

ENLIGHTENMENT AND REVOLUTIONS

Enlightenment is humanity's departure from its self-imposed immaturity.
Immanuel Kant, *What is Enlightenment?* (1784)

In 1784, the German philosopher Immanuel Kant was one of many thinkers observing developments in the nascent United States of America, where some of the political theories of the European Enlightenment were receiving their first pragmatic applications. Kant and many others believed that a new era was emerging, in which human reason would reshape the world. Inspired in part by the scientific revolution, Enlightenment thinkers questioned the traditional social institutions of their world, searching for the "natural laws" of social and political organization. Denis Diderot, editor of the famous *Encyclopédie* which attempted to categorize human knowledge, based his philosophical ideas on the natural sciences. He also encouraged the contributions of Jean-Jacques Rousseau, whose *Discourse on Inequality* (1754) had described the natural state of humans as innocent and virtuous ("noble savages") until corrupted by society. "Écrasons l'infame!" ("Crush the infamous!") was the rallying cry of the provocative Voltaire. By "infamous" he meant any superstitious or religious intolerance, including that of established religions such as the Catholic Church. Voltaire believed, with many other Enlightenment philosophers, that religious beliefs that could not be sustained by reason merely perpetuated human ignorance. Education became an important preoccupation of Enlightenment thinkers, as they debated the appropriate means to create a natural, reasonable society.

THE AMERICAN REVOLUTION

Almost inadvertently, the rebellion of the English colonies in North America became a testing ground for Enlightenment political theories. What began as a demand for equal representation as full-fledged English citizens soon became a political experiment, full of dangers but also opportunities, as many new Americans were aware. Radical notions, such as separation of religion from state institutions, sovereignty of the people, a written government constitution to which leaders and citizens would be held accountable, and systematic checks and balances in the arrangement of government could be explored more fully in the new United States than had been possible in any European country, precisely because of its relative lack of history and tradition.

If George Washington was the commanding general of the American revolution, and Ben Franklin its genial elder statesman, then Thomas Jefferson was its wordsmith. He wrote the initial draft of the Declaration of Independence in 1776, later amended in consultation with Franklin and John Adams, and also modified by the Congress. Jefferson recognized that the Declaration was indebted to previous thinkers, but nonetheless unique: "Neither aiming at originality of principle or sentiment, nor yet copied from any particular and previous writing, it was intended to be an expression of the American mind." In spite of holding many public offices (including the presidency), at his own request Thomas Jefferson is remembered on his tombstone for only three accomplishments: authorship of the Declaration of Independence and of the statute for religious freedom in Virginia, and as the founder of the University of Virginia. Each of these reflects Enlightenment values, and Jefferson believed that Americans had been the first to achieve these in practice. He wrote to James Madison when the Virginia statute for religious freedom finally passed in 1789: "It is honorable for us to have produced the first legislature who had the courage to declare that the reason of man may be trusted with the formation of his own opinions."

THE FRENCH REVOLUTION

Jefferson was U.S. minister to France in 1789, and witnessed the beginnings of the French Revolution. France had aided the American revolutionaries, and there was a lively exchange of ideas between the two countries. Jefferson, however, doubted that France, with its very different history and traditions, could or should try to emulate the Americans.

The French Revolution began modestly, with a meeting of representatives of the Estates General in May of 1789. (Traditional French society was divided into three "estates" or groups: the powerful minorities of the nobility and the clergy, and the "third estate," comprising most of the population.) King Louis XVI reluctantly agreed to the innovation of a written constitution, but the terrible economic conditions in France encouraged demands for still more radical change. In August the Constitutional Assembly issued the Declaration of the Rights of Man and Citizen, modeled on the American Declaration of Independence, which demanded civic equality for all citizens.

From these beginnings the Revolution soon entered a far more extreme phase. The king was arrested in 1792 and executed in early 1793. Horrified European states formed a coalition against France, where a wartime tribunal, the Committee for Public Safety, took charge of the government. In its zeal to establish an Enlightened and perfectly egalitarian society, the Committee introduced reforms such as the metric system and a new calendar designed to reflect the seasons of nature rather than religious dates. Church property was expropri-

American artist John Trumball depicted the 1776 signing of the Declaration of Independence approximately fifteen years after the event. The tall red-haired man near the center of the painting is Thomas Jefferson, the author of the Declaration.

ated, and Notre Dame cathedral was transformed into a "Temple of Reason." Objections to such radical changes were answered by the executions of thousands of "counter-revolutionaries." Maximilien Robespierre, the Committee's ruthless leader, explained: "If the mainspring of popular government in peacetime is virtue, amid revolution it is at the same time virtue and terror: virtue, without which terror is fatal; terror, without which virtue is impotent. Terror is nothing but prompt, severe, inflexible justice; it is therefore an emanation of virtue." These excesses were Enlightenment values carried to their extreme. A reaction was inevitable. Ultimately Napoleon seized control of the chaos, re-establishing a regime that was authoritarian but which also reflected the changes wrought by the Enlightenment in innovations such as the Napoleonic Code. *S.I.*

5000	2000	1000	500	AD1	400	600

The French Revolution

The most seismic event in modern European history broke out on 14 July 1789 with the storming of the French prison in Paris, the Bastille. The Estates-General, an assembly of aristocrats and notables, had been in session since the spring. It mutated into the National Assembly and enacted radical reforms: abolishing feudal privileges, issuing a Declaration of the Rights of Man, establishing a constitution and limiting royal power. In 1792 a counter-revolutionary coalition of European powers threatened France and the situation further radicalized. The First Republic was declared, the monarchy abolished and the king and queen executed. The army saved the revolution but the Terror of 1793-4 brought a reaction that produced first the Directory and later Napoleon. Monarchy had yielded to republic which yielded to empire. Despite its excesses, the French Revolution is associated with modern concepts of democracy, popular sovereignty and egalitarianism now taken for granted in Europe, but revolutionary in their time.

The showing of the head to the crowd at the execution of King Louis XVI on 21 January 1793, Paris.

South Africa: First "Kaffir" War

In 1779, Boer settlers moving north and east from the Cape Colony encountered Bantu peoples migrating south. There followed the series of skirmishes known as the First Kaffir War, "kaffir" being a white pejorative term for blacks. The settlers, with their superior weaponry, were victorious in most of the actions. Moreover, their cause was helped by tribal disagreements among blacks, who were by no means a cohesive force. San, Nguni and Khoikhoi never made common cause. Indeed, there were instances of white commandos supported by Khoikhoi retaliating against the San for livestock raids. But in essence this was the first black-white contest for land in southern Africa. White notions of individual ownership and economic exploitation of the land were utterly opposed to the traditional ideas of communal ownership held by black African societies of every kind.

The Great Fish River, the Bantu kingdom boundary, was the scene of many skirmishes in the First Kaffir War.

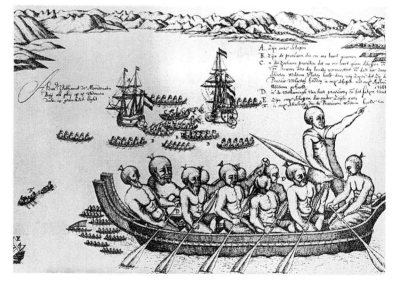

Tasman's drawing of Tasmanians, natives of the island that would be named first after his patron Van Diemen, then after himself.

Australia

In 1642 a Dutch sailor, Abel Tasman, discovered Tasmania and New Zealand and later Fiji and Tonga. But the Dutch did not follow up these discoveries. It was not until 1770, when Britain's Captain James Cook sailed into Botany Bay, on the east coast, that the island continent was formally discovered by Europeans. Having discovered it, the British were at a loss to know what to do with it. It was a remote and unattractive destination for settlers, although a steady trickle made their way out from earliest times. Then in 1788, the first penal colonies were founded, making a virtue of the continent's isolation. With the end of the American War of Independence, North America could no longer be used, as it had been, as a dumping ground for English criminals. Australia replaced it in this dubious role for nearly a century.

American Independence

The revolt of the English colonies in North America produced consequences that were, in the long run, as momentous as those of the French Revolution. In the second half of the eighteenth century, England's American colonies chafed increasingly under rule from London. Their concerns focused on taxation, especially excise, and the absence of parliamentary representation. In 1775, the British turned the troops against them. In 1776, colonist losses at the Battle of Bunker Hill led to calls for outright independence, and a declaration to that effect was drafted by Thomas Jefferson and adopted by the Continental Congress on 4 July 1776. Eventually, with French help, the colonists won the war and later constituted themselves as a federal nation. Their military leader, George Washington, was elected first president of the republic in 1789. The new country tested the ideals of the Enlightenment that would soon galvanize European politics.

The American Declaration of Independence: a bill poster with the text.

Opening up Siberia

With the collapse of the Mongol empire and the rise of the Russian state, the colonization of Siberia began. As early as the 1580s, Yermak Timofeyevich crossed the Urals and established himself in southwestern Siberia. Others followed and by the middle of the seventeenth century Russians had reached the Pacific coast. They built a string of forts to protect their gains from native tribesmen. But it was in the eighteenth century that the exploitation of the huge region began in earnest. In particular, the fur trade drew many who were attracted by the enormous potential profits. Siberia later became a dumping ground for Russian political prisoners and was not really opened up to the outside world until the building of the Trans-Siberian Railway in the late nineteenth century.

A copper engraving showing three Siberians, one attended by walruses, made by a German visitor in the eighteenth century.

- 1751 China invades Tibet.

- 1756 Seven Years' War (-1763): Britain defeats France and Prussia retains Silesia.

- 1757 Burma united by warlord Alaungpaya.

- 1757 Battle of Plassey: Clive defeats Nawab of Bengal, establishes British in India.

- 1758 China occupies eastern Turkistan.

- 1759 British gain Quebec from the French.

- 1762 Catherine II, the Great, assends the Russian throne (r.-1796).

- 1763 Indian adventurer Hyder Ali (1722-1782) conquers Kanara, Mysore.

- 1764 Confiscation of Church lands in Russia.

- 1767 Mason-Dixon line marks border between Pennsylvania and Maryland.

- 1768 Russian-Turkish war (-1772) leads to huge Russian gains.

- 1769 Burma repels Chinese invasion.

- 1770 Englishman Captain James Cook discovers east coast of Australia.

- 1772 First partition of Poland: gains for Russia, Prussia and Austria.

- 1773 Boston Tea Party: protest against tea duty.

- 1776 America declares independence from Britain.

- 1777 Sidi Mohammed ends slavery in Morocco.

- 1779 First Kaffir War (-1781) as Boers meet Xhosa tribe resistance.

- 1780 Rebellion in Peru against Spanish rule.

- 1781 Cornwallis surrenders at Yorktown: decisive British defeat in American war.

- 1783 Peace of Versailles: Britain recognizes American independence.

- 1788 First British penal colony established in New South Wales.

- 1789 George Washington first president of the United States.

- 1789 Start of the French Revolution.

- 1792 Abolition of the French monarchy; year 1 of the French republic.

- 1793 Execution of King Louis XVI and Marie Antoinette of France.

- 1793 Second partition of Poland.

- 1793 First free British settlers reach Australia.

- 1794 Reign of Terror in France ends.

- 1794 Agha Mohammed founds the Kajar dynasty in Persia.

- 1795 The Directory takes over government of France (-1799).

- 1795 Third partition of Poland.

- 1795 Britain occupies Cape of Good Hope, South Africa.

- 1798 Napoleon's Egyptian campaign: success on land.

- 1798 At sea, Nelson destroys French fleet at the Battle of the Nile.

- 1798 Wolfe Tone organizes revolt against British rule in Ireland.

- 1799 Napoleon overthrows Directory, establishes Consulate.

- 1799 Civil war in Tonga.

5000	2000	1000	500	AD1	400	600

Benjamin Franklin, Writer and Scientist

His many writings testify to Ben Franklin's cheerful and witty personality, making him one of the most likable characters in colonial American history. Franklin blended a strong ethical sense inherited from his Puritan parents with a lively intellectual curiosity and belief in tolerant rationality inspired by Enlightenment values. During his long life (1706-90), he pursued a number of careers, as essayist, publisher, scientist, postmaster, and statesman. Although he had only two years of formal schooling, he was a voracious reader, devouring works by John Bunyan, Plutarch, Daniel Defoe, Cotton Mather, and (his favorite) Joseph Addison in his youth. In 1732 he began publishing the popular *Poor Richard's Almanack*, with pithy advice such as "Early to Bed and Early to Rise, Makes a Man Healthy, Wealthy, and Wise." Franklin also invented the widely used Franklin stove. His scientific experiments included the extremely dangerous flying of a kite in a thunderstorm in order to demonstrate that lightning was actually electricity. Franklin lived for a time in France, where he was popular as "le Bonhomme Richard," after his almanac persona. Shortly before his death he wrote optimistically to friends there that American "Experiments in Politicks" were "getting into good order very fast."

Franklin's vacuum pump, used in some of his electrical experiments, with a French edition of his writings open in front of it.

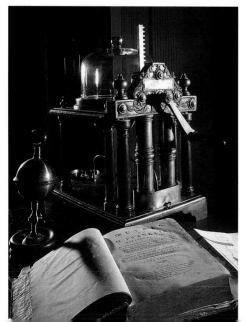

British East India "Company Style"

As rivalries and combat drained the treasuries of various competing Indian kingdoms, artists saw their traditional patronage evaporate. Eventually, however, Indian artists found new patrons among the English. When Sir Charles Malet visited the ancient monumental sculptures in the Ellora caves, he commissioned an Indian artist to make sketches for him. The British East India Company had by now established an important presence in India, and members of the company also became sponsors of the arts, to such an extent that it is possible to speak of "Company Style." Indian artists attempted to accommodate the demands for naturalism made by their English patrons. In this process they learned to incorporate perspective and other techniques foreign to traditional Indian art in their work. Examples of Company Style include the drawings of natural historical subjects made by Indian artists that hang in the India Office Library in London. In Calcutta, one of the principal locations of the company, there was also a flourishing bazaar trade in lively paintings depicting daily relations between the English and the Indians. The neoclassical architecture favored by the company was also adopted, as private villas in this style were built first by the English and then by wealthy Indians.

European Influences

By the mid-eighteenth century, a European presence was well established around Africa's coasts. Primarily motivated by commerce, Europeans had early adopted a missionary purpose. For over a century, Portuguese Catholicism had influenced society and art in East Africa, Congo and Benin while Dutch Protestants had settled in the Cape. Before 1750, European schools had been founded at, e.g., El Mina and Accra. Various factors facilitated expansion of European interests in the later eighteenth century. Droughts in West Africa prior to 1756 and the Cape's smallpox epidemics of 1755 and 1767 decimated regional populations. Political disorder weakened the great empires of Ethiopia and Congo and the Muslim lordships of the Maghreb. The slave trade may well have sapped the creative energies of equatorial Africa. Experiencing industrial revolution and economic growth, Europe sought raw materials. Until this, Europeans were familiar only with Africa's coasts; "interior parts" remained unknown. From c. 1790, expeditions sought to ascertain geographical features and to locate resources and potential markets. So far, conquests had been limited. Napoleon invaded Egypt in 1798 only to be dislodged by Britain, but this foreshadowed future developments.

"Interior parts unknown;" a European perspective on Africa c. 1800.

An example of "Company Style" c. 1760

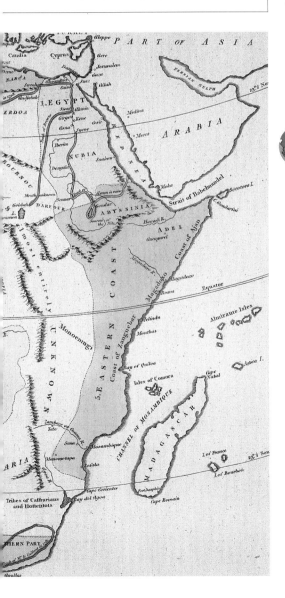

European Art and Literature

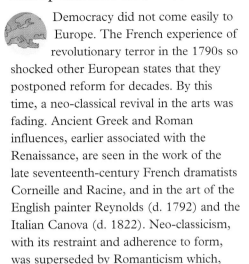
Democracy did not come easily to Europe. The French experience of revolutionary terror in the 1790s so shocked other European states that they postponed reform for decades. By this time, a neo-classical revival in the arts was fading. Ancient Greek and Roman influences, earlier associated with the Renaissance, are seen in the work of the late seventeenth-century French dramatists Corneille and Racine, and in the art of the English painter Reynolds (d. 1792) and the Italian Canova (d. 1822). Neo-classicism, with its restraint and adherence to form, was superseded by Romanticism which, inspired by the social and political change of the day, allowed for the emotion and imagination of the English poets such Wordsworth (1770-1850) and Coleridge (1772-1834) and the German critics and poets August (1767-1845) and Friedrich (1772-1829) von Schlegel, who formulated and publicized the ideas of the Romantics. The great German composer Beethoven (1770-1827) bridged the Classical and Romantic traditions in music.

Cupid and Psyche by Canova, 1787-93

Admitting (and Rejecting) the "Barbarians"

East Asian countries responded differently to an increasing European presence. Japan under the Tokugawa shogunate controlled its ports so strictly that it remained virtually isolated from Europeans until the mid-nineteenth century. The Ch'ing emperors in China were initially more interested in a smooth transition from Chinese to Manchu rule, incorporating Chinese bureaucracy into their government while preserving their own Manchurian heritage. The Manchu emperors were at first tolerant of Christian missionaries and intrigued by Jesuit scientists. Jesuits remained in China for over a century, a conduit for ideas that created a vogue for *chinoiserie* in European architecture and interior design and influenced European philosophy. Voltaire was among the European philosophers who admired the "natural morality" of Chinese society as portrayed by the Jesuits. Meanwhile, the emperor Chi'en Lung built a summer palace in European style. The "Middle Kingdom" was too powerful to fear the European "barbarians," although their presence was controlled. Christianity came to Yi dynasty Korea (1392-1910) from China, but it was rejected as incompatible with a Confucianist state, and persecuted into the nineteenth century. Thailand, however, pursued a uniquely successful course. A series of Thai Buddhist kings avoided European conquest while showing adroit interest in Europe: their country was the only one in Southeast Asia never colonized by Europeans.

An example of the Chinese textile designs that became part of the chinoiserie *vogue in Europe during the late eighteenth century.*

125

5000	2000	1000	500	AD1	400	600

British India

Neither the failing Mughal empire nor the Maratha confederacy were strong enough to control all of subcontinental India. By the end of the eighteenth century, the British had established themselves as the most potent European power in Indian affairs, having disposed of their French rivals. The East India Company, reconstituted in 1773 as an arm of government, was the instrument of British advance. Military strength, bribery and the shrewd exploitation of internal differences between rival kingdoms carried British power relentlessly across the subcontinent until by 1818 Britain was the effective master of India. Further annexations followed later—Burma and the Punjab, for instance—but by the second decade of the century the main job was done. British India, the Raj, the jewel in the crown of empire, was established. It was to last just over a century, only a moment in the long history of India.

A British East India Company official astride an elephant with an escort of foot soldiers and Indian retainers, late eighteenth century.

■ **1801** Union of Britain and Ireland creates United Kingdom.

■ **1803** Louisiana Purchase: France sells Louisiana to the USA.

■ **1804** Napoleon I, Emperor of the French (-1815).

■ **1805** Nelson's victory at the Battle of Trafalgar ensures British supremacy at sea.

■ **1805** Napoleon captures Vienna and defeats an Austro-Russian army at Austerlitz.

■ **1805** Mohammed Ali achieves effective Egyptian independence from Turkey.

■ **1806** Formal dissolution of Holy Roman Empire.

■ **1807** Britain first European nation to abandon the slave trade.

■ **1812** French suffer disastrous reverse in Russia.

■ **1812** War between Britain and the United States (-1814).

■ **1814** Allies occupy Paris; Napoleon abdicates.

■ **1815** The Hundred Days: Napoleon returns.

■ **1815** Battle of Waterloo: Wellington defeats Napoleon.

■ **1816** Independence of Argentina.

■ **1818** Independence of Chile.

■ **1818** Britain establishes effective control over most of India.

■ **1819** Spain cedes Florida to the United States.

■ **1819** Stamford Raffles founds Singapore.

■ **1821** Independence of Mexico.

■ **1821** Death of Napoleon on St. Helena.

■ **1822** Pedro I, emperor of newly independent Brazil.

■ **1822** Foundation of Liberia by freed American slaves.

■ **1823** Monroe Doctrine declares North America a zone free of European colonial interest.

■ **1823** Egypt conquers the Sudan, founds Khartoum.

■ **1823** First Anglo-Burmese war (-1826), as Britain seeks to contain Burmese expansionism.

■ **1825** Decembrist rising in Russia.

■ **1828** Andrew Jackson, seventh president of the United States.

■ **1829** George Stephenson's "Rocket," first commercially successful passenger steam locomotive.

■ **1830** July revolution in Paris brings Louis-Philippe to power (-1848).

■ **1830** Polish revolt against Russian rule.

■ **1830** Greek independence from Turkey.

■ **1830** Independence of Belgium.

■ **1830** French capture Algiers, overthrow *bey*.

■ **1832** Great Reform Act extends franchise in Britain.

■ **1833** First Carlist War in Spain (-1838).

■ **1836** Great Trek of the Boers from Cape Colony across the Orange River.

■ **1836** Texan independence from Mexico; independent republic (-1845).

■ **1837** Accession of Queen Victoria (r. -1901).

■ **1839** Chartist agitation in Britain.

■ **1839** Anglo-Chinese opium war (-1842).

■ **1845** Great Irish Famine (-1849): 2 million die or emigrate.

■ **1846** Repeal of the British Corn Laws opens free trade era.

■ **1846** Mexican-American war (-1848).

■ **1848** Year of revolutions in Europe.

■ **1848** Publication of the *Communist Manifesto* by Karl Marx.

800	1000	1200	1400	1600	1800	2000

Louisiana Purchase

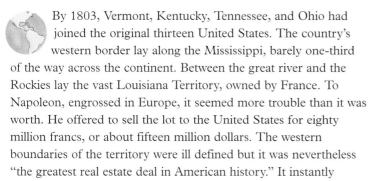

By 1803, Vermont, Kentucky, Tennessee, and Ohio had joined the original thirteen United States. The country's western border lay along the Mississippi, barely one-third of the way across the continent. Between the great river and the Rockies lay the vast Louisiana Territory, owned by France. To Napoleon, engrossed in Europe, it seemed more trouble than it was worth. He offered to sell the lot to the United States for eighty million francs, or about fifteen million dollars. The western boundaries of the territory were ill defined but it was nevertheless "the greatest real estate deal in American history." It instantly

doubled the size of the country—all at a cost of four cents an acre. The purchase led to friction between the United States and the Spanish southwest. It eventually tripped off the Mexican War (1846-8) which drove the Mexicans out of the region and cleared the way for continental unity.

The Louisiana Purchase treaty of 1803. The background document is a map of New Orleans.

Napoleon: Revolutionary Messenger

The Napoleonic Wars continued the French Revolutionary Wars that had started in 1792. From 1797 to 1812, Napoleon was invincible on land. In successive campaigns, he defeated every major continental power. By 1808, Europe from Cadiz to Moscow was under French control, directly or through alliances. Only British naval mastery denied France complete hegemony. Eventually, the Peninsular War and the Russian campaign of 1812 broke the back of the Grand Armée and Waterloo in 1815 ended the Napoleonic era. But even in defeat, his legacy was immense and was felt everywhere. Napoleon tamed the French Revolution and turned it into a conquering imperium while

carrying its modernizing and egalitarian spirit across the continent. He rationalized the chaotic map of Germany and abolished the Holy Roman Empire. The post-war settlement formally restored the *ancien régime* but the revolutions of 1830 and 1848 demonstrated the undiminished potency of the French Revolutionary legacy.

Napoleon Enthroned by the French artist Ingres, c. 1806.

Hong Kong

The Industrial Revolution created a huge growth in British trade. With its total command of the seas, Britain sought convenient refueling stations for its ships around the world. In East Asia, Singapore—founded in 1819—and Hong Kong were acquired for this purpose. However, Hong Kong soon developed a less savory role. Its position made it ideal for the import and distribution of Indian opium into China. This trade was illegal in Chinese law but enormously profitable. In 1839, the Chinese commissioner at Canton, Lin Tse-hsu—acting directly on the orders of the emperor—confiscated opium warehouses belonging to British traders. There followed the First Opium War between Britain and China, which Britain won in short order. Hong Kong was part of the settlement. A second war was fought twenty years later with similar results. The fabled island started life as a government-backed *entrepôt* for illegal drug importers.

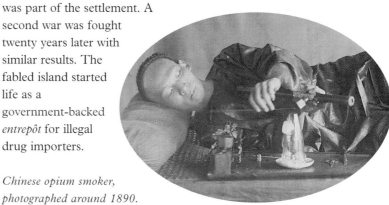

Chinese opium smoker, photographed around 1890.

The Boers' Great Trek

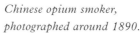

When the Cape of Good Hope passed from Dutch to British control in 1795, it made no immediate difference to the Boers or Afrikaners. But gradually British policy became more liberal. Missionary societies and the effects of the anti-slavery movement introduced a more benign regime towards black Africans. This irked the Boers. In 1836, parties of Voortrekkers began to leave the colony, crossing the Orange River and placing themselves beyond the reach of the British. Some settled in the Transvaal, others in Natal. The latter were attacked by Zulus, against whom they won a sensational victory at the battle of Blood River in 1838. When Britain annexed Natal in 1843, many Boers retreated to the interior and founded the Orange Free State. In all, this series of migrations known as the Great Trek took the Afrikaners to the Limpopo, a vast distance, and established them in the South African interior.

Part of the Laager Wall of Sixty-four Wagons at the Voortrekker Monument to the Great Trek, Pretoria, South Africa.

5000	2000	1000	500	AD1	400	600

The tragic end of Sir John Franklin's expedition to find the Northwest Passage, depicted in a painting from 1895.

Later Exploration of North America

Explorers continued to search for the elusive Northwest Passage in the nineteenth century. The mandate of the expedition headed by Meriwether Lewis and William Clark, which set out from St Louis in 1804, was to discover "water communication across this continent." Finding the route westward more difficult than foreseen, the expedition wintered with the Mandan Indians of North Dakota. From there, Lewis and Clark set out with a new guide and interpreter, a Shoshoni woman named Sacajawea (Bird Woman). Although the expedition failed to find the Northwest Passage, during the three years it took to travel to the Pacific and back, much new information about the lands and peoples of western North America was collected. Westward expansion of the United States was greatly encouraged by the discovery of gold in northern California in 1848, which attracted thousands of adventurers, followed by merchants, artisans and farmers. At that time the fate of the expedition which actually did discover the Northwest Passage (in 1847) was still unknown. Evidence of the tragic death of British explorer Sir John Franklin and his men in the Arctic (and of their discovery) was not confirmed until 1859.

Asian Nomads

Nineteenth-century paintings by the Russian artist Vassili V. Vereshchagin preserve an impression of the life of central and northern Asia that must have seemed very exotic to many Europeans. Many parts of Asia were (and sometimes still are) populated by nomadic tribes of distinctive cultural heritages. The Mongols of northeastern Asia are perhaps the most famous of these, no doubt because of their extraordinary conquests throughout Asia and Europe in the thirteenth century under the initial leadership of Ghengis (Chingis) Khan. Many of the remaining Mongols live today in the Republic of Mongolia; a substantial number also live in China. The religion of the eastern Mongols is Lamaist Buddhism, which is also the usual religion of the central Asian Buryat people, although some who live west of Lake Baikal now practice Russian Orthodox traditions. The Huns were also central Asian Mongols. A mix of Turkish and Mongol nomads led to the Turkic-speaking Muslim Tatars. The Khirghiz are a similar Muslim group who were later absorbed into the now defunct USSR. Many of these peoples still pursue their traditional life. Their homes are tents called yurts, from Russian *yurta*, in turn derived from Turkish *yurd*, meaning domicile, nation, or estate.

A painting by Vereshchagin of a traditional Khirghiz yurt, a circular tent made of felt stretched over a wooden frame. The floor would be covered with carpets and felt pads.

| 00 | 1000 | 1200 | 1400 | 1600 | 1800 | 2000 |

Not all Maori peoples rebelled during the Maori Wars. Queen Victoria presented this statue of herself to the Awara people in appreciation of their loyalty.

Pacific Colonialism

European exploration of the Pacific was furthered by the English Captain James Cook, a skillful navigator and chartist. Cook rediscovered New Zealand more than a century after Tasman had left, and unknowingly repeated the early voyage (*c.* 950 AD) of the Maori navigator Kupe, sailing around the coasts of the North and South Islands. Continuing his first voyage (1768-1771), Cook charted and claimed the eastern coast of Australia, and his positive report was influential when England sought new penal colonies after the American War of Independence. It was Matthew Flinders, however, who first circumnavigated Australia in 1802-1803, and suggested its name from the long-rumored *Terra Australis Incognita*. The first convicts had already arrived in Australia by 1788; in 1793 the first free settlers arrived. Farming and ranching eventually superseded the penal colonies, and tragically interfered with the lives of the Aborigines. The discovery of gold in 1848 brought a huge influx of adventurers. New Zealand was first colonized by Christian missionaries, as were many of the Pacific islands throughout this period. Systematic farm settlement of New Zealand began in 1840. Although some 500 Maori chiefs signed a treaty with Britain in that year, by 1843 disputes over territory erupted into the first Maori War. A second war broke out in 1860.

The Egyptian Khedives

French intervention in Egypt, undermining Mameluke rule, enabled army officer Mohammed Ali to emerge as khedive with effect from 1811. Nominally viceroys of the Turkish sultan, the khedives amounted to independent kings. Mohammed Ali sought to modernize Egypt. He reformed the army, and strove to improve education and technology. He founded a state printing press and secular schooling, promoted irrigation and introduced textile, glass and chemical industries. Unfortunately, the native business classes were bypassed by most of these developments. Aside from a growing bureaucracy, the main

Mohammed Ali (above), from a portrait (c. 1840). Emerging in 1805, he ruled as khedive from 1811 to 1849.

beneficiaries were European commercial interests. Meanwhile, Europe's dominance in trade, facilitated by African middlemen, continued to increase. The transport revolution, a product of Europe's industrial growth, along with the emergence of the United States, brought an increasing share of commerce into the Atlantic sphere. Before the mid-century, riverboats enabled European trade to reach inland Africa. Even exporting a wider range of produce—timber, gum and manufactured cloth—the African economies could not compete. In 1830, debt-ridden Algiers was taken into French control, and by the 1850s some 130,000 colonists were settled there.

Social Problems in Europe

The relative political stability from 1815 favored the spread of the Industrial Revolution. Popular notions of progress fostered enterprise, which often turned to exploitation, widening the gulf between employer and worker. For the first time, Europe saw the emergence of an urban working class as masses flocked to the cities to live in poor, cramped housing and to labor long hours for small wages in conditions often unsafe and unhealthy. The misery of such workers motivated Karl Marx, a German-born Jew, to produce his *Communist Manifesto* in 1848. Marx inherited the idealist tradition of Hegel

Children working in German mines.

(d. 1831), who had advanced an organic theory of the state. Developing Hegel's earlier line of thought Marx rejected religion. Viewing established religion as an obstacle to be overcome, Marx argued that the proletariat (working class) would *inevitably* wrest economic and political control from the bourgeoisie (middle class), initiating a classless society. The first half of the century saw Germany replace France as the cultural center of Europe, with middle classes debating philosophy, reading the literary works of Goethe, and enjoying the symphonies of Beethoven.

THE TRANSPORT REVOLUTION

... the traveler who proposes to make a trip across Asia when the great highway really is completed need not be discouraged.

Harper's New Monthly Magazine, 1898

Even before the middle of the nineteenth century, the steam engine had been pressed into transport service throughout Europe. Ever since James Watt's development of the rotative beam principle had enabled steam engines to directly drive machinery, Great Britain had produced a number of pioneering engineers who experimented in parallel with the application of steam power to maritime and overland transport. Prominent among these pioneers were George Stephenson (1781-1848) and Isambard Kingdom Brunel (1806-1859).

SHIPPING

The early nineteenth century had seen rapid development in marine engines as the still sail-dependent paddle steamer, like the Savannah which crossed the Atlantic in 1819, gave way to screw-propeller craft. From 1838 Brunel was actively involved in the design of ocean-going steamships. Brunel's *Great Britain* was the first propeller-driven trans-Atlantic vessel, but his greatest contribution to ship design was the *Great Eastern* of 1856. Powered by screw-propeller and paddles, the *Great Eastern* was an impressive 695 feet long. Her record as the largest vessel in the world would stand for half a century. While screw-propeller craft soon dominated trans-oceanic shipping, paddle steamers would become a particular feature of North American and African riverways in the second half of the nineteenth century. Advances in motive power and design, however, do not entirely explain the rapid growth of international shipping that would see British merchantmen carry over 6,000,000 tons by 1875 and French tonnage

exceed the 1,000,000 mark. Ship canals would greatly reduce journey times and facilitate communications between the continents. The French-backed Suez Canal, opened in 1869, shortened the sea-route to India by 4,000 miles. The Panama Canal, initially proposed by Brunel but after many delays and setbacks completed with American support only in 1914, would reduce the journey from the west coast of the USA to Europe by 6,000 miles.

THE RAILWAY

Meanwhile, steam traction had been applied with equal determination to overland transport. Early experiments with road locomotives having proved impractical, Richard Trevithick demonstrated the first railway locomotive at a Merthyr Tydfil coalfield, Wales, in 1804. The potential of this new form of transport soon became apparent. Development of industry in Great Britain and elsewhere in Europe necessitated haulage of coal, ore, and other raw materials to factories along with distribution of manufactured goods. Industrialized cities increasingly depended on agricultural produce transported from their hinterland. Road communication was as yet insufficiently developed and inland waterways had obvious limitations. The principle of rail haulage was long understood, but had lacked suitable motive power. Many historians consider that the railway locomotive transformed what would otherwise have merely been industrial change into industrial revolution for Europe. Before the nineteenth century ended, the railway had facilitated social and economic transformation in every continent. Much credit for locomotive

development is due to George Stephenson, who built Britain's first public railway in 1825. From the 1830s onwards, Stephenson locomotives featured outside Britain as railways got under way in France, Russia and the United States. Brunel's contribution related more to line construction, especially tunneling and bridge-building. He was engineering consultant for railways in Europe and India. By 1854, Europe had 14,000 miles of line connecting most of the major cities. Railways were by this time well established in the USA and had already appeared in India and Australia. European and American locomotives were exported worldwide; in many other parts of the world locomotive building only got under way in the twentieth century. The United States was crossed in 1869 and Canada in 1885; the

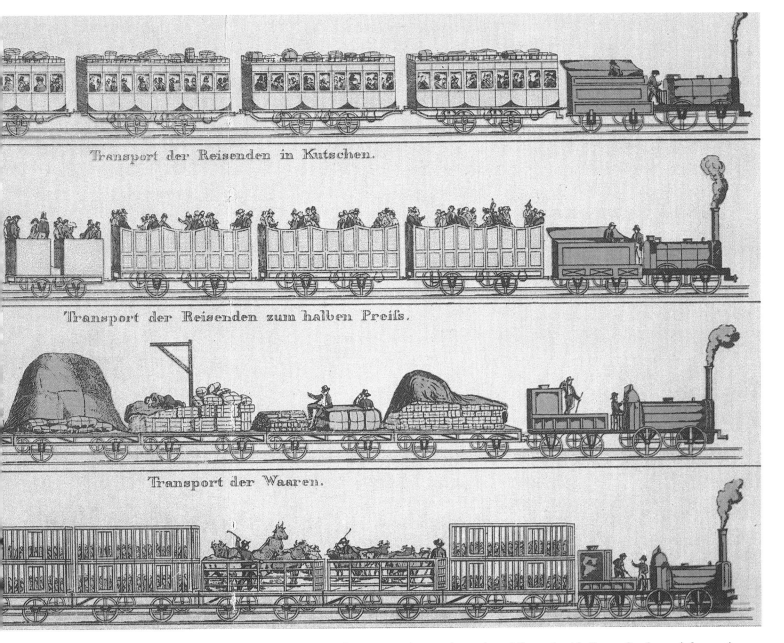

Transport der Reisenden in Kutschen.

Transport der Reisenden zum halben Preifs.

Transport der Waaren.

A contemporary etching of the Manchester-Liverpool railway line transporting people, goods and livestock with George Stephenson's locomotive.

Trans-Siberian was all but complete by 1898 and the crossing of Australia would not be long delayed. In contrast to the "Old World" where railways followed the cities, it was not uncommon for "New World" cities to follow the railway. In many parts of Africa, where construction commenced in earnest around the end of the nineteenth century, railways became a tool of European colonialism, their very routing giving arbitrary political boundaries a semblance of reality. By c. 1880, Europe and North America had effectively finished building main lines. The later stages of construction focused more on narrow-gauge light railways, reaching into less accessible parts of the country. In addition, the application of the railway was extended. Development of specialized adhesion systems and such engineering improvements as jackshaft drive facilitated the production of small locomotives for the logging roads of North America, and for sugar and other plantations in countries as far apart as Paraguay and Indonesia.

METROPOLITAN TRANSPORT

IIn metropolitan areas of Europe and North America, passenger transport soon became a greater priority than haulage of goods. In London, metropolitan lines had already appeared as early as 1863, using cut-and-cover techniques to run below street level. The following decade saw elevated railways appear in New York and in other American cities. In many towns of size, suburban tramways were laid alongside public roads. All of these strategies posed challenges to locomotive designers, as steam was still the only available motive power. However, at the Berlin Trades Exhibition of 1879, Werner von Siemens demonstrated an experimental electric locomotive. London acquired its first electric underground railway in 1890; Paris and Berlin had followed by the turn of the century. Electric street tramways had by this time made an appearance. What one might with some justification call the first phase of a transport revolution, that concerned with public systems, was (for most of the world) already over.

A.M

5000	2000	1000	500	AD1	400	600

Bismarck and German Unification

Napoleon, the very embodiment of the strong state, destroyed the old Germany. In his wake, Prussia modernized quickly, creating an efficient and meritocratic bureaucracy and an outstanding educational system, both civil and military. Through the Zollverein, a customs union based on Prussia but including most of Germany except Austria, it anticipated unification. This came in 1871, accomplished by Bismarck, the Prussian chancellor. In the 1860s, he engineered wars against Denmark, Austria, and France in turn, winning them all. The victory over France made Prussia irresistibly strong in Germany, ensuring unification under her aegis. But Bismarck's concern, in Prussia and Germany alike, was to maintain the social and political influence of the landed aristocracy. He succeeded, disappointing liberals who had looked to Prussia for leadership in the new Germany. The German empire, now the most powerful state in Europe, was led not by modernizers but by a reactionary elite.

A contemporary portrait of Otto von Bismarck.

Scramble for Empire

In 1880, little more was known of Africa than in 1680. The Ottomans controlled most of the Mediterranean shore apart from French Algeria; there were traditional trading contacts along other coasts; the Portuguese had colonies in Angola and Mozambique; the British and the Boers were in the Cape Colony; Ethiopia was remote and independent. The rest of the vast continent was unknown and unexplored. Yet on the eve of the First World War, thirty-four years later, only Ethiopia remained in African control. Britain, France, Belgium, Germany, Italy, Spain and Portugal had colonized the rest. The scramble had been started unwittingly by the Scottish missionary David Livingstone, who had appealed to the conscience of Christian Europe to end African slavery. At a conference in Berlin in 1885, the European powers agreed to partition the continent between them. Instead of missionaries, Africa got hard-eyed opportunists bent on glory and enrichment.

The ivory stocks of the Arab chieftain Tippu-Tip at Stanley Falls. It was wealth like this that set off the European "scramble for Africa."

India: the Sepoy Mutiny

In 1857, soldiers of Britain's Indian army, called *sepoys*, mutinied. The remote causes included British failure to respect traditional distinctions of religion and caste. The proximate cause was the issue of new rifle cartridges with greased ends. It was rumored that the grease was animal fat, and since the ends had to be bitten off, this was potentially offensive to Hindus—who feared it might be cow fat—and Muslims who feared it might be pork fat. The sepoys, who vastly outnumbered their officers, captured Delhi and Cawnpore and besieged Lucknow. Many atrocities were committed: they were answered in kind once the British restored order in 1858. It was not a national rising, being confined to north-central India, but nevertheless it is sometimes referred to as the first national war of independence. It resulted in the administration of India being transferred from the East India Company to the Crown.

After the mutiny, British reprisals were pitiless. These ex-soldiers were tied to artillery pieces and blown to atoms.

End of the Shoguns

In 1853 Commodore Matthew Perry of the US Navy sailed into Tokyo Bay with a squadron of ships. He was not the first overseas visitor to Japan—the ban on foreigners had been repealed as long ago as 1720—but he was the most significant. He concluded a trade treaty with the Japanese. It was agreed to exchange ambassadors. Soon Japanese trade missions were visiting Europe. In 1867, the last shogun resigned: the emperor regained personal power. He abolished feudalism and began a rapid program of modernization in education, industry and the military. Japan modernized by borrowing ideas from Europe and America lest it fall victim to imperial conquest. It succeeded so well that it developed its own empire instead. The war with China in 1894-5, fought over expansion in Korea, was easily won. Ten years later, the defeat of Russia announced Japan's arrival as a great regional power.

A contemporary Japanese woodcut of a Japanese attack on Ping-Yang in Shanxi Province, China, during the Sino-Japanese War.

| 800 | 1000 | 1200 | 1400 | 1600 | 1800 | 2000 |

- **1850** Taiping rebellion in China (-1864) major challenge to Manchu dynasty.

- **1850** Foundation of University of Sydney, Australia's first.

- **1852** Establishment of French Second Empire under Napoleon III (-1870).

- **1853** US Navy anchors in Tokyo Bay, to negotiate trade treaty with Japan.

- **1854** Crimean War (-1856), in which Anglo-French forces defeated Russia.

- **1856** David Livingstone completes crossing of the African continent.

- **1857** Indian Army Mutiny.

- **1860** Italian Risorgimento: Garibaldi's Redshirts invade the south.

- **1861** Proclamation of the Kingdom of Italy.

- **1861** Emancipation Edict of Tsar Alexander II liberates Russia's serfs.

- **1861** Outbreak of American civil war (-1865).

- **1863** Emancipation Proclamation ends slavery in the United States.

- **1863** Second Polish Revolution (-1864) suppressed with great brutality by Russians.

- **1865** Assassination of Abraham Lincoln.

- **1865** War between Paraguay and Brazil, Argentina, and Uruguay (-1870).

- **1867** Following defeat by Prussia, Hapsburg empire becomes Austro-Hungarian empire.

- **1867** Formation of Dominion of Canada.

- **1868** Rama V ascends throne of Siam at sixteen; founder of the modern Thai nation (r. -1910).

- **1869** Opening of the Suez Canal.

- **1870** Rome becomes capital of Italy to complete unification process.

- **1870** Franco-Prussian War.

- **1870** Establishment of French Third Republic (-1939).

- **1871** Germany united under imperial rule of Prussian royal house; Bismarck chancellor.

- **1871** Feudalism abolished in Japan.

- **1873** Establishment of the Spanish First Republic.

- **1876** Porfirio Diaz dictator of Mexico (-1911).

- **1876** Little Big Horn: General Custer's 7th US Cavalry annihilated by Sioux-Cheyenne forces.

- **1878** Congress of Berlin provided basis of Balkan settlement until 1914.

- **1881** Assassination of Tsar Alexander III.

- **1884** Establishment of French empire in Indo-China.

- **1885** Foundation of Indian National Congress.

- **1886** Upper Burma seized by Britain.

- **1888** Kaiser Wilhelm II emperor of Germany (-1918).

- **1889** Promulgation of first Japanese constitution.

- **1894** Arrest of Capt. Alfred Dreyfus on false charges of espionage.

- **1895** Defeated in Sino-Japanese War, China forced to accept independence of Korea.

- **1898** Outbreak of Boer War (-1902) between Britain and the Boers of South Africa.

- **1898** Spanish-American War marks the emergence of the United States on the world stage.

American Civil War

The civil war was fought on the issue of states' rights versus those of the federal government. This larger issue focused on the question of slavery, the South's "peculiar institution." The election to the presidency of the anti-slavery candidate Abraham Lincoln in 1860 provoked the secession of eleven southern states which formed a Confederacy. This action led to war. There were two main theaters: in Virginia and along the Mississippi. The civil war was therefore fought in the Confederacy. The South's early successes were reversed first at Shiloh and Antietam (1862) and crucially at Gettysburg (1863). In 1863, Lincoln abolished slavery. The end-game was a bloody Union progress through the Confederacy, resulting in a wholesale destruction of life and property. More Americans died in the civil war than in both world wars combined. Afterwards, the North enjoyed an unprecedented economic boom; the South faced a century of sullen stagnation.

Lincoln in City Point, *a contemporary allegorical depiction of Lincoln freeing the slaves.*

5000	2000	1000	500	AD1	400	600

Woodblock printing became a characteristic Japanese art in the eighteenth and nineteenth centuries. This print depicts a wealthy European gentleman with his Japanese wife, who is wearing European fashions.

The Meiji Restoration

In the nineteenth century, European and American traders sought to ease Chinese trade restrictions and to open Japanese ports, and their governments were prepared to use their superior naval technology to accomplish this. In Japan, although resistance was initially greater, eventually the transition to a modern state was easier. Even during the years of isolation, there was some curiosity about "western" science: in 1811, the shogunate had established an office to translate foreign books. By 1857 this had become a school of science and languages known as the Institute for the Investigation of Barbarian Books. As the Tokugawa shogunate crumbled, internal revolution eventually resulted in the Meiji Restoration in 1868 when the fourteen-year-old Emperor Mutsuhito became an important symbol of modern Japan, a country which sought knowledge "throughout the world so as to strengthen the foundations of imperial rule," as the new Charter Oath put it. This included scientific fields previously unknown in Japan. In 1877 Edward S. Morse, who taught zoology at Tokyo University, gave the first lecture in Japan on Darwinian theory, noting in his journal that the audience was apparently "keenly interested" and also that it was a pleasure to lecture to a group free of "theological prejudice."

The Independent Kingdom of Siam

Thailand (Siam) alone among Southeast Asian countries maintained its independence throughout the period of European colonization. This was due to skillful diplomacy and a genuine interest in European science and technology by a series of strong Thai rulers. Avoiding the pitfalls of the region's traditional ethnic and religious conflicts, which led directly to the French protectorate over Cambodia and the British annexation of Burma, the Thai Buddhist kings took the initiative in opening relations with Europe and America early in the nineteenth century, and had concluded important trade treaties with Britain, the United States, France, and other countries by about the middle of the century. These were the work of Rama IV (King Mongkut), who had studied western governments as a Buddhist monk before becoming king. His policies were continued by his son Rama V (King Chulalongkorn), who came to the throne in 1868 and ruled until 1910. Rama V abolished the remnants of the feudal system and slavery in Thailand, established centralized administration, reformed the tax system, and started a postal service. His interest in technology as well as political science led to the introduction of the telegraph (1883) and the opening of the first railway (1893) in Thailand.

The King and Queen of Siam adorn the cover of a French journal. Rama V (r. 1868-1910) extensively modernized his country, with administrative reforms, the establishment of postal and telegraph services, and the first railway.

Popular Arts During and After the Civil War

The ethical dilemmas of slavery found expression in popular arts and literature as well as in political speeches. *Uncle Tom's Cabin*, a fictionalized treatment of slavery published by Harriet Beecher Stowe in 1852, was so popular that it is sometimes reckoned as one of the causes of the Civil War. Narratives by freed or escaped slaves were also published and recited in public. Frederick Douglass became such a remarkable orator for the cause of abolition that some doubted his slave background, which, in turn, inspired him to write his autobiography. Other arts developed with the Civil War: the battlefield and camp photographs taken by Matthew Brady and his team revealed the experience of war in an entirely new,

| 800 | 1000 | 1200 | 1400 | 1600 | 1800 | 2000 |

The vast scope of the American landscape captured artistic imaginations as Americans continued to expand westwards. This chalk lithograph from 1866 shows the Rocky Mountains towering over a wagon train of emigrants.

brutal, and intimate fashion. One of Brady's photographers, Timothy H. O'Sullivan, later went to work for the US Geographic Survey, documenting the vast landscapes of the still incompletely charted West. As Americans continued to push westwards, such landscapes also became the subject of painters, giving rise to a new American genre. Native Americans, too, captured the imagination of artists and photographers even as native homelands were threatened.

African Jihads

 Jihads or "holy wars" in West Africa were primarily aimed at establishing a purified Islam and were directed against rulers considered insufficiently Islamic and too tolerant of animism. Shehu Usman dan Fodio initiated a Fulani jihad against the Hausa states in northern Nigeria and established a Fulani empire by 1812. Al-Hajj Umar's jihad of 1852 coincided with French penetration of Senegal and brought him into conflict with the colonial power when he attacked the French at Bakel in 1855 and Madine in 1857. Conflict with the French continued intermittently until Umar's son was finally defeated in 1893. Yet the most famous African jihad is that of Mohammed Ahmad who saw visions in 1881 telling him he was to be *Mahdi*, a "messiah" of the whole Islamic world. At that time Egypt, with the help of British officials, was attempting to control the Sudan. The Mahdi's call for a jihad was received favorably and by 1882 he had a well-organized army in the province of Kordofan. British advisers to the khedive saw that it would be impossible to hold on to the Sudan, and in 1884 General Gordon was sent to Khartoum to organize the evacuation of Egyptian troops. Before military support could arrive he was overwhelmed by the Mahdi's forces and killed, much to the horror of the general public in Victorian England.

General Gordon, whose death in 1885 in the Sudan made him a notable victim of the Mahdi's Muslim "holy war."

The French novelist Émile Zola in his study, painted by the Impressionist Edouard Manet.

Social Reform

The railway, a product of the Industrial Revolution, became a major agent of social change. By 1850 most European cities were linked by rail, facilitating transport of goods and mobility of persons. People could live further from their workplace and commute. Holidays had become popular and seaside towns developed particularly in northern Europe, from Brighton in England to Sopot in Poland. From *c.* 1850, social reform, especially in Britain and Germany, began gradually to improve housing, public amenities and working conditions. Demand for radical change, mounting in eastern Europe, may have been softened in the west but social difficulties increased, especially those arising from urbanization, and concerns arising therefrom found expression in art and literature. The novels of Émile Zola, published between 1871 and 1893, typify the French school of naturalism, with their rather deterministic representation of man trapped in circumstances beyond his control. Northern European dramatists, including the Norwegian Ibsen (d. 1906) and the Swede Strindberg (d. 1912) were radical in addressing previously taboo social issues of *fin de siècle* urbanism such as public corruption, women's emancipation, and marital breakdown.

5000	2000	1000	500	AD1	400	600

1900 Boxer uprising in China suppressed with foreign help.

1901 Establishment of Commonwealth of Australia, ending system of autonomous colonies.

1901 Ancient Ashanti kingdom annexed by Britain, attached to its Gold Coast colony.

1903 United States recognizes the independence of Panama from Colombia.

1903 First ever airplane flight by Wright Brothers at Kitty Hawk, North Carolina.

1904 Russian-Japanese War (-1905) results in stunning Japanese victory.

1905 Norwegian independence from Sweden.

1905 Workers' revolt in Russia crushed after year-long disturbances.

1907 New Zealand given dominion status within British Empire.

1908 Austria-Hungary annexes Bosnia-Herzegovina.

1910 Insurrection in Lisbon; king flees abroad; declaration of Portuguese republic.

1910 Union of South Africa comes into being.

1910 Japan annexes Korea.

1911 Overthrow of Porfirio Diaz in Mexico; many years of revolution and disorder.

1911 Manchu dynasty ends as boy emperor abdicates; proclamation of Chinese republic.

1912 First Balkan War between Bulgaria, Serbia, and Greece against Turkey, which loses territory.

1912 Second Balkan War: Bulgaria attacks Serbs and Greeks but is repulsed.

1914 Opening of the Panama Canal.

1914 Assassination of Archduke Franz Ferdinand of Austria-Hungary in Sarajevo.

1914 Outbreak of the First World War (-1918).

1916 Easter Rising in Dublin begins process that leads to Irish independence.

1917 United States enters the war.

1917 Bolshevik Revolution in Russia brings Lenin to power.

1917 Balfour Declaration states British government support for Jewish homeland in Palestine.

1918 Defeat of Central Powers in First World War; collapse of German, Austro-Hungarian, and Turkish empires.

1918 Czechoslovakia declares its independence. Establishment of Yugoslavia.

1918 Civil war in Russia (-1920) ends in Bolshevik victory.

1919 Treaty of Versailles agrees post-war settlement and establishes League of Nations.

1919 Germany adopts the constitution of the Weimar republic.

1919 The Volstead Act inaugurates the prohibition era in the United States (-1933).

1919 Amritsar massacre in which British Gurkha troops kill 379 civilians.

1921 Anglo-Irish treaty establishes effective independence of most of Ireland, following partition.

1922 Mussolini and his *fascisti* march on Rome and seize power.

1922 Egypt achieves sham independence: British retain ultimate control.

1923 Occupation of the Ruhr by Franco-Belgian troops.

1923 Munich Beer Hall putsch: Hitler attempts to overthrow the Bavarian government.

1923 Spanish military coup brings General Primo de Rivera to power (-1930).

1923 Turkish republic declared under presidency of Mustapha Kemal.

1923 Transjordan, formerly part of the Ottoman empire, an independent state.

1924 Death of Lenin ends first phase of the Communist era in Russia.

1924 Indian leader Gandhi released from prison on health grounds.

Theodore Roosevelt

 The Spanish-American war of 1898 made the United States an imperial power. It gained the Philippines, Puerto Rico and Cuba from Spain. Theodore Roosevelt, at that time Assistant Secretary of the Navy, raised a volunteer cavalry troop known as the Rough Riders whose Cuban exploits gained him a national reputation. In 1900, he won the vice-presidency and in 1901 found himself president following McKinley's assassination. Roosevelt greatly expanded the role of the United States in international diplomacy, moderating its traditional isolationism. He expanded the armed forces, especially the navy. His corollary to the Monroe Doctrine facilitated active US intervention in Haiti and the Dominican Republic. He provided the political will to build and control the Panama Canal. He also negotiated the end of the Russo-Japanese war, for which he won the Nobel Peace Prize, and helped to defuse the Morocco crisis of 1906. Roosevelt made America a significant international force.

Theodore Roosevelt

Union of South Africa

Ever since the Great Trek, there had been periodic tensions between the British authorities in South Africa and the Afrikaners. In the 1850s, the British had recognized the autonomy of the Orange Free State and the South African Republic beyond the Vaal. The discovery of gold and diamonds in the Transvaal caused relations to sour: the Afrikaners or Boers taxed the mining companies heavily and discriminated against immigrant workers. The resultant tensions sparked the Boer War (1899-1902). The Boers fought pluckily but lost. Transvaal and the Free State were briefly ruled as crown colonies, but self-government was restored in 1906. In 1910, Britain created the Union of South Africa as a dominion within the empire, comprising Transvaal, the Orange Free State, Natal and the Cape Colony. The tensions between Boers and non-Boers were not resolved but the Union survived until the declaration of a republic by the apartheid regime in 1961.

The English forcing Boer general Pieter Cronje to surrender at Paardeberg, 1900. The Boers were governing themselves again by 1906.

Balfour Declaration

On 11 December 1917, General Edmund Allenby led his British troops into Jerusalem, succeeding where Richard the Lionheart had failed more than seven hundred years earlier. Two days earlier, the Turkish army had slipped away. But just five weeks before this dramatic event, the British Foreign Secretary, Arthur Balfour, had said in a letter to Lord Rothschild that the British government "view[s] with favor the establishment in Palestine of a national home for the Jewish people … it being clearly understood that nothing will be done which may prejudice the civil and religious rights of existing non-Jewish communities." On taking up the mandate to administer Palestine after the war, Britain attempted to act on the declaration by encouraging Jewish settlement. But the twin contradictions were not—could not be—reconciled. The Balfour Declaration was, however, an important signpost on the road to a Jewish state in Palestine.

The Last Emperor

Attempts around the turn of the century to introduce reforms into China along Japanese lines had led to a reactionary movement called the Boxers, who attacked foreigners and missionaries. In 1900, an international expeditionary force was sent to Peking (Beijing) to quell the Boxer rebellion. The Boxers had had encouragement from close to the imperial throne, especially from the dowager empress, Tz'u-hsi, who had been the effective ruler of the country for over thirty years. In 1905, limited reforms were proposed but it was too little, too late. In 1911 rebellion broke out and spread, being harnessed by republican revolutionary groups under the leadership of the western-educated Sun Yat-sen. The imperial army should have been able to crush the rebels but its leader, General Yuan, suddenly offered to defect in return for the presidency of the Chinese republic. The boy emperor P'u-I, the last of the Manchus and the last of all the emperors, abdicated.

The Dowager Empress Tz'u-hsi, a painting based on a photograph of 1903.

The Great War

Apart from the crucial involvement of the Americans after April 1917, the First World War of 1914-18 was an almost wholly European affair. Following early reverses, the entente powers—France, Britain and Italy—gained the upper hand on the western front in 1917-18. Germany's defeat destroyed its empire and those of its two principal allies, Austria-Hungary and Turkey. Russia, an entente ally, lost on the eastern front. Its empire also collapsed, to be replaced by the Bolsheviks. The victors, France and Britain, were exhausted – especially the French, on whose land the western front lay. Verdun, the bloodiest battle of the war, cost 650,000 lives. Over 310,000 died at the Somme. In all, nine million died. They were victims of an industrial military technology which delivered enormous firepower but little mobility: the tank and the airplane were in their infancy, so that much of the war was an attritional slaughter.

Battle of Cambrai, on the western front, November 1917: British machine-gunners in a captured trench.

Tin Lizzies and Flappers

Technological innovations continued to change American lives. By 1900, the telephone, the incandescent lamp, and the phonograph were increasingly common. In 1903, the Wright brothers performed their brief but historic airplane flight at Kitty Hawk. In 1908, Henry Ford (1863-1947) began manufacturing the ungainly but practical and affordable Model T, affectionately called the "Tin Lizzie." By 1919 half the cars in the world were Model Ts. Ford pioneered the moving assembly line, which attracted international attention. Nineteenth-century experiments in photography led to the "moving picture" and the storefront nickelodeon, where a customer could see a collection of short films for a nickel. D.W. Griffith inaugurated the feature film with his three-hour Civil War epic, *The Birth of a Nation*, in 1915. The first film studios were established in the obscure town of Hollywood, and by 1918, America's two favorite stars, Mary Pickford and Charlie Chaplin, each signed million-dollar contracts. In the 1920s, jazz music, with its early roots in black spirituals and slave songs, began to become widely popular. The "Jazz Age" was epitomized by the flapper with bobbed hair and short skirt in the early works of F. Scott Fitzgerald, and not at all inhibited by the establishment of Prohibition in 1920.

The film star Mary Pickford was known as "America's Sweetheart."

The Rise of the Afrikaans Language

Although Afrikaans was the spoken language of Afrikaners in South Africa during the nineteenth century, it was seldom written before a group led by S.J. de Toit launched the First Afrikaans Movement in 1875. Use of Afrikaans as a symbol of national identity intensified after the Boers' defeat by the British in 1902 and the latter's attempts to anglicize the former republics. In reaction a movement for national education established schools teaching in Afrikaans. Afrikaans was ignored by the Act of the Union of 1909 but was acknowledged by the Provincial Councils in 1914, which led to its introduction into state schools. The second Afrikaans Movement was largely fueled by the strong sense of nationalism manifested by many Afrikaners on the outbreak of the First World War. It produced authors of distinction such as Totius, Cellier and Langeshoven, one of whose poems later became the anthem of the republic. In 1917 Afrikaans was allowed to be used in services of the Dutch Reformed Church, although a translation of the Bible did not occur until 1933. Afrikaans finally received full recognition as a state language when the Nationalist government decided it should replace Dutch for all official purposes in 1925.

The Afrikaans Monument, built to commemorate the establishment of the Boer language, Paarl, South Africa.

Technology and Conflict

 The continuation of the French *Belle Époque*, grounded in the previous decade's naturalistic and Impressionist aesthetic movements, into the 1900s fostered an image of this as a halcyon period for Europe, with the continued popularity of artists like Renoir, writers such as Maupassant and composers of the caliber of Bizet, Strauss and Dvořák. Meanwhile, technological development accelerated, with the internal combustion engine helping wealthy citizens to "discover" motoring, and electricity bringing lights and tramcars into most European cities by *c.* 1910. Dramatic advances in science included the discovery of radioactivity by Poland's Marie Sklodowska and her French husband Pierre Curie, and the formulation of the theory of relativity (1905) by the German Albert Einstein. Glorification of technology inspired a new movement in the arts, for which the Italian poet Marinetti (d. 1944) coined the term Futurism. Its exponents, including Marinetti himself, the Italian painter Boccioni and Russian poet-dramatist Mayakovsky, often graduated from praise of mechanization to praise of warfare—several prominent futurists became involved in the Fascist or Bolshevik movements.

Marie Sklodowska-Curie in her laboratory, the Nobel prize winner for physics in 1911.

A European cartoon of Russia, Britain, Japan, France, and Germany clawing pieces of China.

China in Crisis

 Internal revolts, a troubling dependence on foreign opium, defeat in war, and an increasing European presence in the region led to unprecedented crisis in China in this period. Internal and external demands for change brought varying responses. The Boxer Rebellion of 1900 was led by a group of young men who sought a return to traditional values. Steeped in ritual practice of the martial arts ("boxing"), members of the secret "Society of Harmonious Fists" believed that through Taoist sorcery and magical incantations they could become impervious to the bullets of the foreign enemies—both Europeans and (initially) the Manchu emperors—whom they sought to expel. A different solution was proposed by some Chinese educators, who sought to reform the traditional education system and incorporate western learning. The author Lin Shu popularized Chinese versions of the works of Dickens, Dumas, Scott, Balzac, and others from oral translations. Yen Fu, who traveled the world as a member of the Chinese navy, produced literate translations of and commentaries upon those European authors whose liberal principles he felt would be useful in China, such as Adam Smith, John Stuart Mill, and Montesquieu. These aims failed; in 1911 the boy emperor abdicated, and China fell into warlordism that lasted until 1928.

The Father of the Turks

Many goals of the Young Turks who attempted to reform the ailing Ottoman Empire in 1908 were ultimately achieved by Mustafa Kemal, who became the first president of the newly proclaimed Turkish Republic in 1923. Believing in western democratic principles and science, Kemal undertook an ambitious reform program intended to bring an ancient state into the twentieth century. He established religious tolerance, and separated the education and court systems from Islamic control, demanding instead "modern scientific civil codes." Kemal also initiated the creation of a new alphabet using Roman characters instead of Arabic script, which he felt was inadequate to express modern ideas. When he had himself mastered these characters, Kemal traveled throughout Turkey with a blackboard, demonstrating the proper formation of the new letters to his audiences. Kemal also encouraged both men and women to wear western clothing, a startling innovation in a culture which traditionally demanded that women be veiled and covered from head to toe. He built schools for girls, and opened the professional world to women. He also granted women the vote, first locally (1929), and then nationally (1934). Kemal is the founder of modern Turkey, reflected in the name by which he is widely known: "Atatürk"—"Father of the Turks."

Mustafa Kemal, Turkey's first president.

IDEOLOGY AND CONFLICT

If Social Democracy is opposed by a doctrine of greater truth, but equal brutality of methods, the latter will conquer though this may require the bitterest struggle.

Adolf Hitler, *Mein Kampf*

It is to a degree ironic that Communism and Fascism, viewed as opposite poles of the political spectrum, should share certain common features. Diametrically opposed in ideological terms, as systems of government both are totalitarian in character and result in single-party states. Compliance from the population at large is usually achieved through a combination of repression and propaganda. In both systems, parades and mass rallies are among the mechanisms used to generate and maintain popular support.

THE EMERGENCE OF COMMUNISM

Following the October Revolution of 1917, a Communist government under Vladimir Ilyich Lenin extended its authority over the former Russian empire. Compared with right-wing doctrines, Communism, a revolutionary form of socialism, had a firmer ideological basis. Rooted in the teachings of Karl Marx, Russian Communism stressed the necessity of state control of all industry and commerce. Condemning private ownership of the means of production, it attacked the bourgeoisie (capitalist middle class). Communism's revolutionary character was reflected in an aspiration to overthrow the existing order through class struggle which, because doctrinaire Marxism assumed consistency of class attitudes and was historically deterministic, would "inevitably" lead to victory of the proletariat (working class). Through Marxist influence, Communism also rejected religion. The message appealed particularly to urban working classes and in Russia, which had seen little social reform, distribution of wealth up to the 1920s was more uneven than in the west. Moreover, Communism was "international," reaching out to workers worldwide. Western concern,

therefore, was fired less by the revolution which created the Soviet Union than by the rapid westward spread of Communism. Soon local Communist organizations had emerged, achieving public office or staging revolts in Finland (a former Russian province), Hungary, Bulgaria, Yugoslavia, Czechoslovakia, Germany and Italy. Communist parties were also formed in Spain, France and Britain, even if these exercised little influence. The movement also spread into Asia, with the formation of a Chinese Communist party in 1921.

THE EMERGENCE OF FASCISM

A right-wing movement, which sometimes exhibited traits of national socialism (as opposed to social democracy), Fascism demanded subordination to the state which in turn had direct involvement in the economy. State industries and social schemes were a feature of Fascism, but the system backed the concept of private property and capitalist forces were expressly courted. There was no particular class focus and religion was in principle upheld. Lacking a clear ideology, although the German Nazi Party sought philosophical justification, Fascism was largely a reaction against Communism. Certain conservative elements had long scorned social democracy, claiming that it was detrimental to the national economy. Then, in the aftermath of the Great War, left-wing revolts and widespread clamor for socialism caused panic, especially in Germany and Italy. Both countries had experienced defeat, disillusionment, economic crisis and an apparent failure of parliamentary democracy. Now, the "Red Flag" threatened. In Italy, local soviets were formed in 1919 and disturbances ensued,

with a particularly paralyzing strike in 1922. This apparent westward spread of Communism prompted right-wing reaction. That year, Mussolini and his Fascist Party orchestrated their "March on Rome." The attitude of King Victor Emmanuel II, who apparently viewed Mussolini's actions as patriotic, was crucial to Fascism's early success in Italy. In Germany, Hitler faced a longer struggle for acceptance after the ignominious failure of a coup in 1923. It took the Wall Street Crash and a complete collapse of the German economy for the second time since the Great War to secure Nazi support. Given the "international" character of Communism, it is not surprising that Fascism should have cultivated a chauvinistic form of nationalism. In Germany, Hitler took this further, adopting racial superiority theories then current in certain schools of social science. Although directed against various minorities, this racism particularly took the form of anti-Semitism. Far from being confined to Germany, anti-Semitism was quite widespread in Europe, owing more to xenophobia and resentment of Jewish economic prosperity than to religion. However, a more visible Jewish presence due to recent immigration, and revival of traditional fears, made it easier to fan the embers of anti-Semitism in Germany. The Nazis realized that internal unity could profit from direction of energies against perceived external threats, and Hitler's irrational equation of Jews with Communists did much to ensure their victimization. Clearly, the nightmare of persecution and genocide that followed was facilitated by widespread support for Nazi ideals across the continent. Notwithstanding Nazi exploitation of anti-Semitism, however, hatred of Jews was not essential to

A militaristic Nazi poster of the 1930s featuring the stern, determined face of Adolf Hitler. It carries the message "Long Live Germany."

Fascism as such. As a bulwark against Communism, Fascism was deemed quite respectable in many European and South American countries, including Argentina and Brazil. Chauvinistic nationalism fostered by Fascism undoubtedly contributed to the outbreak of the Second World War. At that stage, however, support among right-wing states for the war effort of the Axis powers (German-Italian alliance) varied; encouraged by its Fascist movement, Finland joined the invasion of Russia for its own reasons. In Norway and Romania, Fascist governments supported the Nazis, having been brought to power by Hitler. Other Fascist-style governments included Portugal and Spain, which had come to power in the context of anti-Communist struggle, and remained neutral throughout the war. In Brazil, the Fascist-style government of Vargas declared war on the Axis powers in 1942. Significantly, these last three governments survived the war. Meanwhile, the Soviet Union seemed to have emerged as the net beneficiary of Fascist defeat. Western fears of Communist expansion, far from being allayed, became intensified, only now they found a new form of expression. With the United States having emerged from isolation to become involved in European affairs, the stage was set for the ideological conflict of the Cold War.

A.M

5000	2000	1000	500	AD1	400	600

- 1925 Reza Khan proclaimed Shah of Persia, founder of Pahlavi dynasty (-1979).

- 1925 Treaty of Locarno attempts to settle post-war boundary disputes in Europe.

- 1926 Stalin comes to power in Russia (-1953).

- 1926 Foundation of the kingdom of Saudi Arabia.

- 1927 Abolition of slavery in Sierra Leone.

- 1927 Canberra new federal capital of Australia.

- 1928 Salazar finance minister in Portugal, later premier and effectively dictator (-1968).

- 1929 Vatican City established as independent state.

- 1929 Wall Street crash inaugurates world economic depression.

- 1931 King Alfonso XIII flees Spain; declaration of the Second Spanish republic.

- 1931 Japanese occupation of Manchuria; establishment of puppet state.

- 1932 Chaco war between Paraguay and Bolivia (-1935).

- 1933 Hitler comes to power in Germany.

- 1934 Long march of the Chinese Communists (-1935).

- 1935 Beginning of Stalinist show trials in Russia.

- 1936 Germany re-occupies the Rhineland in defiance of the Versailles treaty.

- 1936 Italy invades and conquers Ethiopia (Abyssinia).

- 1936 Spanish Civil War (-1939) in which Franco's Nationalists defeat Republicans.

- 1937 Sino-Japanese War (-1945).

- 1938 Munich crisis: Britain and France capitulate to German demands over Czechoslovakia.

- 1938 Anschluss (union) of Germany and Austria; Hitler returns in triumph to Vienna.

- 1939 Germany invades Poland: start of the Second World War.

- 1940 Fall of France and Battle of Britain.

- 1941 Germany attacks Russia.

- 1941 Pearl Harbor: Japan and the United States now at war.

- 1942 Stalingrad: Germans suffer shattering defeat in Russia.

- 1942 Singapore falls to the Japanese, who also overrun Indo-China.

- 1944 D-Day: Allied landings in Normandy.

- 1945 Allied victory in Europe; death of Hitler and destruction of German Third Reich.

- 1945 American victory in Asia: first atomic bombs dropped on Hiroshima and Nagasaki force Japanese capitulation.

- 1945 San Francisco conference leads to formation of the United Nations.

- 1945 Potsdam conference effectively divides Europe into western and Russian spheres.

- 1946 Juan Peron comes to power in Argentina (-1955).

- 1947 End of British Raj: India and Pakistan separate and establish independent states.

- 1947 Marshall Plan for the economic renewal of Western Europe.

- 1948 Burma achieves independence.

- 1948 Establishment of the state of Israel; first Arab-Israeli war.

- 1948 Nationalists win election in South Africa; start of apartheid era.

- 1948 Assassination of Gandhi, India.

- 1949 Foundation of NATO.

- 1949 Communists proclaim People's Republic of China under Mao Zedong.

Russia's Great Patriotic War

In June 1941—with Germany triumphant in the west, except for Britain—Hitler invaded the Soviet Union. German armies swept east to the Volga, with Stalin frantically retreating as his country was cut in two. Ukrainians and others welcomed the Germans as liberators. The advance faltered before Leningrad, which survived a horrific siege of over 900 days in which one and a quarter million died. In the south the tide was finally turned at Stalingrad in February 1943 when the German Sixth Army surrendered. This had been the biggest and most decisive battle of the war on any front. The Germans lost 300,000 men. The city was flattened. Thereafter, the Soviets' counter-offensive carried them westward to meet the advancing Anglo-American troops who had landed in Normandy in June 1944. By April 1945, the Russians were in Berlin, the Third Reich was destroyed and the shape of Cold War Europe was visible.

The Soviet flag flies over the Reichstag's ruins, Berlin, May 1945, signaling the end of the Second World War in Europe.

| 800 | 1000 | 1200 | 1400 | 1600 | 1800 | 2000 |

Communist China

The Chinese Communist Party was founded in 1921. Mao Zedong was a founder member. The Kuomintang, or Nationalist Party, under the energetic leadership of Chiang Kai-shek, ended the post-imperial chaos and controlled the government by 1928. Chiang purged Communists from the party. They retreated to the countryside where they mobilized a peasant army. In 1934, when Nationalist troops destroyed their base in Jiangxi, they made the celebrated Long March of over 5,000 miles to safety in Shanxi. Chiang still faced problems from warlords in the more remote provinces, which were compounded by the devastating Japanese invasion of Manchuria and northern China in 1937. A Nationalist-Communist alliance was formed to face the Japanese threat, but their mutual hostility resumed in 1945. Another civil war followed, which the Communists won. Chiang was banished from the Chinese mainland and in 1949 the People's Republic of China was proclaimed, with Mao at its head.

Mao Zedong with Lin Biao in Tienanmen Square, Beijing, celebrating the twentieth anniversary of the People's Republic of China, 1969.

Indian Independence and Partition

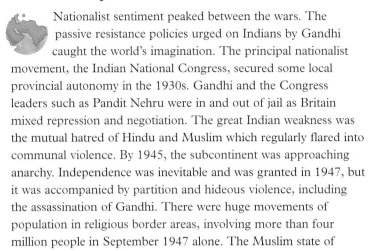

Nationalist sentiment peaked between the wars. The passive resistance policies urged on Indians by Gandhi caught the world's imagination. The principal nationalist movement, the Indian National Congress, secured some local provincial autonomy in the 1930s. Gandhi and the Congress leaders such as Pandit Nehru were in and out of jail as Britain mixed repression and negotiation. The great Indian weakness was the mutual hatred of Hindu and Muslim which regularly flared into communal violence. By 1945, the subcontinent was approaching anarchy. Independence was inevitable and was granted in 1947, but it was accompanied by partition and hideous violence, including the assassination of Gandhi. There were huge movements of population in religious border areas, involving more than four million people in September 1947 alone. The Muslim state of Pakistan, under Mohammed Ali Jinnah, was formed from the old provinces of Baluchistan, Sind and parts of the Punjab.

Lord Mountbatten (center), Pandit Nehru (white hat, left) and M. A. Jinnah (right) during partition discussions, June 1947.

Depression and New Deal

In 1929, Wall Street suffered the greatest fall in its history. Tens of thousands of investors, who had borrowed heavily to finance stock purchases, were ruined. The crash triggered an economic depression. Banks and businesses failed, mortgages were foreclosed and commodity prices plummeted. By 1932, more than 10 million were unemployed. The incoming president, Franklin Roosevelt, proposed a "new deal" to stabilize and stimulate the economy and to secure basic social reforms. Its hallmark was the active involvement of the federal government in economic activity. The Agricultural Adjustment Acts (1933, 1938) provided subsidies to farmers to curtail production in order to boost market prices. The federally funded Tennessee Valley Authority dammed the river to improve navigation, control flooding, and provide hydroelectricity. Through such public works, the New Deal broke with traditional economic orthodoxy. By involving Washington in direct social and economic management, it laid the foundations of American big government.

Shareholders following price movements on the New York stockmarket during the Wall Street Crash in October 1929.

Apartheid

In the 1948 general election, the Nationalist Party in South Africa won an overall majority for the first time. The Nationalists were the party of the Afrikaners or Boers, whose anti-British feeling was exceeded only by their racist contempt for blacks. Their policy was called *apartheid* or separate development. This was simply a polite term for the most severe racial discrimination against non-whites, the overwhelming majority of the population. There was open discrimination in employment, in public housing, in education provision and in land allocation. Interracial marriage was banned. Pass laws inhibited freedom of movement for non-whites. Apartheid was designed to produce not just white supremacy but Boer supremacy. This vicious system—much more systematic than the traditional forms of South African racism—was practiced for over forty years until its collapse.

Armed police with dogs in the black township of Soweto near Johannesburg, South Africa.

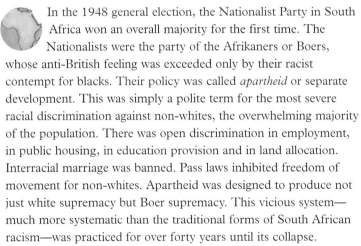

5000	2000	1000	500	AD1	400	600

Mahatma Gandhi, India's spiritual politician.

Mahatma Gandhi

The slight, bespectacled Mohandas Karamchand Gandhi was called "Mahatma," or "Great Soul" by his followers. Ghandi fostered a sense of Indian national identity as much through his personal philosophy and ethics as through his more overtly political actions. His influence as a figure of principled non-violence was profound inside and outside India. Intelligent and idealistic, Gandhi adapted his Indian heritage and English education into a unique blend of ethical pragmatism. Deeply imbued with the Jainist doctrine of *ahimsa* (non-violence), Gandhi's views were also shaped by Christianity and the ideas of the great Russian novelist Leo Tolstoy, the English critic John Ruskin, and the American social critic Henry David Thoreau. He won the affection of many Hindus by his refusal to accept the restrictions of caste and by his insistence on equality. Compassion for the impoverished led him to reject western comforts. Perhaps no action earned him more admirers in India than his sincere but strategic rejection of European dress (and, implicitly, the values of industrialized society) in 1921. Henceforward he wore the homespun loincloth and shawl of a peasant, and the image of Gandhi at his spinning-wheel became inextricably associated with the simple, ethically principled life he advocated.

His tolerance toward Muslims led to Gandhi's tragic assassination by a Hindu fanatic in 1948.

Gangsters, Talkies, and Jazz

The United States' "noble experiment" of Prohibition, which forbade the import, manufacture or sale of alcohol, had little effect on the social ills caused by drink, and instead inspired a thriving trade in bootleg liquor, managed by gangsters like "Scarface" Al Capone. Prohibition was officially repealed in 1933. Meanwhile, the Depression years influenced popular culture. President Franklin D. Roosevelt's innovative and controversial Works Progress Administration sponsored art projects, including large public murals inspired by those of Rivera, Orozco, and Siquieros in Mexico. John Steinbeck's poignant novel *The Grapes of Wrath* (1939) depicted the plight of the farmer. Many Americans escaped to the movies, which, in spite of scandals and censorship, enjoyed a "golden age." Sound, introduced in 1927, was improved, and color was incorporated in the '30s and '40s. Romantic adventures and musicals were popular, as well as "tough guy" films inspired by the novels of Dashiell Hammett and Raymond Chandler. In 1941, Orson Welles produced the film *Citizen Kane* after critically acclaimed stage work in New York, where the brooding plays of Eugene O'Neill also drew attention. Jazz music grew in popularity, featuring singers such as Ella Fitzgerald and Billie Holiday, and also developed new forms, such as swing and bebop.

Much beloved for his trademark grin (from which he earned the nickname "Satchmo," short for "Satchelmouth") as well as for his musical skills as a jazz trumpeter and singer, the American Louis Armstrong was popular in Europe as well as in his native land.

Pablo Picasso in his studio with his model Sylvette David, 1954.

African Music

Since the 1950s, African music has been influenced by technical innovations as well as by far-reaching political and social changes. Radio, the phonograph, audio cassettes and western instruments together with urbanization have all been major factors. Further experimentation and adaptation of music which originally came from Africa fused with local traditions. Thus jazz, rumba, rhythm and blues, reggae and rap have led to soukous, highlife, Afro beat, Juju, *makossa* and *mbaqanga*. The origins of current African pop also lie in these developments. *Chimurenga* music from Zimbabwe is a good example of a style produced directly by a liberation movement, while traditional elements such as praise-singing, philosophical reflections and sharp social commentary have often been retained within the new forms. Little wonder that some musicians are unpopular with governments! Notable African musicians include the pianist Dollar Brand; singers Miriam Makeba, Thomas Mapfumo; trumpeters E.T. Mensah, Hugh Masekela; saxophonists (the late) Fela Anikulapo-Kuti, Manu Dibango; guitarists Tabu Ley, Sunny Ade; reggae artists Alpha Blondy, Lucky Dube; "world music" favorites Angelique Kidjo, Youssou N'dour, Baaba Maal, Papa Wemba; bands like OK Jazz, Osibisa and cappella groups like Ladysmith Black Mambazo.

Prosperity and Disillusionment

Perhaps the experience of the Great War prompted Europe's younger generation of the 1920s to break with "established tradition." While musical composition of this period tends towards the experimental, the masses of the 20s and 30s were more taken with jazz and swing. Such American influences were easily spread through phonograph and radio, not to mention cinema, although by 1930 many European countries were developing domestic film industries, that of France receiving particular recognition. These cultural developments reflected a new prosperity; middle-class consumerism was emerging. This is further illustrated by the popularization of motor transport as mass production was adopted by car manufacturers such as Renault in France and Hanomag in Germany. Parallel to such prosperity, anxieties grew as mechanization created unemployment and Fascism caused storm clouds to gather over Europe. On a popular level, "primitive rhythm" music and "dark" cinema may reflect growing disillusionment; intellectual life was increasingly taken with a self-conscious modernism, reflected in the subjective art of Spain's Picasso (d. 1973) and in the existentialism of French thinkers Sartre (d. 1980) and Camus (d. 1960). Focus on the existence of the individual promoted a growing pessimism among Europe's intelligentsia.

Success and Devastation in Japan

Throughout the Meiji period the Japanese adapted European political and economic models with a success that eluded its former mentor, China. Victory over the Russians in a territorial war in 1904-5 had established Japan as an international presence. Joining the Allies in the First World War required little effort, and extended Japan's regional influence when they acquired former German territories. In the 1920s, mass culture evolved in Japan with the aid of the phonograph, radio, and cinema. The Japanese developed a love of baseball, and began to create distinctive films. In the thirties, however, an increasingly militant presence in the government and external pressures from Russia and China drew Japan into an unproductive conflict with China and distanced it from its former European allies. Japan began to pursue an aggressive expansionist policy aimed at including not only China, but also Southeast Asia, the Pacific islands, Australia, and New Zealand under its dominion in a "Greater East Asia Co-Prosperity Sphere." Unprepared for the Japanese attack on Pearl Harbor, the United States was slow to mobilize in the Pacific during the Second World War, but the turn in Japan's fortunes was drastically confirmed by the horrific damage inflicted by the atomic bombs dropped on Nagasaki and Hiroshima in 1945.

The atomic bomb dropped on Hiroshima in August 1945 was a weapon of unprecedented destruction. The loss of life was devastating, and the city was left in ruins.

5000	2000	1000	500	AD1	400	600

■ **1950** Start of the Korean War (-1953).

■ **1952** Inauguration of the European Coal and Steel Community.

■ **1954** Vietminh troops defeat the French at Dien Bien Phu.

■ **1955** Formation of the Warsaw Pact, the Communist bloc's answer to NATO.

■ **1955** US Supreme Court rules racial segregation in public schools unconstitutional.

■ **1956** Suez Crisis: US and USSR force Britain and France to abandon military attacks on Egypt.

■ **1956** Hungarian uprising against Communist rule crushed by Soviet tanks.

■ **1956** Sudan gains independence.

■ **1957** Treaty of Rome establishes the European Economic Community, later the European Union.

■ **1957** Sputnik: USSR launches first spacecraft.

■ **1958** Former British colony of the Gold Coast becomes independent republic of Ghana.

■ **1958** Charles de Gaulle returns to power in France; launches fifth republic.

■ **1958** Chinese "Great Leap Forward" leads only to mass starvation.

■ **1958** Successful revolution in Cuba brings Fidel Castro to power.

■ **1960** Former Belgian Congo (Zaire) gains independence.

■ **1961** Yuri Gagarin first man in space.

■ **1961** First US "military advisors" sent to South Vietnam.

■ **1962** Cuban Missile Crisis, in which US forced USSR to dismantle nuclear bases in Cuba.

■ **1962** End of French war in Algeria, which wins independence.

■ **1963** Foundation of Organization of African unity by 32 newly independent states.

■ **1963** Assassination of US President John F. Kennedy at Dallas, Texas.

■ **1964** North Vietnamese attacks on US ships; retaliatory bombing by USAF; effective start of Vietnam War.

■ **1964** China explodes its first nuclear bomb.

■ **1964** After many years of racial protest, Civil Rights Act passed by US Congress.

■ **1965** Coup brings Sese Seko Mobuto to power in the Congo (Zaire).

■ **1966** Beginning of Cultural Revolution in China.

■ **1967** Civil war in Nigeria (-1970) as eastern Biafra region attempts secession.

■ **1967** Stunning Israeli victories over Egypt, Syria, and Jordan in the Six-Day War.

■ **1968** Prague Spring: liberal Communist regime in Czechoslovakia overthrown by Moscow.

■ **1968** Assassinations of Martin Luther King and Robert Kennedy.

■ **1969** After months of tension, widespread civil unrest in Northern Ireland; beginning of the "Troubles."

■ **1969** Neil Armstrong becomes the first man on the moon.

■ **1973** Ceasefire agreed in Vietnam War; US withdraws.

■ **1973** Rising international oil prices end post-war economic boom in developed world.

■ **1973** Army coup in Chile under Pinochet: President Allende murdered.

■ **1974** Turkish troops invade Cyprus and partition island.

■ **1974** US President Richard Nixon resigns after exposure of Watergate scandal.

■ **1974** Military uprising in Portugal ends dictatorship, reinstates democracy.

The State of Israel

In the 1930s, European Jews fleeing from the Nazis settled in Palestine, encouraged by the Balfour Declaration: the Holocaust quickening demands for a fully independent Jewish state. Most of the long-standing Muslim population of Palestine was opposed to this. In 1947, Britain ceded its interest in Palestine to the United Nations which partitioned the territory, creating the state of Israel. In effect, the Jewish independence campaign presented the UN with a *fait accompli*. The new state was attacked simultaneously by Egypt, Jordan, Syria, Lebanon, Iraq and Palestinian guerrillas. Israel survived and immigrants poured in during the 1950s. The second Arab-Israeli war in 1956 was mixed up with the Suez Incident and left things much as before. Only in 1967 did Israel acquire secure borders: her breathtaking victories in the Six-Day War against Egypt, Jordan and Syria gained east Jerusalem, the west bank of the Jordan, and the Golan Heights.

The Dome of the Rock in Jerusalem symbolizes the modern Arab-Israeli division: here Muhammad ascended to heaven; here Abraham offered Isaac to God. It is land sacred to both sides.

African Decolonization

The post-war years brought rapid African decolonization. Economic development and colonial education spread political awareness. The first country to gain independence was Libya in 1951, benefiting from Italy's defeat in the war. More significant was the independence of Sudan in 1956 and especially that of Ghana in 1957: the former Gold Coast had a tradition of statehood going back to the Ashanti kingdoms. The first crack in French West Africa came in 1958 when Guinea voted for independence. The next six years brought decolonization to its peak, sometimes marred by tragedy as in the vicious Algerian war of independence and the chaotic slaughter that accompanied the end of the Belgian Congo. By the early 1970s, only the old Portuguese colonies of Angola and Mozambique and the rebel white regime in Southern Rhodesia held out. None survived the decade. Neo-colonialism—economic domination without political ties—remained a problem.

Kwame Nkrumah (left) who became president of an independent Ghana in1957, with Sékou Touré, president of Guinea.

Civil Rights

Following the US civil war, African Americans in the South still suffered widespread discrimination. In 1896, the Supreme Court approved the segregation of railroad passengers. By the 1950s, the climate had changed. President Truman had integrated the armed forces in 1948. In 1946, Jackie Robinson became the first black man to play major league baseball, a particularly symbolic moment. In the South, however, race remained an urgent problem. A 1954 Supreme Court judgment overturned the 1896 ruling and outlawed segregation in public schools. President Eisenhower sent federal troops to Little Rock, Arkansas, to enforce this ruling. In the 1960s, a mass campaign for civil rights, under the leadership of Rev. Martin Luther King, led to the Civil Rights Act of 1964. A Voting Rights Act followed in 1965. Together with public protests against US participation in the Vietnam war, the race issue made the 1960s one of America's most troubled decades.

The Rev. Martin Luther King Jr., the Baptist clergyman who won the Nobel Peace Prize for his black civil rights campaign.

European Union

The European Coal and Steel Community was formed in 1952 to facilitate Franco-German economic co-operation. It was the product of post-war idealism, intended to bind the old enemies to each other in peace. Six years later, the Treaty of Rome broadened the idea by creating the European Economic Community, an internal free trade area embracing France, Germany, Italy and the three Benelux countries. Britain stayed pointedly aloof from this process but eventually joined in 1973. The community gradually developed more powers and became the European Union in 1993. In its first twenty years it functioned mainly as the free trade area it was originally designed to be, benefiting from the effects of Marshall Aid and the prolonged international post-war boom. It later sought to expand its powers in a more obviously political direction, most notably in the development of a single European currency.

The Council of Europe building in Strasbourg, seat of the European Parliament and the Council of Europe.

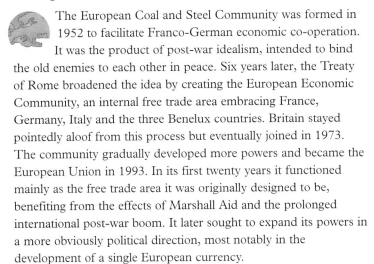

Vietnam

The Japanese overran Southeast Asia in the Second World War. The French empire in Indochina was restored in 1945. But a Vietnamese nationalist movement developed under the leadership of the Communist Ho Chi Minh and his brilliant military chief Vo Nguyen Giap. They defeated the French at Dien Bien Phu in 1954. A peace settlement followed which partitioned the country. North Vietnam became Communist. The south was backed first by the French and later by the Americans.

In 1963, North Vietnam began a war against the south with the aim of re-uniting the country. But the United States saw this as a test case in the Cold War to contain global Communism and committed troops in ever-increasing numbers. In fact it was a nationalist more than a Communist war. The North Vietnamese won, sweeping the Americans out in a humiliating defeat and reuniting the country in 1975.

Ho Chi Minh

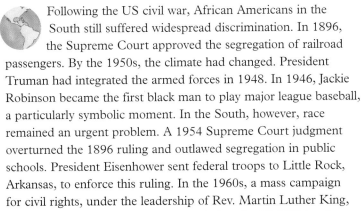

A Divided Continent

As East-West relationships worsened and Europe became a focal point of the Cold War, the people of a divided continent experienced a sense of anxiety fueled by propaganda. However, the emergence of the West's European Economic Community (EEC) from 1958 promoted increased prosperity and rising standards of living. Television stations were set up across the continent and soon this medium assumed a dominant role. Indeed, the mass-media had already influenced the development of an American pop-art movement, using collage and silk-screen techniques. European pop-art's leading figures include Britain's Peter Blake (b. 1932). By the same token, the rising profile of technology underlay the work of Frenchman Edgar Varèse (d. 1965) in electronic music. Student protests of 1968 against the Vietnam War and Russia's invasion of Czechoslovakia prompted youth rebellion across the continent. This trend found expression in French new wave cinema, which depicted young people as living lives of existential amoralism. In Britain, youth rejection of society's values inspired experimental novels like those of Anthony Burgess, featuring amoral teenage gangs speaking a futuristic language.

A German television station, c. 1960

This Chinese woodcut, a piece of propaganda art from c. 1949, depicts Chinese peasants on a collective farm "receiving a tractor," an agricultural advance that was intended to be lauded as an example of the benefits to ordinary people brought by the then new Communist regime.

Mao Zedong

In October 1949, Mao Zedong (Mao Tse-tung) declared the formation of the People's Republic of China and inaugurated a new epoch in China. The social reorganization spearheaded by Mao was one of the most sweeping in history, and sometimes led to disaster. After the failure of the agricultural reforms of the "Great Leap Forward," which ended in drought and famine that claimed twenty million lives by 1962, Mao sought to regroup his forces. The "little red book" of *Quotations from Chairman Mao* (authored by his friend and ally Lin Biao) appeared in 1963 and functioned effectively as propaganda for Mao.

The "Great Proletarian Cultural Revolution," launched in 1965, was a further attempt to renew the spark of revolution. Young Red Guards campaigned militantly against the four "olds" of tradition: old ideas, customs, culture, and habits. Foreign influences of any kind and any intellectual activity that did not further the aims of the socialist revolution were discouraged, often through public humiliation and frequently with violence. The Red Guards were disbanded in 1968 and, with China on the brink of civil war, the Cultural Revolution declared officially ended the following year. Nonetheless, persecutions and executions continued until Mao's death in 1976, ultimately claiming thousands of lives.

Nigerian writer Wole Soyinka

Black African Literature

Black African literature developed rapidly during the 1950s. Chinua Achebe's novels show Ibo society changing from its first contact with Europeans until the military coup in 1966. His most famous, *Things Fall Apart*, 1958, was the first novel by an African to attain the status of a contemporary classic. Wole Soyinka, also from Nigeria, draws inspiration from Yoruba mythology for his plays and novels. His plays are widely performed and include *Death and the King's Horseman*. He became the first black African writer to be awarded the Nobel Prize for literature. From East Africa, Ngugi wa Thiong'o describes Kikuyu society from before the Mau-Mau Emergency until after independence: *A Grain of Wheat* (1967) and *Petals of Blood* are among his best novels. Francophone Africa produced equally fine works. The Senegalese statesman and poet Leopold Senghor embodied specifically African experiences in his poetry. From Guinea, Camera Laye gave an honest depiction of traditional African society in his autobiography *The African Child* (1953). Very different was the powerful attack on French colonialism and missionary activity by the Cameroonian writer Mongo Beti in *The Poor Christ of Bomba*, a novel banned in French West Africa.

New Literary Traditions in Asia

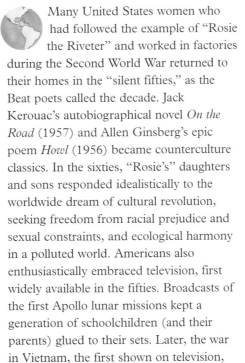

Literary expression in twentieth-century Asia has been characterized by various responses to western influence. In India, these reactions began in the nineteenth century, when dismissive scorn of Indian literary traditions by the British adviser Thomas Babington Macaulay provoked a strong reaction in favor of Indian literature and vernacular languages. Prominent among the writers of this Indian renaissance was the famous poet Rabindranath Tagore, who won the Nobel Prize in 1913, and also introduced the short story form into Indian vernacular writing. Nonetheless, English schools have promoted a new Indian tradition in English; the influential autobiographies of Ghandi and Jawaharlal Nehru were written in this language. The fiction of R.K. Narayan treats the struggle to accommodate tradition with western values with a gentle irony that has been compared with that of Chekhov. The novels and stories of Raja Rao also deal with aspects of the search for identity. The ancient traditions of Persian literature also felt the impact of western influence in the early twentieth century. Mohammed Ali introduced the short story form, and the poet Nima Yushij broke completely with traditional forms in the 1920s, although these forms still persist in the work of others. Yushij's successors continue to experiment with new forms.

Culture and Counterculture

Many United States women who had followed the example of "Rosie the Riveter" and worked in factories during the Second World War returned to their homes in the "silent fifties," as the Beat poets called the decade. Jack Kerouac's autobiographical novel *On the Road* (1957) and Allen Ginsberg's epic poem *Howl* (1956) became counterculture classics. In the sixties, "Rosie's" daughters and sons responded idealistically to the worldwide dream of cultural revolution, seeking freedom from racial prejudice and sexual constraints, and ecological harmony in a polluted world. Americans also enthusiastically embraced television, first widely available in the fifties. Broadcasts of the first Apollo lunar missions kept a generation of schoolchildren (and their parents) glued to their sets. Later, the war in Vietnam, the first shown on television,

became a focus of protest. Meanwhile, a flurry of distinctive prose and poetry from different South American authors won international acclaim. Pablo Neruda of Chile, known for his epic poem of the Americas, *Canto General*, was awarded the Nobel Prize in 1971. Jorge Luis Borges (Argentina), Gabriel García Márquez (Columbia), also a Nobelist (1982), and Mario Vargas Llosa (Peru) were only some of the distinguished authors to emerge in this period. Notable also was the innovative architecture of, among others, Lucio Costa and Oscar Niemeyer, designers of Brasilia, the new capital of Brazil.

Edwin E. "Buzz" Aldrin, one of the two Apollo 11 astronauts to walk on the moon in July 1969, in a photograph taken from the spaceship. The first lunar mission captured the imagination of the American public.

5000	2000	1000	500	AD1	400	600

The Reagan "Revolution"

Ronald Reagan was the first president seriously to challenge the post-Roosevelt consensus. On taking office in 1981, he forced through a series of budget and tax cuts. The top tax rate dropped from 70% to 37.5%. Although overall federal spending did not shrink, it slowed significantly. The exception to this was the defense budget, which Reagan expanded. The result was an ever-growing budget deficit. The defense strategy forced the Soviet Union to match American spending levels, with fatal consequences for the battered Soviet economy. Reagan hastened the fall of Communism in Europe. Elsewhere, his fervent anti-Communism produced the Iran-Contra scandal. The administration secretly sold arms to the bitterly anti-American regime in Iran and used the proceeds to aid Contra guerrillas in Marxist Nicaragua. In all, Reagan led a retreat from big government, oversaw the collapse of Communism and left America as the world's only superpower.

Ronald Reagan

- **1975** Death of Franco followed by successful transition to democracy in Spain.

- **1975** Angola declares its independence as Portuguese troops leave.

- **1975** North Vietnam conquers south, reunites country under Ho Chi Minh.

- **1975** Khmer Rouge under Pol Pot come to power following victory in Cambodian civil war.

- **1975** Pathet Lao Communists win Laotian civil war.

- **1975** Assassination of President N'Garta Tombalbaye sets off civil war in Chad.

- **1975** Start of long civil war in Lebanon (-1991).

- **1976** Deaths of Mao Zedong and Zhou Enlai, leaders of the Chinese revolution.

- **1976** "Dirty war" against dissidents in Argentina; thousands murdered.

- **1977** Army coup in Pakistan ousts government of Zulfikar Ali Bhutto.

- **1978** Egypt and Israel sign Camp David accords to normalize relations.

- **1978** Sandinista revolutionaries seize power in Nicaragua.

- **1979** Margaret Thatcher British prime minister

- **1979** Iranian revolution deposes shah and establishes a Shi'ite Islamic state.

- **1979** Soviet troops intervene in Afghan civil war.

- **1979** Vietnamese troops conquer Phnom Penh, ousting Pol Pot.

- **1980** Outbreak of Iran-Iraq war (-1988).

- **1980** Newly independent Zimbabwe elects Robert Mugabe to power.

- **1981** Ronald Reagan President of the United States (-1989).

- **1981** Assassination of President Sadat of Egypt.

- **1981** Civil war in Sri Lanka between Tamils and Singhalese.

- **1982** Britain recaptures Falkland (Malvinas) islands following Argentinian invasion.

- **1982** Israeli invasion of Lebanon; establishment of UN peacekeeping force.

- **1983** American invasion of tiny Caribbean island of Grenada.

- **1984** Indian prime minister Indira Gandhi assassinated.

- **1985** Mikhail Gorbachev secretary-general of Soviet Communist party.

- **1986** Overthrow of the Marcos dictatorship in the Philippines.

- **1988** Soviet troops withdraw from Afghanistan.

- **1988** Beginning of the *intifada*, mass Palestinian uprising against Israel.

- **1989** Following the end of the Angolan civil war, SWAPO wins elections.

- **1989** Collapse of Communism throughout eastern Europe; fall of the Berlin Wall.

- **1989** Massacre of protesters in Tienanmen Square in Beijing, China.

- **1989** Overthrow of regime of Alfredo Stroessner, dictator of Paraguay for 35 years.

- **1990** Boris Yeltsin elected president of the Russian Federation.

- **1990** Yugoslavia begins to fall apart as Slovenia declares its independence.

- **1990** After 27 years in prison, Nelson Mandela, leader of African National Congress, is released.

- **1991** Gulf War: United States, France and Britain shatter Iraqi army.

- **1991** Yeltsin replaces Gorbachev as Soviet Union breaks up.

- **1991** Yugoslavia disintegrates: Serbia and Croatia at war.

- **1991** Civil war in Somalia; power vacuum leads to total anarchy.

- **1992** Assassination of Rajiv Gandhi, Indian prime minister.

- **1992** President Fujimori assumes dictatorial powers in Peru.

- **1992** Reunification of Germany.

- **1994** Nelson Mandela elected president of post-apartheid South Africa.

800	1000	1200	1400	1600	1800	2000

Iranian Revolution

The Pahlavi dynasty in Iran was not ancient, dating only from 1925. By the 1970s, the shah—Mohammed Reza Pahlavi—seemed impregnable on the Peacock throne. He was a modernizer; Iran was prospering from abundant oil revenues and he had a strong ally in the United States. Yet he had implacable enemies among the conservative Shi'ite Islamic clergy, of whom the most virulent was Ayatollah Ruhollah Khomeini, whom he had exiled. Public protests against the harshness of the police were supported by some sections of international liberal opinion but were also manipulated by the clergy. Popular discontent with the shah's regime suddenly spiraled out of control in 1978, part of a growing nationalist and anti-western movement in the Islamic world generally. He was forced to flee and Khomeini returned to Iran in 1979 amid scenes of delirious public adulation to establish an Islamic republic.

Ayatollah Khomeini

Collapse of Communism in Europe

Communism had dominated Europe in one form or another since the Bolshevik revolution of 1917. After the Second World War, Russia made huge gains in Eastern Europe, with client Communist states established everywhere. Occasional revolts in East Germany, Hungary, Poland and Czechoslovakia were crushed, sometimes with Russian tanks. But the Soviet Union was facing financial ruin because of an escalating arms race with the United States, and in 1985 Mikhail Gorbachev, the new Soviet leader, attempted to liberalize his regime. Instead, the whole edifice collapsed. Sensing lack of Russian resolve, people across Eastern Europe protested in the streets in an obvious display of contempt for their Communist overlords. The Russians did not intervene. Communist regimes were swept away in the heady year of 1989. The Berlin Wall, symbol of a divided Europe, was torn down and Germany reunited. Finally, in 1991, Russia itself abandoned Communism.

Mikhail Gorbachev with the East German leader Erich Honneker shortly before the fall of the Berlin Wall.

Mandela's Triumph

Nelson Mandela was born in 1918, the son of a Thembu chief. He practiced as a lawyer and joined the African National Congress. In 1964, he was sentenced to life imprisonment for offenses against the regime. He spent twenty-seven years in jail, an outrage to world opinion. South Africa was increasingly regarded as a pariah state. Eventually, in 1990 he was released. What astonished the world was the generosity and lack of bitterness of this remarkable man. He assumed the leadership of the ANC and began the process that led to democracy. Along with F. W. de Klerk, the leader of the Nationalist Party who managed the dismantling of apartheid with great skill, he negotiated a new, democratic South Africa with majority rule, but with safeguards for the minority whites. In 1994, he was elected president. Mandela was not just an outstanding political leader: he was a symbol of optimism.

Nelson Mandela

Towards an Australian Republic

The last quarter of the twentieth century has witnessed a steady drift away from Australia's traditional ties with Britain. In 1972, the Labor Party under Gough Whitlam returned to office after a gap of twenty-three years. Three years later, his government was dismissed by the governor-general—the representative of the Crown—in a dispute between the federal government and the states. The states objected to Whitlam's attempt to force through welfare increases in an economic depression. Constitutionally, the governor-general was within his rights but it was a seminal moment. Labor regained office under Bob Hawke in 1983 and kept it for thirteen years. Under Hawke, and particularly under his abrasive successor Paul Keating, Labor moved steadily towards a fundamental constitutional change. This republicanism reflects Australia's growing multiculturalism: the country looks ever more to Asia and the United States rather than to Britain.

The Australian Parliament House in Canberra.

5000	2000	1000	500	AD1	400	600

The Japanese film director Akira Kurosawa is sometimes inspired by Shakespearean themes. This still is from Ran *(1986), which is loosely based on the tragedy* King Lear.

East Asian and Pacific Arts

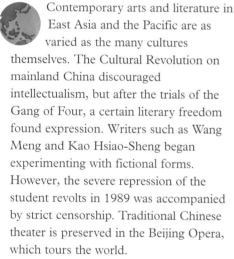

Contemporary arts and literature in East Asia and the Pacific are as varied as the many cultures themselves. The Cultural Revolution on mainland China discouraged intellectualism, but after the trials of the Gang of Four, a certain literary freedom found expression. Writers such as Wang Meng and Kao Hsiao-Sheng began experimenting with fictional forms. However, the severe repression of the student revolts in 1989 was accompanied by strict censorship. Traditional Chinese theater is preserved in the Beijing Opera, which tours the world.

In Japan, Kawabata Yasunari was the first Japanese author to win the Nobel Prize, in 1968. Playwright and novelist Mishima Yukio earned international fame for his despairing, erotically charged work, even before his shocking suicide. Film director Akira Kurosawa, who first garnered international fame with *Rashomon* (1950), produced the epics *Kagemusha* and *Ran* in the eighties. Nagisa Oshima (*In the Realm of the Senses*, 1976) has been compared with French director Jean-Luc Godard, and Juzo Itami produces comedies (*Tampopo*, 1987, and *A Taxing Woman*, 1988) that are popular in the west as well as Japan.

The Australian novelist Patrick White received the Nobel Prize in 1972, while a generation of Australian directors and actors have produced very distinctive films.

The Arts in Africa

By 1975 formal western-style art training and institutions in Africa meant modern artists felt a tension between the demands of tradition and the projection of new, more forward-looking views. Various art movements tried to find forms of expression that were uniquely African. Erstwhile anti-colonial literature turned to the paradoxes of post-colonial realities. Zimbabwean Tsitsi Dangaremba won global recognition for her novel *Nervous Conditions* (1989) and Ben Okri won the Booker Prize (1991). Theater groups juxtapose indigenous elements with modern concerns, as did Ngugi wa Thiongo's experiments with peasant theater. The notable musicians Angelique Kidjo, Youssou N'Dour and Salif Keita were inducted into the global musical aesthetic through "world music." African film-making grew in sophistication, recognition, and representational concerns, while cheaper video technology triggered frenetic production activity. This period clearly marked a shift of emphasis for African cultural production. If economic crises, political instability, and the need for survival led to the forced exile of writers like Ngugi wa Thiongo and Nigerian Wole Soyinka, and voluntary exile for musicians, artists and film-makers, the challenge for African artists now is to find new reference points and frameworks to articulate today's realities of economic decline, emigration, and multi-racial, multi-belief societies.

Multiculturalism

Apparently monolithic mass communications media, such as the hundreds of curiously similar channels available through cable and satellite television, may be one impetus behind the emphasis on multiculturalism that seems characteristic of recent arts and literature in the United States. Many artists reject the notion of a single cultural identity, instead seeking to characterize diversity in a world that appears increasingly contracted by technology. Some works refine concerns important in the sixties, such as issues of feminism and race. Toni Morrison and Alice Walker write novels focusing on black women that also touch many readers of other races and gender. Morrison's evocative *Beloved* (1987) won a Pulitzer Prize, and she was awarded the Nobel Prize in 1993. Walker's novel *The Color Purple* (1982), also a Pulitzer winner, was transformed into a film by director Stephen Spielberg. Yet Spielberg is better known for his large-scale movies with extraordinary special effects such as *Raiders of the Lost Ark*, *E.T.*, and *Jurassic Park*, which are phenomenally successful in box-office terms around the world. Does the global popularity of these movies, with their advanced computer-generated technology and sentimental emphasis on traditional American values, contradict the necessity of recognizing difference and multiplicity insisted upon by some other artists? Or will new technologies offer increased diversity? Answers may lie in the next millennium.

Poster for Steven Spielberg's film E.T.

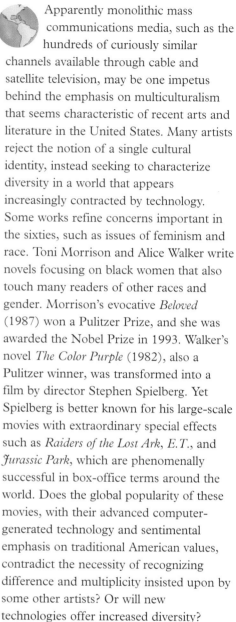

A still from the notable Indian director Satyajit Ray's film Ashani Sanket.

New Arts and Literatures in Old Civilizations

Ancient traditions in Asian literatures wrestled with reviving old forms, as well as experimenting with new ones introduced from the west. Arabic literature has re-established itself in inventive ways. The Egyptian playwright and novelist Tawfiq al-Hakim promoted a dramatic tradition in a culture that previously had very little drama. The Syrian Adonis (Ali Ahmad Said) is an innovative and challenging essayist and poet. Another Egyptian, Naguib Mahfouz, who is perhaps best known for his sweeping *Cairo Trilogy*, was awarded the Nobel Prize in 1988; but his work is banned in some Arabic-speaking countries because of his support of Sadat's peace treaty with Israel. Another Muslim writer, who is a native of India and writes in English, has also suffered Islamic condemnation. Salman Rushdie's 1989 novel *The Satanic Verses* provoked the Ayatollah Khomeini into offering a reward for the author's assassination. Another Indian author, the poet-politician P.V. Narasimha Rao, became India's ninth prime minister in 1991. He writes in several languages. The variety of India, with its many cultures and languages, is perhaps united only by the Indian love of the cinema. Most of the many films produced in India are unremarkable, but the films of Satyajit Ray have won international acclaim.

Towards a United Europe

A gradual easing of East-West tensions in the 1970s, accelerating with Gorbachev's administration in the USSR from 1985, introduced a more confident era in Europe. To a degree, this new confidence is reflected by postmodernism in architecture and in the arts. This term, gaining popularity from the mid-1970s, describes a movement which rejects the "modern" preoccupation with form. Postmodern architecture has drawn inspiration from the Baroque and Classical buildings of the past, applying these styles to spare modern outlines. Musical composition had, by the 1980s to '90s, adopted influences from non-European cultures and from popular culture including rock, as instanced by the work of Turnage (b. 1960). The prosperity of this age, however, has fostered a "consumer society" throughout western Europe which, since the demise of Communism, is becoming manifest in the east, especially in the Czech Republic and Hungary. Across the continent, economic and social problems, including long-term unemployment and social disadvantage, pose a serious challenge. Reaction against this dehumanizing "consumer society" is, however, gathering pace; a prominent critic of current trends is Irish-born Charles Handy, formerly professor of economics at the London Business School, whose *Age of Unreason* appeared in 1990.

The Pompidou Center, Paris. This typical "postmodern" building consists of a glass façade supported totally by an external steel skeleton. It is the most visited attraction in the capital.

NEW FRONTIERS

"Toto, I have a feeling we're not in Kansas anymore."
The Wizard of Oz (MGM, 1938)

In the "global village," Canadian educator Marshall McLuhan (1911-1980) claimed, "the medium is the message." These frequently reiterated phrases continue to suggest the opportunities and quandaries posed by developing communications technologies. McLuhan's theories, originally applied to film and television, argued that the *forms* of electronic communications were more influential on human beings than the ostensible contents. McLuhan's theories are related to the work of the American mathematician Norbert Wiener (1894-1964), who coined the term "cybernetics" to describe the analysis of systems of communications and control in humans, machines, and organizations. The strange frontier of relations between humans and increasingly complex and pervasive technologies continues to provoke questions and controversy today.

COMPUTERS

Computers, considered simply as machines capable of complex arithmetic, are actually very old. The ancient abacus is a computer. The seventeenth-century scientist-philosophers Blaise Pascal (1623-1662) and Gottfried Wilhelm Leibnitz (1646-1716) each invented computers independently; a mechanism created by Leibnitz is still in use. However, computers first became generally important in the nineteenth century, when complex mathematical and physical equations were essential for solving design and construction problems posed by the transportation revolution, such as determining stress distribution and center of gravity. Electronic computers were first used during the Second World War to aid weapon design. Small versions of electronic computers developed rather slowly in the early 1970s and their potential was largely unrealized. Initially the personal computer was a "do-it-yourself" kit marketed to hobbyists with some expertise. Yet when more "user-friendly" computers developed, their popularity soon exceeded all expectations, forming a multi-billion-dollar industry.

The increasing use of these small computers in education raises interesting issues about how thinking and the acquisition of knowledge may change in the future. The multimedia capabilities of computers—the incorporation of film or audio clips, for example—offer an experience substantially different from reading a book. Reading is a cumulative process; computer learning is a process of juxtapostion. Will the use of computers effect widespread social change of the sort initiated by the printing press, which eventually made widespread literacy thinkable and even essential?

Computer networks also raise intriguing social questions. Networks offer a global, nearly instantaneous, sustained flow of information that is almost (humanly) impossible to assimilate or control. This potentially volatile but steady stream of information demands highly flexible responses in the world marketplace, affecting the labor force as well as the stock market. The networks also raise issues of privacy, intellectual property rights, and rights of access. It undoubtedly brings people together who might not otherwise meet. It offers immediate "publication." It can be anonymous, but also offers convenient tracking of users. Should this be regulated? How is it possible to regulate it? It will be interesting to see how this new medium takes shape in the immediate future. Like early television, it has already begun to attract commercial, political, and civic interest. Who will determine the ultimate form (and thus the content, according to McLuhan) of the inter-computer networks?

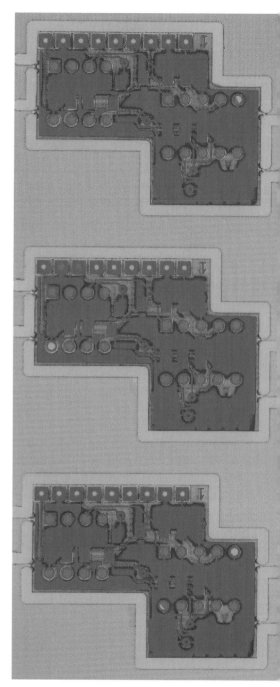

CYBERSPACE, CYBORGS, AND CHROMOSOMES

Although cybernetics is no longer considered a discipline in itself, it has been absorbed into many other fields of study, as the prevalence of the prefix "cyber" suggests. "Cyberspace" is where the flow of information in computer networks "exists." It is also a synonym for "virtual reality," or the space where human beings can interact with three-dimensional "virtual" images. Wearing special gloves and headgear, a person can now "see," "touch," and sometimes "hear" objects that aren't "really" there. A favorite science-fiction topic, virtual reality may also be useful in long-distance

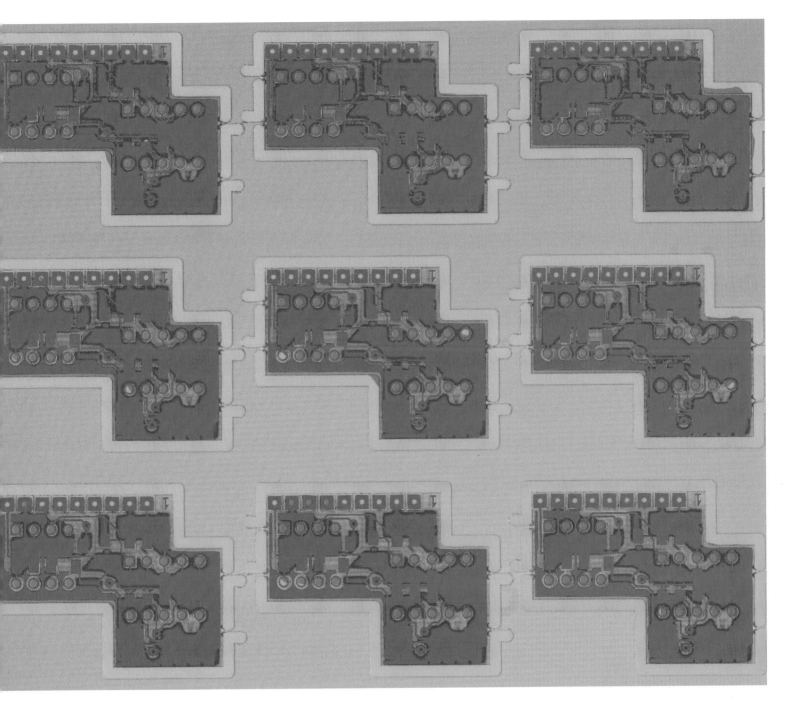

Magnified microchips—the essence of the computer. The next century presents an intriguing future for its increased "interaction" with humans.

manipulation of robots performing dangerous tasks, or may help stroke victims recover the use of their limbs.

"Cyborg," an abbreviation of "cybernetic organism," can be defined as simply a human being with an artificial body part, such as a plastic heart valve. Medical science has been eroding the boundaries between the "natural" body and "artificial" replacement parts for some time now, and new research will undoubtedly produce biotechnology that is increasingly indistinguishable from, or even better than, the "original." Worldwide research on the Human Genome Project, intended to discover the secrets of each human gene and "map" the complete genetic creation of human beings, will undoubtedly contribute to this rapidly unfolding future. Very recently, scientists created an artificial human chromosome that shows potential as a means of delivering gene therapy to treat genetic disorders. Someday, will humans be able to change their personalities as well as cure disease through this technology? Cloning is another biotechnological process that is moving rapidly from the realm of science fiction to science fact, as the recent birth of a cloned sheep named Dolly in Edinburgh demonstrated to the world.

There is great potential for relief of human suffering and intriguing new possibilities for human development in these scientific frontiers as the second millennium approaches. At the same time it is plain that exploring these frontiers also poses profound challenges to current systems of human ethics, and even to the very definition of "human."

S.I.

INDEX

BIBLIOGRAPHY

GENERAL

Cipolla, C.M. *The Fontana Economic History of Europe* 5 vols. London, 1978

Ellis, H. *The Pictorial Encyclopedia of Railways* London, 1968

Forde-Johnson, J. *History from the Earth: An Introduction to Archaeology* London, 1974

Kennedy, P. *The Rise and Fall of the Great Powers* London, 1988

Roe, D. *Prehistory: An Introduction* London, 1970

Cotterell, A. ed. *The Penguin Encyclopedia of Ancient Cultures* London: Penguin Books, 1988

Gowing, Sir L. ed. *A History of Art* New York: Barnes & Noble, 1995

Grolier Multimedia Encyclopedia Version 7.0.2. Computer software. Grolier Incorporated, 1995

Ralph, P. L., Lerner, R.E., Meachum, S., and McNall Burns, E. *World Civilizations: Their History and Culture* 8th ed. 2 vols. New York: W.W. Norton & Company, 1991

WESTERN AND CENTRAL ASIA

Basham, A.L. *The Wonder That Was India* 3rd ed. New York: Taplinger, 1968

Embree, A.T., ed. *The Hindu Tradition: Readings in Oriental Thought* New York: Vintage, 1972

Gray, J. *Near Eastern Mythology* London: Hamlyn, 1969

Koller, J.M. *Oriental Philosophies* New York: Charles Scribner's Sons, 1970

Pal, P. *"May the Immeasurable Wealth of Your Dance Fill My Consciousness:" Dancing Deities of India* Orientations 28.7 July/August 1997

Rawlinson, H.G. *India: A Short Cultural History* New York: Frederick

A. Praeger, Inc., 1954

Renou, L. ed. *Hinduism* New York: George Braziller, 1962

Spear, P. *A History of India* 2 vols. Harmondsworth: Penguin, 1982

Watson, F. *A Concise History of India* London: Thames and Hudson, 1979

EAST ASIA AND THE PACIFIC

Barclay, G. *A History of the Pacific* London: Sidgwick & Jackson, 1978

Bellwood, P. "Ancient Seafarers" Archaeology 50.2 March/April 1997

Blunden, C. and Elvin, M. *Cultural Atlas of China* New York: Facts on File, 1989

Clark, C.M.H. *A History of Australia* 6 vols. London: Cambridge UP, 1987

Duus, P. *The Rise of Modern Japan* Boston: Houghton Mifflin, 1976

Edwards, W. "Japan's New Past" Archaeology 50.2 March/April 1997

Fairbank, J.K., Reischauer, E.O. and Craig, A.M. *East Asia: Tradition and Transformation* Boston: Houghton Mifflin, 1978

Osborne, M. *Southeast Asia: An Introductory History* 6th ed. St. Leonards NSW: Allen & Unwin, 1995

Tiedemann, A.E. ed. *An Introduction to Japanese Civilization* New York: Columbia UP, 1974

Varley, H. P. *Japanese Culture* 3rd ed. Honolulu: U of Hawaii Press, 1984

THE AMERICAS

Bakewell, P.J. *A History of Latin America: Empires and Sequels 1450-1930* Oxford: Blackwell, 1997

Brine, L. *The Ancient Earthworks and Temples of the American Indians* 1894. Hertfordshire: Oracle, 1996

Current, R.N., Williams, T. H. ,

Freidel, F. and Brinkley, A. *American History: A Survey* 6th ed. 2 vols. New York: Alfred A. Knopf, 1979

Gyles, A.B. and Sayer, C. *Of Gods and Men: The Heritage of Ancient Mexico* New York: Harper & Row, 1980

Moseley, M.E. *The Incas and Their Ancestors* London: Thames and Hudson, 1994

Pike, D.G. *Anasazi: Ancient People of the Rock* New York: Crown Publishers, 1974

Tenenbaum, B.A. ed. in chief. *Encyclopedia of Latin American History and Culture* 5 vols. New York: Charles Scribners' Sons, 1996

Waldman, C. *Atlas of the North American Indian* New York: Facts on File, 1985

"Special Issue: The Year in Science 1997" Discover 18.1 January 1998

Brown, D.M. series ed. *Egypt: Land of the Pharoahs. Alexandria*, VA: Time-Life Books, 1992

EUROPE

Bieler, L. *Ireland: Harbinger of the Middle Ages* London, 1963

Green, V.H.H. *Medieval Civilization in Western Europe* London, 1971

Haussig, H.W. *A History of Byzantine Civilization* English trans. London, 1971

Mayer, H. E. *The Crusades* Trans. John Gillingham. 2nd ed. Oxford, 1988

Meldgaard, J. et al. *Viking Voyages to North America* Roskilde, 1993

Pounds, N.J.G. *An Economic History of Medieval Europe* 2nd ed. London & New York, 1994

Wilson, D. M. *The Viking Achievement* London, 1970

Cameron, E. *The European Reformation*

Oxford, 1991

Dukes, P. *A History of Russia: Medieval, Modern and Contemporary* revised ed. London, 1990

Fowkes, B. *The Rise and Fall of Communism in Eastern Europe* London, 1993

Green, V. H.H. *Renaissance and Reformation* New ed. London, 1991

Hosch, E. *The Balkans: A Short History from Greek Times to the Present* London, 1972

Kann, R. *A History of the Hapsburg Empire 1526-1918* Berkely & Los Angeles, 1974

Treasure, G. *The Making of Modern Europe* London, 1985

Wandycz, P.S. *The Price of Freedom: A History of East Central Europe from the Middle Ages to the Present* London, 1992

AFRICA AND THE MIDDLE EAST

Armajani, Y. *The Middle East Past and Present* Englewood Cliffs, N.J., 1970

Curtin, P. et al. *African History from Earliest Times to Independence* 2nd ed.London & New York, 1995

Goldschmidt, A. *A Concise History of the Middle East* Boulder, Colorado, 1979

Ki-Zerbo, J. et al. (eds.) *UNESCO General History of Africa* 8 vols. Paris, 1981-1993

Gifford, P. & Louis, W.R. *The Transfer of Power in Africa* 2 vols. New Haven & London, 1988

Sluglett, P. and Sluglett, M.F. *The Middle East: The Arab World and its Neighbours* London, 1991

Wesseling, H.L. *Divide and Rule: the Partition of Africa 1880-1914* Westport, Connecticut, 1996

PICTURE ACKNOWLEDGMENTS

Key: t=top, l=left, r=right, c=center, b=bottom, so tl=top left etc.

Nat. = National, Mus. = Museum

All photographs are reproduced by permission of AKG London, except for the following, which are reproduced by permission of: Aquarius Library, London 152t, 153t; Australian Tourist Commission, London 151br; Copyright ©1998 by Universal City Studios, In. Courtesy of Universal Studios Publishing Rights, a division of Universal Studios Licensing, Inc. All rights reserved 152b; Digital Vision, London 154-155; Format, London 154c; Photo Access, South Africa p113c, 122b, 127br; Werner Forman Archive London, p7, 13, 14, 16both, 17t, br, 18b, c, 19br, 23c, bl, 24all, 26bl, c, 27bl, 28both, 32tl, 33tl, br, 34bl, br, 35t, 36b, 39t, 42both, 43b, 44c, 45both, 46both, 47tl, 48both, 49t, 51, 53c, b, 54t, bl, 55t, 56, 57t, 58all, 59b, 63all, 64tr, b, 65t, br, 66tl, 66-7c, 68b, 69all, 73br, 74both, 75tl, 77tr, br, 78b, 79t, 82, 83br, 84b, 86c, 87b, 88all, 92, 93tr, br, 95t, 99tr, 102bl, 103l, 104tl, br, 105b, 107bl, 109t, c, 113t, 114c, 116c, 118t, 119t, bl, 125tl, 126, 129t, 134tl, 137tr.

Additional acknowledgments: Royal Ontario Mus. 14; Field Mus. of Natural History, Chicago 26b, 35t; American Mus. of Natural History 117c; Anthropology Mus., Berlin 46t, 48b, 74t, 87b, 88b, 106tl; Anthropology Mus., Munich 36t; Anthropology Mus., Vera Cruz Uni., Jalapa 24c; Archaelogical Mus., Ephesus 38c; Archaelogical Mus., Istanbul 29bl; Archaelogical Mus., Naples 30-31; Archaelogical Mus., Athens 29br; Arizona State Mus. 62t; Army Mus., Paris 127bl; Art and History Mus., Shanghai 19br; Art Institute, Chicago 99tr; Bibliotheque Nationale, Paris p70-1, 73t, 102t; British Library, London 24t; British Mus., London 17t, 33tr, 58c, 64b, 84-5, 105b, 109c, 119bl, 134tl; Burke Collection, New York 79t; Central History Mus. P'Yongyan, N. Korea 43bl, David Bernstein Fine Art, New York 28tr; De Young Mus., San Francisco 75tl; Entwhistle Gallery, London p77br, 93tr; Erich Lessing 1, 5, 11, 8, 22, 23b, tr, 25both, 27r, 29all, 37t, 38t, c, 39t, 41both, 43br, tr, 44b, 47tr, 52b, 53tl, 62, 73br, 66c, 79br, 82, 83bl, 89b, 93tl, 99b, 104-5, 108t, 114b, 123tl, 124bl, 125tr, 127tl, 146, 153b; European Parliament 147tr; Franco-American Mus. of Friendship, Blerancourt 124bl; Galerie des Batailles, Versailles 96c; Gisbert Bauer 47b; India House Office Library, London 111; Iraq Mus., Baghdad 26tl; Islamic Arts Mus., Cairo 51; J. Paul Getty Mus., California 36b; Kolomenskoje Open Air Mus., Moscow 116b; Laurenziana Library, Florence 102br; Louvre, Paris 29t, 44b, 75tr, 114b, 125tr, 135tr; Maxwell Anthropology Mus., Albuquerque 65t; McGregor Mus., South Africa 6; Metropolitan Mus. of Art, New York p38-9b, 68b; Mrs Bashir Mohamed Collection 88t; Musée d'Orsay, Paris 52b; Musée Guimet, Paris 34br, 43tr, 53tl, 75b, 83bl, 89b; Mus. of America, Madrid 96t, 117t; Mus. of Anthropology, British Columbia 16t; Mus. of Mankind, London 58t, 77tl; Mus. of the American Indian, New York 56, 115t; Nat. Anthropology Mus., Mexico 78c; Nat. Gallery of Scotland 119br; Nat. Library, Madrid 98b; Nat. Maritime Mus., London 128t; Nat. Mus. of Mankind, Ottawa 32l; Nat. Mus. of Rome 42t; Nat. Mus., Beijing 8, 38t, 41t; Nat. Mus., Delhi p24b, 65b; Nat. Mus., Kyoto 64tr, 103r; Nat. Mus., Stockholm 54t; Nat. Mus., Tokyo 66bc; Nat. Palace Mus., Taipei 59b; Natural History Mus. of Vienna 11, 41b, 99b; Naval Mus., Genoa 93bl; Palazzo Ducale, Urbino 79bl; Pennsylvania University Mus. 19t; Philip Goldman Collection, London 119t; Prince of Wales Mus., Bombay 118t; Punjab Govt. Mus., Simla 49t; Robert Aberman 95b; Rockefeller Mus., Jerusalem 5; Romanian History Mus., Bucharest 25t; Royal Library, Turin 94t; San Francisco Mus. of Asiatic Art 55t; Schloss Ambrass Collection, Innsbruck 79br; Seattle Art Mus. 48t; Smithsonian Institute, Washington 18-19b; State Library, Dessau 98-9; Tanzania Nat. Mus. 7; Tapestry Mus., Bayeux 62; Tokapic Palace Library, Istanbul 95t; Tretyakov Gallery, Moscow 128b; Victoria and Albert Mus., London 78b, 97, 117b, 125tl, b, 126; Viking Ship Mus., Bygdoy 53b; W. Munsterberger Collection 34bl; Wallace Collection, London 116t; Warsaw Mus. 27r; Washington Nat. Gallery of Art 108b; Yale University Art Gallery, New Haven 121. **Cover:** castle, bull, stone circle: Tony Stone Images, London; explosion: Science Photo Library, London; Civil War soldier: Library of Congress; stained glass: Quadrillion Publishing; space images and astronaut: Digital Vision, London; all others: AKG London.

EDITOR'S ACKNOWLEDGMENTS

The general editor would like to thank all who assisted her with this book, including all its authors. Special thanks are due to Susan Imhoff for her high degree of involvement with the project overall, and to Kevin Repp for her encouragement and help. Thanks are extended to Julia Hardiman, Ute Krebs, Andrew Fleming and the staff at AKG London, as well as Barbara Heller of the Werner Forman Archive, for their patience and assistance. Thanks are also due to colleagues at Quadrillion Publishing, in particular Bron Kowal, Jane Alexander and Suzanne Evins, for their support throughout the work.